Oregon Legal Research

Carolina Academic Press
Legal Research Series

Tenielle Fordyce-Ruff, Series Editor
Suzanne E. Rowe, Series Editor Emerita

❧

Arizona, Third Edition — Tamara S. Herrera

Arkansas, Second Edition — Coleen M. Barger, Cheryl L. Reinhart &
Cathy L. Underwood

California, Fourth Edition — Aimee Dudovitz, Sarah Laubach & Suzanne E. Rowe

Colorado, Second Edition — Robert Michael Linz

Connecticut — Jessica G. Hynes

Federal, Second Edition — Mary Garvey Algero, Spencer L. Simons,
Suzanne E. Rowe, Scott Childs & Sarah E. Ricks

Florida, Fourth Edition — Barbara J. Busharis, Jennifer LaVia & Suzanne E. Rowe

Georgia — Nancy P. Johnson, Elizabeth G. Adelman & Nancy J. Adams

Idaho, Third Edition — Tenielle Fordyce-Ruff

Illinois, Second Edition — Mark E. Wojcik

Iowa, Second Edition — John D. Edwards, Karen L. Wallace & Melissa H. Weresh

Kansas — Joseph A. Custer & Christopher L. Steadham

Kentucky, Second Edition — William A. Hilyerd, Kurt X. Metzmeier & David J. Ensign

Louisiana, Third Edition — Mary Garvey Algero

Massachusetts, Second Edition — E. Joan Blum & Shaun B. Spencer

Michigan, Third Edition — Cristina D. Lockwood & Pamela Lysaght

Minnesota — Suzanne Thorpe

Mississippi — Kristy L. Gilliland

Missouri, Third Edition — Wanda M. Temm & Julie M. Cheslik

New York, Third Edition — Elizabeth G. Adelman, Theodora Belniak,
Courtney L. Selby & Brian Detweiler

North Carolina, Third Edition — Brenda D. Gibson, Julie L. Kimbrough,
Laura P. Graham & Nichelle J. Perry

North Dakota — Anne Mullins & Tammy Pettinato

Ohio, Second Edition — Sara Sampson, Katherine L. Hall & Carolyn Broering-Jacobs

Oklahoma — Darin K. Fox, Darla W. Jackson & Courtney L. Selby

Oregon, Fourth Edition, Revised Printing — Suzanne E. Rowe & Megan Austin

Pennsylvania, Second Edition — Barbara J. Busharis, Catherine M. Dunn,
Bonny L. Tavares & Carla P. Wale

Tennessee, Second Edition — Scott Childs, Sibyl Marshall & Carol McCrehan Parker

Texas, Second Edition — Spencer L. Simons

Washington, Second Edition — Julie Heintz-Cho, Tom Cobb & Mary A. Hotchkiss

West Virginia, Second Edition — Hollee Schwartz Temple

Wisconsin — Patricia Cervenka & Leslie Behroozi

Wyoming, Second Edition — Debora A. Person & Tawnya K. Plumb

❧

Oregon Legal Research

Fourth Edition,
Revised Printing

Suzanne E. Rowe

Megan Austin

Tenielle Fordyce-Ruff, Series Editor
Suzanne E. Rowe, Series Editor Emerita

CAROLINA ACADEMIC PRESS
Durham, North Carolina

ISBN: 978-1-5310-1668-5
The Library of Congress has cataloged the 2018 printing as follows:

Library of Congress Cataloging-in-Publication Data

Names: Rowe, Suzanne E., 1961- author. | Austin, Megan, author.
Title: Oregon legal research / by Suzanne E. Rowe, Megan Austin.
Description: Fourth edition. | Durham, North Carolina : Carolina Academic Press, LLC, [2019] | Series: Legal research series | Includes bibliographical references and index.
Identifiers: LCCN 2018030139 | ISBN 9781531009632 (alk. paper)
Subjects: LCSH: Legal research--Oregon.
Classification: LCC KFO2475 .R69 2019 | DDC 340.072/0795--dc23
LC record available at https://lccn.loc.gov/2018030139

e-ISBN 978-1-5310-1669-2

CAROLINA ACADEMIC PRESS

700 Kent Street
Durham, North Carolina 27701
Telephone (919) 489-7486
Fax (919) 493-5668
www.cap-press.com

Printed in the United States of America.

Summary of Contents

Contents

List of Tables and Figures

Tables

Figures

Series Note

The Legal Research Series published by Carolina Academic Press includes titles from many states around the country as well as a separate text on federal legal research. The goal of each book is to provide law students, practitioners, paralegals, college students, laypeople, and librarians with the essential elements of legal research in each jurisdiction. Unlike more bibliographic texts, the Legal Research Series books seek to explain concisely both the sources of legal research and the process for conducting legal research effectively.

Preface and Acknowledgments

The primary audience for this fourth edition of *Oregon Legal Research* continues to be the law student, paralegal, or layperson who is learning the sources and processes for conducting research in Oregon law. Experienced researchers and librarians may find this book a helpful reference to Oregon legal resources and current research techniques.

The fourth edition welcomes Megan Austin as a co-author. Her vast experience teaching legal research and her deep knowledge of research techniques are visible throughout the book. Three changes will be evident to those who have used prior editions. First, the chapters have been organized to align with the steps of the fundamental research process. This means secondary sources appear earlier in the book, just as they often do in the research process. Enacted law is presented next, followed by judicial opinions. One chapter now covers both an overview of judicial opinions and courts as well as case law research. Second, information about federal legal research has been compiled in a new appendix, rather than being introduced in each chapter. Third, the research process has been condensed from seven steps to six. The extra step of reading authorities, and particularly cases, was a remnant of print research, which required moving to a different set of books to read cases. We still stress the importance of reading legal authorities carefully.

As with prior editions, the premier online providers of legal research are still Lexis and Westlaw,[1] but high quality legal material is increasingly available for free. While books still have an important place in legal research, many traditional tools have been replaced by online counterparts.

---

1. For readability, throughout this text we use the shortened "Westlaw" for Thomson Reuters Westlaw Edge. We omit the registered trademark symbols for that term as well as for Lexis, Lexis Advance, and Shepard's. We are grateful for the permission of these publishers to include small excerpts to illustrate their products to readers.

The fourth edition continues to use primarily Oregon citation form, as explained in the *Oregon Appellate Courts Style Manual*, because that is the form researchers are likely to encounter in Oregon legal documents and resources. There are subtle differences between the state's citation style and the national citation format of *The Bluebook: A Uniform System of Citation* and the *ALWD Guide to Legal Citation*. Oregon style uses shorter abbreviations for state sources (e.g., abbreviating the state's statutory code as "ORS" rather than "Or. Rev. Stat.") and deletes periods in reporters (e.g., abbreviating *Oregon Reports* as "Or" not "Or.") and other abbreviations (e.g., "edition" is abbreviated "ed" without a period).

Many people have contributed their expertise to the four editions of this book. We are grateful for the assistance of Caulin Price, Zachary Sykes, and Jessica Hong in finalizing this fourth edition. For the third edition, Elizabeth Ruiz Frost, Stephanie Midkiff, Angus Nesbit, Megan McCombs Hays (Lexis) and Jessica Greathouse (Westlaw) provided feedback on chapters and answered many questions. Additional contributions were made by Jaye Barlous, Ryan Hall, Kyung Duk Ko, Lindsay Massara, Lauren Russell, Alice LaViolette, Jerry Curry, Layne Sawyer, Elayna Zammarelli, Nicole Mortemore, Ashley Wong, Zach Conway, and Michael Schneider. For the second edition, those making substantive and editorial suggestions included Harvey Rogers, Angus Nesbit, Dan Barerra, Katie Green, Jeff Hinman, Kyra Patterson, and Donna Williamson. For the first edition, guidance and insights came from Dennis Hyatt, Sam Jacobson, Steve Johansen, Joan Malmud Rocklin, Angus Nesbit, Amy Sloan, Kyu Ho Youm, David Olsson, David Schuman, Stephanie Midkiff, Michael Moffitt, Carl Bjerre, Greena Ng, Jennifer Hisey, Marcus Reed, Tim Hering, and Donna Williamson.

Suzanne Rowe
Megan Austin

May 2019

Oregon Legal Research

Chapter 1

The Research Process and Legal Analysis

I. Legal Research and Legal Analysis

A client enters a lawyer's office with a problem; the lawyer must know the controlling law in order to solve the problem.

A lobbyist prepares for a hearing before a legislative committee; the lobbyist must explain why current statutes are insufficient to address an important issue.

A scholar is intrigued by a policy question; the scholar must know the existing law and related commentary to be able to advocate for a better policy outcome.

In each of these instances—and in myriad other examples—lawyers conduct legal research to assist clients and to influence the development of the law. Legal research is the process of finding relevant authorities for a particular legal issue. The most important authorities are constitutional provisions, statutes, administrative rules, and judicial opinions. Researchers locate these authorities primarily by creating word searches or by scanning topical outlines and indexes.

Legal analysis is interwoven throughout this process, raising challenging questions. How will you frame the legal issue you must research? How will you decide which searches will produce the most comprehensive and relevant research results? How will you know from skimming a results list which documents deserve more attention? When you read the text of a document, how will you determine whether it is relevant? How will you learn whether more recent material changed the law or merely applied it in a new situation? The answer to each of these research questions requires legal analysis. This intersection of research and analysis can make legal research very difficult, especially

Table 1-1. Examples of Authority in Oregon Research

	Mandatory Authority	Persuasive Authority
Primary Sources	Oregon's constitution Oregon statutes Oregon Supreme Court cases	Indiana's constitution California statutes Washington Supreme Court cases
Secondary Sources	—	Practice guides Treatises Law review articles Legal encyclopedias

for the novice. While this book's focus is legal research, it also includes the fundamental aspects of legal analysis required to conduct research effectively.

II. Types of Legal Authority

Legal authorities are often divided along two lines. The first line distinguishes primary sources from secondary sources. *Primary authority* is law produced by government bodies with law-making power. Legislatures write statutes; courts write judicial opinions; and administrative agencies write rules (also called regulations). *Secondary sources*, in contrast, are materials that are written about the law, generally by practicing attorneys, law professors, or legal editors. Secondary sources include treatises, law review articles, practice guides, and legal encyclopedias.

Another division is made between mandatory and persuasive authority. *Mandatory authority* is binding on the court that would decide a conflict if the situation were litigated. In a question of Oregon law, mandatory or binding authority includes Oregon's constitution, statutes enacted by the Oregon legislature, opinions of the Supreme Court of Oregon,[1] and Oregon administrative rules. *Persuasive authority* is not binding, but may be followed if relevant and well reasoned. Authority may be merely persuasive if it is from a different ju-

---

1. An opinion from the Court of Appeals is binding on the trial courts if the Supreme Court of Oregon has not addressed the particular topic.

Table 1-2. Overview of the Steps in Research

1. Prepare to research. Gather facts, determine the issue, decide which jurisdiction controls, and generate a list of research terms. Then create different types of searches, depending on the results you need.

2. Consult secondary sources, including practice guides, treatises, legal encyclopedias, and law review articles.

3. Find enacted law: constitutional provisions, statutes, or rules.

4. Research case law.

5. Update legal authorities by using a citator such as Shepard's or KeyCite to (a) ensure that an authority is still respected and (b) find additional sources that may be relevant to the research project.

6. Read all relevant legal authorities carefully. Analyze your issue and determine whether more research is needed. End your research when you have no holes in your analysis and when you begin seeing the same authorities repeatedly.

risdiction or if it is not produced by a law-making body. In a question of Oregon law, examples of persuasive authority include a California statute, an opinion of a Washington state court, and a law review article. Notice in Table 1-1 that persuasive authority may be either primary or secondary authority, while mandatory authority is always primary.

Within primary, mandatory authority, there is an interlocking hierarchy of law involving constitutions, statutes, administrative rules, and judicial opinions. The constitution of each state is the supreme law of that state. If a statute is on point, that statute comes next in the hierarchy, followed by administrative rules. Judicial opinions may interpret the statute or rule, but they cannot disregard it. A judicial opinion may, however, decide that a statute violates the constitution or that a rule oversteps its bounds. If there is no constitutional provision, statute, or administrative rule on point, the issue will be controlled by *common law*, also called judge-made law or case law.[2]

---

2. Common law is derived from judicial decisions, rather than statutes or constitutions. *Black's Law Dictionary* 334 (10th ed 2014).

III. Overview of the Steps in Legal Research

Conducting effective legal research means following a process that contains discrete steps. This process leads to the authority that controls a legal issue as well as to commentary that may help you analyze new and complex legal matters. Each step can be completed using a variety of resources and techniques, which will be explained throughout the remainder of the book. The outline in Table 1-2 presents the steps of a basic research process.

If you are unfamiliar with an area of law, you should follow each step of the process in the order indicated. Beginning with secondary sources will provide both context for the issues you must research and citations to relevant primary authority. As you gain experience in researching legal questions, you may choose to modify the process. For example, if you know that an issue is controlled by statute, you may choose to begin with Step 3. Or, if you know a specific case governs, you might begin with Step 4.

IV. Preparing to Research

A. Gathering Facts, Determining the Issue, Deciding Jurisdiction, and Generating Search Terms

The beginning of any research process is to gather the facts of the client's situation and understand the client's issue. In law practice, gathering facts may include interviewing the client, reviewing documents, and talking to colleagues who are also working for the client. Understanding the client's issue contains two parts: knowing what the client hopes to achieve and determining the legal questions that will allow the client to achieve it.

As you are getting started, you must decide which jurisdiction's law controls. This book assumes that the client's situation is controlled by Oregon law, but you must determine whether federal law, the law of another state, tribal law, local law, or even foreign law is binding.

Next, generate a list of research terms. These may be legal terms or common words that describe the client's situation. You will use these terms to create online searches, to review indexes, and to scan tables of contents. To compile a comprehensive list of research terms, some researchers ask the journalistic questions: Who? What? How? Why? When? Where? The resulting terms may relate to the facts, issues, or desired solutions of your client's situation. Include in the list both specific and general words, as well as synonyms and antonyms for each term. Using a legal dictionary or thesaurus may help you generate additional terms. Some search engines suggest additional search terms based on those that you enter.

As an example, assume you are working for a defense attorney who was recently assigned to a burglary case. Around midnight, your client allegedly bent a credit card to spring the lock to a stereo store, where she stole $20,000 worth of equipment. She is charged with first-degree burglary. You have been asked to determine whether there is a good argument for limiting the charge to second-degree burglary based on the fact that she used a credit card and not professional burglar tools. Your list of terms could include burglary, burglar tools, burglar, thief, crime, second degree, and incarceration. As your research progresses, you will learn new research terms. For example, a secondary source may refer to a *term of art*, a word or phrase that has special meaning in a particular area of law. Later in your research, you may read cases that give you insights into the words judges tend to use in discussing this topic. These terms and words need to be added to the list.

B. Creating Effective Searches

Take your search terms and create searches that will be most likely to lead to the documents you need. As explained in detail later in this chapter, some online sources allow you to type a simple question, while others work best when search terms are combined with specific connectors and commands. Pay careful attention to the way different online sources interpret searches, for example, whether a blank space is read as an alternative or a phrase. The search *burglar thief* will retrieve very different results if read as *burglar* or *thief* as opposed to the phrase *burglar thief*. If an online search produces far too many results, review the list for more specific search terms or create more narrow searches. A narrow search may require multiple connectors and terms, for example, *burglar tool /10 second degree*. On the other hand, if the terms you use initially produce no hits, review the list for more general terms or make your searches more broad by removing connectors or terms from the search to produce more results.

C. Selecting Online Sources for Legal Research

To select among available online resources, remember that your goal is to find all relevant material and to ensure that the material is both accurate and authoritative.

- *Authoritative.* Documents written by courts, legislatures, and administrative agencies are "the law." Articles and treatises written by recognized experts in a field are not binding, but they can be very persuasive and are often authoritative. To learn what resources a particular site contains and the dates of coverage, look for a "+" or "i" or "?" icon.
- *Official.* Look for a note on government websites indicating whether its contents are official or authenticated. Often, the print versions of statutes are the official versions, while increasingly a government's online version of administrative rules will be official.
- *Comprehensive.* Much recent material is available on many websites, but some historical material and some important secondary materials may be available only on limited websites or in print.
- *Contextual.* Increasingly, online sources provide a table of contents and other tools that provide context for the reading.[3] These sources are valuable because they aid understanding.
- *Annotated.* While many sites will provide the text of a case or statute, the more helpful research sites will also provide annotations or links to related materials.
- *Current.* Check both to see how recent the available material is and to ensure that the online source covers the period of time relevant to your research (especially when doing historical work). Some online sources are no more current than their print counterparts, and websites may contain outdated material.

---

3. Books tend to provide more context than documents viewed online. Thus, some researchers find that beginning legal research in print is more productive than beginning online. In part, this context is provided through tables of contents that give an overview of the legal area, allowing you to understand the big picture before concentrating on a narrow legal issue. Skimming a table of contents can also help you orient a particular document within the larger legal scheme. In addition, many attorneys find they read more carefully and thoroughly in print than on a computer screen. This may be due to the layout of the print page, the absence of visual distractions (including text notices and advertisements), or personal preference.

- *Cost Effective.* Online sources provided by governments and universities are free and highly reliable. When cost is an issue, consider using these sources first. Online commercial services, on the other hand, can be very expensive. A single research project, poorly conceived and sloppily done, can cost hundreds or even thousands of dollars on a subscription service. Check the billing practices in your office before using commercial online sources. Also, be sure you know your office's policy regarding the printing of documents from commercial service websites, which often brings extra charges.

The best way to find accurate and authoritative material online is by using highly regarded and dependable sites. Some examples of established, reputable online research sites include expensive platforms provided by Westlaw and Lexis; less expensive, but less robust, commercial sites, such as Fastcase; free online providers like Google Scholar; free government websites; and free university and law school library websites.

1. Commercial Providers

Westlaw and Lexis are the largest commercial providers of computerized legal research. Both have reputations for accurate material and user-friendly search techniques. They provide extensive coverage of primary and secondary authority. The current platforms are called Thomson Reuters Westlaw Edge and Lexis Advance. They run searches that are easy to construct and provide tools for narrowing to the most relevant documents.

Other commercial providers of legal materials online include Bloomberg, Casemaker, Fastcase, and VersusLaw. Bloomberg is a relative newcomer to the legal research field, most often helpful in researching issues related to finance and business or in obtaining court documents. The other services tend to be less expensive than Westlaw and Lexis, but they also provide less-extensive coverage and their search engines are not as advanced. Currently, Fastcase is available to members of the Oregon State Bar for free; it provides primary authority, secondary materials, and a basic search engine.

2. Free Online Providers

One of the best free online sources for cases and law review articles is Google Scholar. It is user friendly and searching it can produce good results. The greatest weakness of this source is that it contains only cases and law review articles, not statutes, administrative rules, or other important legal materials.

A good source for law review articles, especially those that have not been published yet, is the Legal Scholarship Network on SSRN (the Social Science

Research Network). Registration is free, and the most recent articles on SSRN often present the most cutting-edge commentary. Often, articles refer to relevant statutes and cases, providing an early boost to any research project.

3. Government Websites

Most states and the federal government provide a plethora of legal material online for free. The primary limitation to these sites is that material may be available only for recent years.[4] Like most states, Oregon maintains its own websites for its primary authority. Although the print versions are the official authority,[5] the online versions are useful for research. You will need to confirm your online research with the official print versions, just as you would with other online research of Oregon law. The following websites link to Oregon's statutes, administrative rules, and appellate cases.

> Oregon Statutes
> https://www.oregonlegislature.gov/bills_laws/Pages/ORS.aspx

> Oregon Administrative Rules
> http://sos.oregon.gov/archives/Pages/oregon_administrative_rules.aspx

> Oregon Appellate Cases
> www.publications.ojd.state.or.us/Pages/index.aspx

4. University and Law School Library Websites

University and law school libraries can be rich sources of free, reliable legal information. The law libraries of the three law schools in Oregon—Lewis & Clark, University of Oregon, and Willamette University—provide helpful material for researching Oregon sources. From each library's home page, look for a link to "Research" or "Research Guides."

Sometimes an academic library provides on-site patrons with access to online services for free. For example, academic versions of Westlaw and Lexis products are sometimes available. Another very valuable site sometimes pro-

---

4. For example, decisions of Oregon's Supreme Court and Court of Appeals are available on the state's website only back to 1998.

5. The Oregon.gov website includes the following and similar disclaimers on a number of pages: "The official record copy is the printed published copy of the Oregon Revised Statutes. The text in the database is not the official text of Oregon law." *E.g.,* http://www.oregon.gov/DAS/EAM/pages/state_statutes.aspx.

Figure 1-1. Finding a Case by Citation on Westlaw

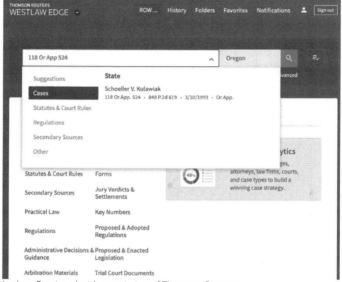

Source: Westlaw. Reprinted with permission of Thomson Reuters.

vided to library patrons is HeinOnline, with extensive coverage of federal documents and law review articles.

5. Gateway Sites

Some libraries contain links to sites with legal material, even when the library itself does not maintain the material. Two examples are Cornell Law School's "Legal Information Institute" at www.law.cornell.edu and Washburn University School of Law's "WashLaw" at www.washlaw.edu. The Oregon segments of those websites have links to Oregon cases, statutes, administrative materials, and more. A similar gateway site is FindLaw at www.findlaw.com.

D. Selecting Online Search Techniques

Each website has a different method for retrieving and displaying information, although all tend to follow the same fundamental search algorithms. Because most websites are constantly being revised and because their platforms change over time, only general information is included here. The following explanations are for Westlaw and Lexis.[6] Much of this information should be easily applied

---

6. In addition, Westlaw and Lexis provide ample training material on their websites. YouTube videos are also available and many are helpful.

Figure 1-2. Finding a Case by Parties' Names on Lexis

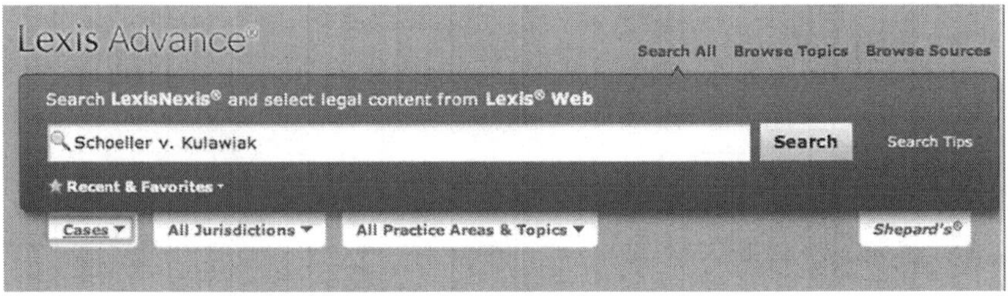

Source: Lexis Advance. Reprinted with the permission of LexisNexis. All rights reserved.

to other online sources. In addition, look for a link such as "Help" or "Searching Hints" to provide information about search techniques for each particular site. Some sites offer online tutorials to introduce their resources and search processes.

1. Beginning Research with a Citation

When you have a citation to a case, statute, article, or other legal source, retrieving that document online is as simple as typing the citation into a designated box on the proper screen. On Westlaw or Lexis, type the citation into the universal search box on the main page. You can also search for a case by party name. See Figure 1-1 for a search for a case found in volume 118 of *Oregon Reports, Court of Appeals*, beginning on page 524. See Figure 1-2 for a search for the same case using the parties' names.

2. Searching with Terms and Connectors

Most search engines allow you to conduct a search simply by typing in a single word. If the word is a term of art like "interpleader" or a cause of action that is less common, for example "kidnapping," this one-word search might be successful. In contrast, if the search is in a broad legal area like "murder" or "jurisdiction," you will need to add more terms to yield successful results.

You can create highly effective searches for specific terms by using Boolean connectors. These connectors tell the computer how terms should be placed in relation to one another in targeted documents, enabling you to more accurately control what the computer searches for.

To create a search query, think of the ideal document you would like to find and try to imagine where your search terms would be located in relation

Table 1-3. Boolean Connectors and Commands

Goal	Lexis	Westlaw
To find alternative terms anywhere in the document	or blank space	or blank space
To find both terms anywhere in the document	and	and &
To find both terms within a particular distance from each other	/p = in same paragraph /s = in same sentence /n = within n words	/p = in same paragraph /s = in same sentence /n = within n words
To find terms used as an exact phrase	put the phrase in quotation marks	put the phrase in quotation marks
To control the hierarchy of searching	enclose terms in parentheses	enclose terms in parentheses
To exclude terms	and not	but not %
To extend the end of a term (e.g., employ!)	! *	!
To hold the place of letters in a term (e.g., wom?n)	?	*

to each other within that document. Would they be in the same sentence? The same paragraph? Table 1-3 summarizes the most common connectors and commands. On Lexis, you can find explanations of commands by clicking "Tips" to the right and above the universal search bar; scroll down to "Common Connectors." On Westlaw, click on "advanced" beside the universal search bar; on the right of the resulting screen, you will see the connectors and expanders.

The ability to use terms and connectors can make the research process both easy and effective, but initially it takes practice. If you enter *adverse possession*, you will find documents that contain either of those terms; to find the specific property claim, enclose the terms in quotation marks as *"adverse possession."*

Consider an example search designed to determine whether a contract containing a covenant not to compete is enforceable against a former employee.

EXAMPLE: Searching terms: *(covenant or contract) /p (noncompetition or "restraint of trade" or compet!) /p employ!*, the computer will look for:

- either the term *covenant* or *contract*;

- within the same paragraph as the term *noncompetition* or the term *restraint of trade* or variations of *competition, compete, competitor*;

- and also in that paragraph variations of *employ, employee, employer, employment*.

Misuse of connectors can produce bizarre search results. If, instead of "/p" in the example above, the researcher used the "or" connector, the results could include (1) a case in which former spies sued the federal government for failing to adhere to a secret *contract*, (2) a case determining whether an implied *covenant* can be read into an oil and gas lease, and (3) a case dismissing a beer importer's unfair *competition* claim.

You can also use connectors to alter the searches you originally created, narrowing results or casting a wider net. After running the search in the example above, you might want to narrow to results that use *"covenant not to compete"* if you find that term is used in the most relevant cases in your jurisdiction.

3. Searching with Natural Language

Natural language searching is the type used most often on Google, Yahoo!, and other general search engines. You simply type in a question or a list of words, and the computer program decides which words are critical, whether the words should appear in some proximity to one another, and how often they should appear in the document. In the previous example, the following sentence could be used as a natural language search: "Is a covenant not to compete enforceable against a former employee?"

Westlaw and Lexis both tout the success of their search engines with these natural language queries. One search explores all of the documents in their databases and returns hundreds of results. The next step, however, is the more difficult one: filtering through all of those documents to find the most relevant. Each platform provides tools for doing so. On Westlaw, these tools appear in the left margin under the heading "Narrow." The filters differ for each type of document. Cases, for example, can be filtered by research term, date, judge, etc. See Figure 1-3. Similar filters exist on Lexis, also in the left margin.

Figure 1-3. Narrowing Filters for Cases on Westlaw

Source: Westlaw. Reprinted with permission of Thomson Reuters.

4. Searching a Table of Contents or Index

A table of contents lists the major concepts of a book, statutory scheme, or other source, in the order that they appear in that source. Online, the broadest concepts often appear on the first screen, and you open to more specific sub-headings by clicking on the concept or an icon next to it. Searching a table of contents provides two benefits. First, skimming a table of contents for your research terms can lead you to relevant portions of the database. Second, examining a table of contents can provide an overview or outline of an area of law. For instance, if you wanted to see the statutes surrounding Oregon Revised Statute 105.620, dealing with adverse possession of property, you could click on the "Table of Contents" link while viewing the statute on Westlaw and scroll through the contents.

An index, in contrast, lists concepts in a source alphabetically. Indexes exist online both for finding sources (e.g., Lexis lists all of its sources alphabetically under a link called "Browse Sources") and for finding material within a source (e.g., a statutory code may have an online index).

5. Searching by Topic

Topic searching is effective when you are familiar with the general area of law involved in your client's issue, but you don't know of relevant statutes or cases.

Westlaw allows topic searching from the "Practice Areas" tab on its main page. Almost thirty broad topics are listed, ranging from Antitrust to Family Law to Tax. To continue with the adverse possession example, you could select the topic "Real Property" and then select the type of documents you want to review (e.g., cases, statutes, secondary sources). Enter the search term *adverse possession* in the search box and use the narrowing options located in the left margin.

On Lexis, searching begins with "Browse," a link at the top of the main page, and then "Topics." From there, you can select from over forty topics listed; they overlap considerably with the topics on Westlaw, but also include Administrative Law, Copyright, Mergers and Acquisitions, Trade Secrets, and others. After selecting a topic like "Workers Compensation," you can open its subtopics (e.g., Benefit Determinations, Coverage) and eventually select "Get topic documents" using a drop-down menu. Another approach is to enter search terms in the box "Search for topics."

Note that, with any platform, topic searching may be useful as a starting point, but it is unlikely to produce a comprehensive list of authorities.

6. Searching Databases, Setting Search Parameters, and Applying Filters

A general search run from the universal search bar could result in thousands of documents, many of which are irrelevant to your work. You can restrict the documents you have to review in three ways: (1) selecting a database; (2) setting pre-search limits from the main page; and (3) using filters after running a search.

Westlaw and Lexis allow — and services like Fastcase require — you to select a database before searching either with terms and connectors or with natural language. Selecting a database really just means restricting the sources that a search will review. Typical databases for Oregon research contain the following: only Oregon cases; Oregon and federal cases; Oregon statutes and court rules; Oregon administrative regulations; and secondary sources, such as law journals from the three Oregon law schools. Even when not required to select a database before running a search, careful researchers often choose to do so.

On Westlaw, you can use the tabs on the main page to restrict sources, a form of database selection. For instance, under "Content types," you could

Figure 1-4. Oregon Sources on Lexis

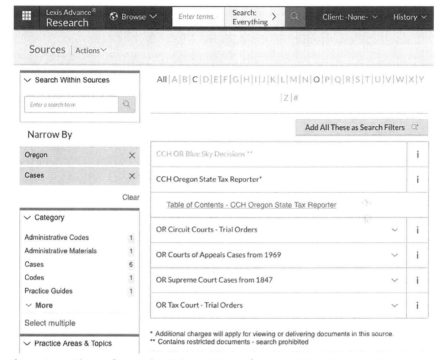

click on "Cases" and then "Oregon" to search only for cases decided by Oregon's courts. On Lexis, use the link at the top of any screen to "Browse" and select "Oregon" as the jurisdiction and "Cases" as the category; then select a source like "OR Supreme Court Cases from 1847" to restrict the sources your search reviews. Figure 1-4 shows the Oregon sources for cases available on Lexis.

Limiting the search's parameters before searching controls the number and relevance of documents a search retrieves. On Westlaw, a drop-down menu to the right of the search bar allows you to select a jurisdiction for your search. On Lexis, tabs under the search bar allow you to restrict by content type (e.g., primary authority, secondary sources, news), jurisdiction, and topic.

After conducting a search, you can still limit the results through the narrowing filters shown in Figure 1-3 and discussed in the accompanying text. Be sure to review filters with each search to ensure that you are using only those that you intend; sometimes filters automatically stay engaged until you change them or disengage them.

7. Using Artificial Intelligence, Data, and Analytics

The most advanced research services have begun providing search options based on artificial intelligence to mine their vast data resources. Lexis now provides these options through Ravel, which it acquired in 2017. In the summer of 2018, Westlaw introduced Westlaw Edge. Both service providers tout these products as providing accurate information more quickly and intuitively. Researchers who have mastered the techniques explained in this book should be able to incorporate into their research process not only these new tools but also future generations of search capacity.

Legal researchers can stay current on cutting edge websites of interest to the legal profession, as well as other legal technology, by accessing blogs such as LawSites Blog, https://www.lawsitesblog.com, which tracks "new and intriguing websites and products for the legal profession." This blog contains reviews of both Westlaw Edge and Lexis Analytics.

8. Working with Documents Online

Westlaw and Lexis allow you to work with and save documents online. You can highlight important provisions, add notes, and save documents in folders that you create for each project. These folders are maintained on the website and accessible from any computer or mobile device. You can share folders with coworkers.

These services also allow you to download, email, or print documents. Printing documents can be very expensive; thus, deciding which key documents to print is important.[7] Most researchers print the key statute and leading cases, keeping these documents close at hand and referring to them frequently.

Most online services save your searches and results, allowing you to run searches again or preventing you from duplicating effort—wasting time and money. On Westlaw and Lexis, use the "History" links to locate past searches. On Westlaw and Lexis, this link is available at the top right of every screen. The period during which the services save searches varies.

---

7. Currently, Westlaw does not provide free printing to law students.

E. Using Print Research Techniques

Because some legal resources are still available only in print, this short section reviews the fundamental techniques for researching with books. Even when resources are available in print and online, some researchers turn to print sources when they become frustrated with online research, perhaps because they are not finding useful material.

First, to find a relevant book in your library, use the online catalog. Be sure to look first for tips on how to construct effective searches, as each library catalog is different. The catalog may include both print and online materials, as well as documents available in microfiche and other formats. Each book will have been assigned a call number that allows you to find it within the library collection. The call number is a series of letters (e.g., KF is the abbreviation for American law) and numbers (e.g., 3700 is the subheading for environmental law) that places the book with others on the same topic. Thus, after you have located one book, scanning the shelves nearby can lead you to additional books that might be more helpful.

Once you locate a book that appears relevant, turn to its table of contents in the first few pages to get an overview of the book's coverage. If your book is part of a series, you might check both the table of contents for the entire series as well as the table of contents for a particular volume. If one of your research terms appears in the table of contents, turn to the portion of the book it references and read the text.

Another effective way to begin working with a book is to turn to the index. Usually, the index appears in the back of the book. In a multi-volume work, the index is likely to be in the first or last volumes, or in soft-cover books shelved with the series. Search the index for your research terms, follow any cross references to other index entries, and record the references to a particular portion of the book. Note that you could be referred to a page, a chapter, a section, or a numbered paragraph.

Some legal books are updated with *pocket parts*, which are additional pages designed to fit into a slot in the back cover of the book. If your book has a pocket part, more current information will appear there. When a pocket part becomes too large to fit inside the book, the publisher may produce a soft-cover supplement. Furthermore, with a series of books, a few soft-cover pamphlets might provide the most recent updates for the entire series. While print material is rarely as current as online sources, these pocket parts and supplements contain the most recent print information.

F. Working with Law Librarians

Often the most valuable tool available to any legal researcher is a law reference librarian in the specific jurisdiction. Many of these professionals have degrees in both law and library sciences, and they are eager to help.

V. Researching the Law

The remainder of this book explains how to conduct legal research in a variety of sources, completing Steps 2 through 6 of the basic research process. Chapter 2 covers secondary sources, and then the book turns to primary authorities. Chapter 3 addresses the Oregon Constitution, which is the highest legal authority in the state. Chapters 4 and 5 describe statutory and legislative history research, respectively. Chapter 6 addresses administrative law. Chapter 7 explains the Oregon court system and the components of a judicial opinion, as well as how to research judicial opinions. Chapter 8 covers citators, particularly KeyCite and Shepard's, which are used to update legal authorities. Chapter 9 demonstrates three different research approaches, pulling together key ideas from throughout the book.

While the chapters are organized according to the steps of the research process, you might want to read them in a different order. Because cases will be referenced throughout the research process, you might want to review Chapter 7 soon after reading Chapter 2, even though researching cases comes later in the basic research process. Readers who benefit from seeing the big picture might want to read Chapter 9 now and refer to it frequently, even though a number of references in it will not become clear until you have read the intervening chapters.

Appendix A introduces federal resources, demonstrating how the research process works in any jurisdiction. Appendix B provides an overview of the conventions lawyers follow in citing legal authority in their documents. Appendix C contains a selected bibliography of texts on legal research and analysis. The general research texts tend to concentrate on federal resources, supplementing this book's brief introduction to those resources. As a final note, because legal research is interconnected, early chapters occasionally refer to concepts that are not fully explained until later in the book. You can always look under "Terms of art" in the index of this book for pages where concepts are introduced.

Chapter 2

Secondary Authorities and Practice Aids

Lawyers use secondary sources to learn about the law and to find references to relevant primary authority. Common secondary authorities include treatises, practice guides, legal encyclopedias, and law review articles. Also under the large umbrella of secondary sources are tools called "practice aids"; they carry no authoritative value but assist lawyers in conducting research, creating documents, and staying current in legal developments. Examples include legal forms, continuing legal education (CLE) publications, and blogs. There is no clear dividing line between secondary authorities and practice aids, and some of the resources discussed in this chapter might be described as both. All of these sources are "secondary" because they are written by law professors, practicing attorneys, legal editors, and even law students; in contrast, primary authority is written by legislatures, courts, and administrative agencies.

Often, beginning a new research project in a secondary source will be more effective than beginning immediately to search for statutes or cases on point. A secondary source may provide an overview of the pertinent issues, aiding in the analysis of the legal problem. The text of these sources may explain unfamiliar terminology and concepts, making it possible to develop a more effective list of research terms. Also, secondary sources and practice aids often provide a shortcut to researching primary authority by including numerous references to cases, statutes, and rules.

This chapter introduces treatises, practice guides, and other books; legal encyclopedias; legal periodicals, including law reviews and bar journals; *American Law Reports*; CLE publications; legal forms; restatements, uniform laws, and model codes; jury instructions and jury verdict information; ethical rules; and current awareness tools.[1] The chapter concludes with a discussion of when and how to use secondary sources and practice aids in legal research.

---

1. This chapter cannot include an exhaustive list of all Oregon secondary sources and practice aids. For additional information, see Stephanie Midkiff & Wendy Schroeder

I. Treatises, Practice Guides, and Other Books

A book on a legal topic can provide an in-depth discussion of the topic and relevant references to primary authority. Legal texts include treatises, practice guides, hornbooks, and *Nutshells*. All of these books share the purpose of covering a particular legal subject, such as contracts or civil procedure. They are distinguished mainly by their level of coverage.

- Treatises are generally considered to be more comprehensive statements on a subject.
- Hornbooks offer a slightly more summarized view of legal subjects.
- Practice guides typically cover an area of law thoroughly, but with a particular focus on the nuts and bolts of practice as opposed to the more theoretical approach of treatises or hornbooks.
- *Nutshells* are a series of books published by West that offer a very condensed explanation of law.

Accordingly, an attorney may use a treatise or practice guide to become familiar with a new area of law, while a law student might typically turn to a hornbook or *Nutshell* to prepare for class, or later to gain a better understanding of a class lecture. This chapter focuses on treatises and practice guides because they are more commonly used in research and cited in documents than are hornbooks and *Nutshells*.

A. Treatises

Some treatises are so well known and widely respected that a colleague or supervisor may suggest that you begin research with a particular title. Examples include Kirkpatrick's *Oregon Evidence* and Wright & Miller's *Federal Practice and Procedure*. The first example covers the law of Oregon evidence in one volume. The second example is a multi-volume treatise. Figure 2-1 provides a sample page from *Oregon Evidence*, as viewed on Lexis.

Many of the more popular treatises are available on Lexis and Westlaw, but some may be available only in print. Online versions are typically updated

---

Hitchcock, *State Documents Bibliography: Oregon* (2009). *See also* Mary Clayton and Stephanie Midkiff's chapter on Oregon practice materials in *State Practice Materials: Annotated Bibliographies* (W.S. Hein 2005); *see generally* Karen S. Beck, *Oregon Practice Materials: A Selective Annotated Bibliography*, 88 Law Libr J 288 (1996).

Figure 2-1. Sample Treatise Page

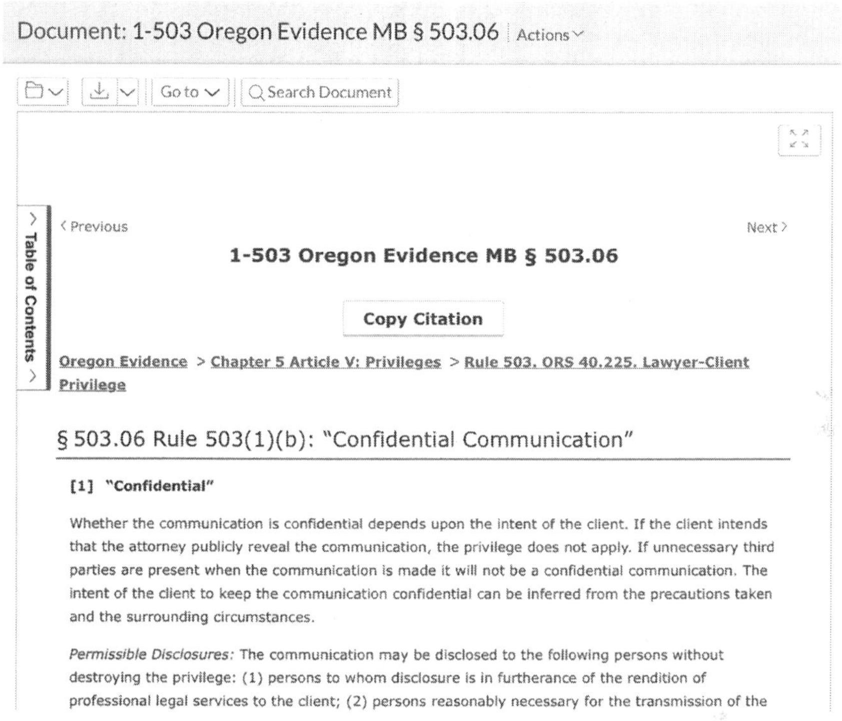

Document: 1-503 Oregon Evidence MB § 503.06 | Actions ⌄

📁⌄ ⤓ ⌄ Go to ⌄ 🔍 Search Document

⟨ Previous   Next ⟩

1-503 Oregon Evidence MB § 503.06

Copy Citation

Table of Contents

Oregon Evidence > Chapter 5 Article V: Privileges > Rule 503, ORS 40.225, Lawyer-Client Privilege

§ 503.06 Rule 503(1)(b): "Confidential Communication"

[1] "Confidential"

Whether the communication is confidential depends upon the intent of the client. If the client intends that the attorney publicly reveal the communication, the privilege does not apply. If unnecessary third parties are present when the communication is made it will not be a confidential communication. The intent of the client to keep the communication confidential can be inferred from the precautions taken and the surrounding circumstances.

Permissible Disclosures: The communication may be disclosed to the following persons without destroying the privilege: (1) persons to whom disclosure is in furtherance of the rendition of professional legal services to the client; (2) persons reasonably necessary for the transmission of the

Source: Lexis Advance. Reprinted with the permission of LexisNexis. All rights reserved.

only when the print version is. Treatises in print are updated in a variety of ways. Bound volumes may be updated with pocket parts or new editions. Some treatises are published in loose-leaf binders, which are updated by replacing outdated pages throughout the binder with current material. Each page is dated to show when it was last updated. Also, new pages at the beginning of loose-leaf binders are often in different colors to draw the reader's attention to the more recent information.

B. Oregon Practice Guides

One of the most helpful secondary sources for Oregon attorneys is the series of practice guides published by the Oregon State Bar (OSB). Each guide covers one area of Oregon law in depth. Titles address administrative law, construction law, environmental law, family and juvenile law, real property, torts, and trial practice, among many other areas of Oregon law. The authors are typically practitioners with extensive experience in the legal area they are writing about. The text is practice-oriented, so it includes explanations, references to primary authority, practice tips, and sample forms. These guides are available for download from the OSB website; in print, they are published as loose-leaf binders. For a list of OSB publications, visit the bar's website at www.osbar.org; click on "CLE/Legal Publications," and then "Log in to BarBooks." BarBooks are available to bar members for free and to others with subscription access.

In addition to the OSB series, West's Oregon Law and Practice series addresses a few topics of Oregon law in a similar manner. In that series, the Civil Procedure title is available on Westlaw. Some libraries have all of the series titles in print.

More general practice guides are published by the Practising Law Institute (PLI), the American Law Institute (ALI), and the American Bar Association (ABA).

C. Finding and Using Legal Books

Treatises, practice guides, hornbooks, and *Nutshells* can be located by using a library's catalog and searching for the general subject matter of a research project. For a well known treatise, include the name of the author as one of your search terms. When searching for practice-oriented material, use the name of the publisher (e.g., Oregon State Bar or American Law Institute). After finding one book on point, scan the other titles shelved around it for additional resources. Increasingly, libraries are showing online availability in their catalogs; thus, a treatise reference in the catalog might send you to an online subscription service the library provides to patrons, which contains the treatise you seek.

To use a treatise or other book, begin with either the table of contents or the index. Both tools are often available online as well as in print versions. In multi-volume treatises, the index is often in the last volume of the series. Locate your research terms and record the references given. A reference may be to a page number, section number, or paragraph number, depending on the publisher. The table of contents or index should indicate which type of number is referenced. Turn to that part of the book, read the text, and note any pertinent primary authority cited in the footnotes.

The authoritative value of a book depends largely on the reputation of the author. Laird Kirkpatrick is a widely recognized expert on Oregon evidence, and his treatise is so respected that it is cited by courts. In contrast, a *Nutshell* on evidence is designed as a study guide for students or a quick overview for practitioners; it is not considered authoritative.

Figure 2-2. Excerpt from CJS on Contracts

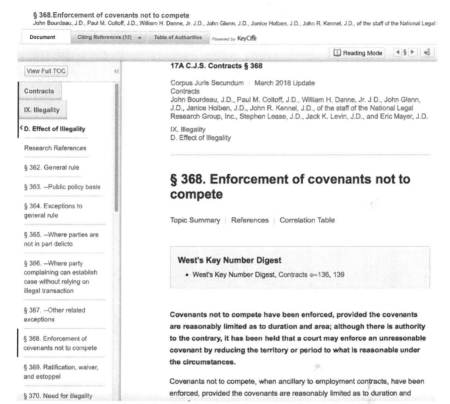

Source: Westlaw. Reprinted with permission of Thomson Reuters.

II. Legal Encyclopedias

Legal encyclopedias provide summarized information on a wide variety of legal subjects. Legal encyclopedias are organized by subject matter under topics selected by the publisher. These topics are presented alphabetically, both in bound volumes and in an online table of contents. The two national legal encyclopedias are *Corpus Juris Secundum* (CJS) and *American Jurisprudence, Second Edition* (Am Jur 2d). Figure 2-2 contains a short excerpt from the topic "Contracts" in CJS, as shown on Westlaw. Some larger states have their own encyclopedias, such as *California Jurisprudence* and *Florida Jurisprudence*. Oregon does not have its own encyclopedia.

On Lexis, use "Browse Sources" to find encyclopedias or type the name of the source into the universal search bar. (Note that Lexis has Am Jur 2d, but not CJS.) On Westlaw, CJS, Am Jur 2d, and similar materials are available under "Content types," "Secondary Sources." Use the filters on the left side to limit "Publication Type" to "Jurisprudence & Encyclopedias." If you know which encyclopedia you want to use, simply type its title into Westlaw's universal search bar. You can search by table of contents or with full-text queries.

To use an online encyclopedia, you might review its index, search its table of contents, or conduct a full-text search. The options available depend on the encyclopedia and the online service you are using. To use an encyclopedia in print, review its softbound index volumes for your research terms. The references will include both an abbreviated word or phrase — the topic — and a section number.[2] The encyclopedia's topic abbreviations are explained in tables in the front of the index volumes. Select the bound volume containing a relevant topic. The spine of each volume includes the range of topics included in that volume.

Whether working online or in print, review not only the sections that result from your search but also those sections just before and after it. Also, skim the material at the beginning of a relevant topic for an overview and general information.

The text of most encyclopedia entries is cursory because the goal of the writers is to summarize the law. Encyclopedia entries will identify significant variations that exist between different jurisdictions, but they do not attempt to resolve differences or recommend improvements in the law.

One potentially helpful feature of an encyclopedia is the list of footnotes accompanying the text. If a footnote refers to recent primary authority from your jurisdiction, you will have made a great step forward in your research. However, because the footnotes in CJS and Am Jur 2d cite to authorities from all American jurisdictions and tend to be dated, you will need to use those cites as a springboard to recent Oregon materials (e.g., using a citator, as explained in Chapter 8).

An encyclopedia may also contain cross references to other sources. For example, CJS includes cross references to West's digests, as shown in Figure 2-2. (Digests are covered in Chapter 7 of this book.)

---

2. Do not confuse these topics and section numbers with the West digest system of Topics and Key Numbers discussed in Chapter 7.

III. Legal Periodicals

A. Law Reviews and Journals

Law reviews and law journals publish scholarly articles written by law professors, judges, practitioners, and students. Each article addresses in detail a specific legal issue. Freed from the constraints of representing a client's interests or deciding a particular case, an author is able to explore whether the laws currently in force are the best legal rules and to propose changes.

Reading articles published in law reviews and journals can provide a thorough understanding of current law because the authors often explain the existing law before making their recommendations. These articles may also identify weaknesses or new trends in the law that might address your client's situation. Sometimes an article compares laws in different jurisdictions, pointing out the benefits or problems in each. The many footnotes in law review and law journal articles can provide excellent summaries of relevant research.

Articles written by students are called "Notes" or "Comments." Although not as authoritative as articles written by recognized experts, student articles can provide clear and careful analysis and their footnotes can contain valuable research leads. Shorter law review pieces, generally written by students, simply summarize a recent case that the publication's editors consider important. These are called "Case Notes" or "Recent Developments." They notify readers of important developments in the law, but do not analyze or critique the case in any depth. They are often not helpful beyond offering a short summary of the case and the court's analysis.

Law reviews and law journals are generally published by law students who were selected according to grades or through a writing competition for membership on the editorial board. Many law reviews have general audiences and cover a broad range of topics. A growing number of other law journals focus on a specific area of law, for example, the *Journal of Environmental Law and Litigation* and the *Columbia Journal of Transnational Law*. Table 2-1 lists law reviews and journals published by Oregon law schools. Still other law journals are "peer edited," meaning that law professors select and edit the articles to be published. Examples of this type of law journal are the *Journal of Legal Education* and *Legal Writing: The Journal of the Legal Writing Institute*.

Law review articles are available on Lexis, Westlaw, HeinOnline, Google Scholar, and other sites, and sometimes on a journal's own website. Many periodicals are published first in soft-cover booklets, which are later bound into a single volume. You will locate articles by volume number, an abbreviation

Table 2-1. Law Reviews and Journals Published by Oregon Law Schools

Animal Law Review — Lewis & Clark Law School

Environmental Law Review — Lewis & Clark Law School

Journal of Environmental Law and Litigation — University of Oregon School of Law

Lewis & Clark Law Review — Lewis & Clark Law School

Oregon Law Review — University of Oregon School of Law

Oregon Review of International Law — University of Oregon School of Law

Willamette Environmental Law Journal — Willamette University College of Law

Willamette Journal of International Law and Dispute Resolution — Willamette University College of Law

Willamette Journal of Social Justice and Equity — Willamette University College of Law

Willamette Law Review — Willamette University College of Law

Willamette Sports Law Journal — Willamette University College of Law

of the name of the journal, and the first page of the article. Even when working online, you will cite articles to print sources.

Law review and law journal articles are not "updated" in the usual sense. You can, however, find out whether an article has been cited favorably or unfavorably by using a citator such as Shepard's or KeyCite, as explained in Chapter 8.

B. Bar Journals

Each state's bar journal contains articles of particular interest to attorneys practicing in that state. The *Oregon State Bar Bulletin*, published ten times each year, contains articles discussing trends in law practice and firm management, analyzing recent Oregon court decisions and legislation, and highlighting important personalities, as well as short columns that appear regularly (e.g., bar counsel, legal writing, disciplinary action). The American Bar Association publishes the *ABA Journal*, which has articles of general interest to attorneys across the nation.

Articles in bar journals are often shorter than the articles published in law reviews and do not have the extensive footnotes found in law review articles. Moreover, the bar journal articles have a practitioner's focus.

C. Locating Articles

Periodical indexes offer the most accurate way of locating relevant articles. These indexes use specific subject headings into which articles are classified. Even novice researchers tend to be successful in searching these index databases using keywords. A popular index of legal periodicals is the *Current Law Index* (CLI). It is available in a database called LegalTrac, which is provided in many law libraries. CLI is also available on Lexis and Westlaw (called "Legal Resource Index"). The coverage of each version varies slightly, but all include articles at least back to 1980. Another important index for legal periodicals is the *Index to Legal Periodicals and Books* (ILPB). A related index called *Index to Legal Periodicals Retrospective* is especially useful in finding older articles because its coverage extends back to the early 1900s. The ILPB products are available online from the H.W. Wilson Company at www.ebscohost.com/wilson. That site contains indexes for non-legal periodicals, too.

Full-text searching for articles is available on Lexis, Westlaw, HeinOnline, Google Scholar,[3] and other services. If you are new to legal research or if you are searching an unfamiliar legal topic, however, full-text searching is likely to produce an unwieldy number of articles, many of which are only tangentially related to your topic. Lexis, Westlaw, and HeinOnline tend to be more helpful when you already have a citation to a relevant article. On Google Scholar, searching with a known article title or author is easiest; in contrast, entering an article's citation rarely produces helpful results.

HeinOnline's search engine is not as sophisticated as those available on Lexis or Westlaw, but it can be effective. One advantage to retrieving articles from HeinOnline is that the text is provided in PDF format, meaning that pagination looks exactly like the print copy (which makes citation of specific pages easier) and footnotes accompany the relevant text (rather than being placed at the end of the article). Many law school libraries subscribe to HeinOnline, making it free to their students and patrons. The website is www.heinonline.org.

Finally, many law journals are posting their own articles on websites. Those can be difficult to search, but they usually provide free access when you already have a citation.

For articles that have not yet been published, the Legal Scholarship Network (the "Law" database) on the Social Science Research Network (SSRN)

---

3. Google Scholar links to the article only if it is available for free on the Internet. If not, you may be directed to a link where you can purchase the article.

provides access through a good search engine. SSRN also provides links to some articles that have already been published. Much of the material on SSRN is available for free, but some fee-based journals are included. To access those journals, you can pay an annual fee, join an organization's site subscription (e.g., through a law school), or request trial access. The website is www.ssrn.com.

IV. *American Law Reports*

American Law Reports (ALR) is a hybrid resource, offering both commentary on certain legal subjects and the full text of published cases on those subjects. Because cases are now so widely available, researchers use ALR almost exclusively for the commentary articles.[4] These articles tend to focus on very narrow topics, take a practitioner's view, and provide a survey of the law in different jurisdictions. Thus, an article on the exact topic of your research is likely to be extremely helpful. Commentary articles are written by lawyers who are knowledgeable but are not necessarily recognized experts.

EXAMPLE: In 1986, Congress passed the *Emergency Medical Treatment and Active Labor Act*, 42 USC § 1395dd (EMTALA). ALR reports a leading EMTALA case, *Thornton v. Southwest Detroit Hospital*, at 104 ALR Fed 157. The official cite for that case is 895 F.2d 1131. Related to the *Thornton* case is an annotation, *Construction and Application of Emergency Medical Treatment and Active Labor Act*, written by a lawyer named Melissa K. Stull. Among some of the topics discussed in this annotation are the reasons Congress enacted EMTALA, the effect of related statutes, the liability imposed on hospitals, and the available remedies. See Figure 2-3 for the first screen of this document. The "Table of Cases, Laws, and Rules" lists related authorities by jurisdiction, making it a powerful research tool. "Research References" include citations for related statutes, encyclopedia entries, treatises, and other sources.

---

4. These articles were called *annotations* until fairly recently, so you might see that term used.

Figure 2-3. Excerpt from ALR Article

Construction and application of Emergency Medical Treatment and Active Labor Act (42 U.S.C.A. § 1395dd)
American Law Reports ALR Federal   Originally published in 1991   *(Approx. 157 pages)*

| Document | History (3) | Citing References (109) ▾ | Table of Authorities | *Powered by* KeyCite |

Part: ◄   1 of 3 ►

104 A.L.R. Fed. 166 (Originally published in 1991)

American Law Reports │ The ALR databases are made current by the weekly addition of relevant new cases.
ALR Federal
Melissa K. Stull, J.D.

Construction and application of Emergency Medical Treatment and Active Labor Act (42 U.S.C.A. § 1395dd)

TABLE OF CONTENTS
Article Outline
Index
Table of Cases, Laws, and Rules
Research References

ARTICLE OUTLINE

§ 1[a] Introduction—Scope
§ 1[b] Introduction—Related matters
§ 1[c] Introduction—Statutory text
§ 2 Background and summary
§ 2.5 Scope of Emergency Medical Treatment and Active Labor Act

Source: Westlaw. Reprinted with permission of Thomson Reuters.

ALR has been published in several series over time. Early series contained both state and federal subjects. Currently, state subjects are discussed in numbered series: ALR3d through ALR7th. Federal subjects are included in *ALR Federal,* now in its third series. A series called *ALR International* began in 2010 and provides analysis of cases from the United States and abroad on selected topics. Lexis has the second through seventh ALR series as well as three federal series. Westlaw provides all of the series; it also has ALR databases for particular practice areas, including admiralty, bankruptcy, and securities.

V. Continuing Legal Education Publications

Attorneys in Oregon are required to attend continuing legal education (CLE) seminars periodically to maintain their membership in the state's bar. The seminars may be held live and last several hours; they may take place during a bar association's lunch meeting; they may be conducted online through webinars; or they may be available through online videos or MP3 downloads. These seminars often present very practical information. Topics range from ethical issues in business law to building a personal injury practice. A CLE seminar may be aimed at new lawyers just learning the fundamentals of practice; however, many CLE seminars are intended to offer new insights on cutting-edge legal issues.

A CLE seminar might be led by a practitioner, judge, or law professor. The person leading the seminar typically prepares materials that include sample forms, sample documents, and explanations. These materials may be available in law libraries; alternatively, the materials (along with audio or video of the CLE seminar) may be purchased. Check the Oregon State Bar's website at www.osbar.org under the "CLE" link.

Some of the largest publishers of similar materials are the Practising Law Institute (PLI), the American Law Institute (ALI), and the American Bar Association (ABA). To locate CLE material, search the library catalog by topic or by author, using the names of the more common CLE publishers as search terms.

VI. Legal Forms

A form can be a great shortcut in drafting a legal document, especially a document you are drafting for the first time in an unfamiliar area of law. A form provides an excellent starting point by keeping you from reinventing the wheel.

Forms are available in a diverse range of sources. Oregon statutes provide forms for some particular situations. To give two examples, ORS 127.531 contains a form for an advance directive concerning health care and ORS 100.740 contains language that must be included in a condominium sales agreement. To find statutory forms, search the ORS General Index under "Forms (Statutory)." For a full-text search, use terms for the substantive content and the term "form" (e.g., *advance directive form*).

Forms may also be found in court rules (discussed in Chapter 4), in practice guides (covered in Part I of this chapter), and CLE materials (discussed in Part

V of this chapter). A "formbook" may provide actual forms or suggested language that you can use in crafting your document. Examples of Oregon formbooks include *Criminal Law Formbook* and *Administering Oregon Estates*. Federal forms are available in numerous titles, including *West's Federal Forms* and *American Jurisprudence Legal Forms 2d*. Search the library catalog by subject for topical formbooks.

The Oregon courts provide a number of litigation-related forms on their website, courts.oregon.gov, in the "Forms Center" under the Forms/Rules/Fees tab. The site has a variety of forms related to family law, stalking orders, name change, and other subjects. The websites of circuit courts in Oregon may contain more forms. In addition, the Oregon State Bar website at www.osbar.org provides a "Forms Library" for forms related to admission to practice law.

Some forms are available on Lexis and Westlaw. For example, Westlaw has a link to "Oregon Form Finder" under the "State Materials" tab and "Oregon" link. Another commercial source for forms is Gale's Legal Forms Library. Many types of forms are included, ranging from business transactions to wills. Contents include forms required by a state entity (i.e., "official forms"), forms drawn from public records, forms drafted by firms for use in a particular state, and generic forms. Check your library to see whether it has a Gale subscription for Oregon forms. If not, you might also try the general form service provided by Gale for a modest fee: U.S. Legal Forms, at http://www.uslegalforms.com/v2/index.html. An additional commercial source is Stevens-Ness Law Publishing, at http://www.stevensness.com/formsdept_main.htm. Under "Legal Forms," click on "Shop for Forms Online," type *Oregon* in the search box, and browse by category to see what is available and the cost.

Take care in using any form. Forms are designed for general audiences, not your particular client or situation. Before using a form, ensure that you understand every word in the form and modify it to suit your needs. Do not simply fill in the blanks and assume that the form correctly represents your client's position or your situation. Unless a particular form is prescribed by statute or by a court, revise the wording to avoid unnecessary legalese.

VII. Restatements and Principles

A restatement is an organized and detailed summary of the common law in a specific legal area. Familiar titles include *Restatement of the Law of Contracts* and *Restatement of the Law of Torts*. Restatements are the results of collaborative efforts by committees of scholars, practitioners, and judges organized by the ALI. These committees, led by a scholar called the *reporter*, draft text that explains the common law in rule format (i.e., they are written with outline headings similar to statutes, rather than in the narrative form of cases). The committees circulate the drafts for review and revision. The restatement that is published by ALI includes not only the text of the rules that embody the common law but also commentary, illustrations, and notes from the reporter.

Restatements were originally intended simply to restate the law as it existed, in an effort to build national consistency in key common law areas. Over time, restatements grew more aggressive in stating what the authors thought the law should be. Presently, ALI produces two series: "Restatements of the Law" state the law as it exists or as it could be interpreted by courts, while "Principles of Law" express the law as the committee thinks it should exist.[5]

A portion of a restatement or principle becomes primary authority for a jurisdiction only if it is adopted by a court in a particular case. After a court has adopted a portion of a restatement or principle, the committee's commentary and illustrations, as well as any notes provided by the reporter, may be valuable tools in interpreting the adopted language. Cases in other jurisdictions that have adopted that language would be persuasive authority.

Restatements and principles are available on Lexis and Westlaw. Print versions can be purchased from the ALI website and are available in some libraries.

VIII. Uniform Laws and Model Codes

Uniform laws and model codes are written by organizations that hope to harmonize the statutory laws of the fifty states. The most active of these organizations is the Uniform Law Commission (ULC), also known as the National Conference of Commissioners on Uniform State Laws (NCCUSL). Much of the work of writing uniform laws and model codes is done by experts who are law professors, judges, legislators, or attorneys.

Familiar examples of these secondary sources include the *Uniform Commercial Code* (UCC) and the *Model Penal Code*. The authors draft statutory language, solicit comments, and then finalize the language. The published uniform law or model code includes both the proposed statutory language and authors' explanatory notes.

---

5. *See* the ALI website for more details: www.ali.org/index.cfm?fuseaction=projects. main.

Generally, you would research a uniform law or model code only after one of its provisions had been enacted by your jurisdiction's legislature. At that point, the provision becomes primary authority and the explanatory notes are very persuasive secondary authority. Reviewing that commentary could help you understand a statute in your jurisdiction that was based on the uniform or model language. For example, every state has adopted a version of the UCC. In researching Oregon's commercial code, you could gain insights from commentary on the UCC that discussed the provisions adopted by Oregon. Additionally, the cases of other states that also adopted the same UCC provisions could be highly persuasive in interpreting Oregon's statute.

Uniform laws and model codes, along with official notes and explanations, are published by their authors. Additionally, commercial versions add commentary and often footnotes with case support. West publishes *Uniform Laws Annotated*, which offers indexing, text, and research annotations to uniform laws prepared under the direction of the ULC/NCCUSL; it is available on Westlaw. The Lexis source is called "Uniform Law Commission Model Acts."

IX. Jury Instructions and Verdicts

At the close of a trial, the judge instructs the jury before it begins to deliberate. These instructions outline the law; in other words, they tell a lawyer preparing for trial what she has to prove in order to prevail. By examining the instructions in advance of trial, an attorney may better be able to present evidence to the jury. Even if a case ends before trial, knowing the instructions a jury would receive may produce more effective research. The Oregon State Bar has committees on uniform jury instructions for both civil and criminal matters. Their publications are entitled *Uniform Civil Jury Instructions* and *Uniform Criminal Jury Instructions*, which are published in loose-leaf binders. They are available on Lexis; go to "Browse" and "Sources" and search for the title.

A very useful piece of information for the lawyer preparing for trial — or hoping to settle a case — is the dollar amount of verdicts or settlements in similar cases in the past. A subscription service called "Jury Verdicts Northwest" provides this information in print and online. It is available on Lexis and Westlaw. On Lexis, you can find additional databases with jury verdict information by going to "Browse" and "Sources," then "Oregon," and then using the filters on the left side of the screen to find the category "Jury Verdicts and Settlements." On Westlaw, begin under "Content types," click on "Jury Verdicts and Settlements," and then select "Oregon." There is one database that combines two services.

X. Ethical Rules

The conduct of lawyers in Oregon is regulated by the Oregon Rules of Professional Conduct, which became effective in 2005. The rules are based on the ABA's Model Rules and cover issues such as the client-lawyer relationship; the lawyer's role as counselor and advocate; limits on a lawyer's transactions with persons who are not clients; and the responsibilities within a law firm of supervising attorneys, junior attorneys, and legal assistants.

These rules are available in a number of places:

- on the Oregon State Bar's website at www.osbar.org (under the tab "For Lawyers," look under "OSB Resources" for the link to "Rules Regulations and Policies")
- on Lexis (in "Oregon Local, State & Federal Court Rules")
- on Westlaw (in the database with statutes and court rules)
- in the West publication *Oregon Rules of Court: State*.

Opinions applying the rules to Oregon attorneys are published in *Oregon Formal Ethics Opinions* and can be searched on the Oregon State Bar's website at http://www.osbar.org/ethics/ethicsops.html.

XI. Current Awareness Aids

Some of the resources discussed earlier in this chapter—notably law journal articles on SSRN and CLE materials—can help attorneys stay current in their particular practice areas. A few other resources deserve note.

A. Bloomberg BNA

Bloomberg BNA offers a wide array of products in specific practice areas that include news; analysis of recent laws; and notices of upcoming cases, hearings, and other events. Topic areas range from antitrust and criminal law to intellectual property and health care. Figure 2-4 shows an example of the Daily Tax Report.

Figure 2-4. Daily Tax Report

Reproduced with permission from Daily Tax Report, Copyright 2018 by The Bureau of National Affairs, Inc. (800-372-1033), http://www.bna.com.

B. Blogs

Blogs can also be very useful in keeping current. Blogs will soon exist for every legal area imaginable. Law blogs are typically called "blawgs," and some are well respected for tracking developments in case law, statutes, and regulatory areas. These are maintained by attorneys or law professors with extensive experience in a particular practice area.

To select a useful law blog, you might begin with the *ABA Journal*'s top 100 blawg list, available at http://www.abajournal.com/blawg100. The list separates the blogs into practice areas, making it easy to find one relevant to your work. Another useful directory of law blogs is BlawgSearch, at http://blawgsearch.justia.com, which organizes thousands of law-related blogs into 75 topical areas.

C. Twitter

Twitter has developed to be a popular platform for breaking news. The *ABA Journal* has a list of the best law Twitter accounts, ranging from the ABA to attorneys who tweet on various legal topics. With Twitter, and any other social media platform, you should be cautious of using the information unless you verify its accuracy.

XII. Using Secondary Sources in Research

As the discussions above suggest, different research projects will benefit from different secondary sources. For a broad overview of an area of law, especially at the beginning of a project, an encyclopedia may be best. For in-depth analysis on a narrow topic, a law review article is more likely to be helpful. On cutting-edge issues, CLE material, SSRN articles, Bloomberg BNA law reports, and blogs will cover new areas of law quickly. In litigation, court-approved forms and uniform jury instructions will be indispensable.

Consider your own background in the subject matter and the goals of your research, and select from these sources accordingly. A source that was not helpful in your last research project may be perfect for the current project. How many secondary sources you use depends on the success of your early searches and the time available to you. It would almost never be prudent to check every source discussed in this chapter.

Despite the value of secondary sources, rarely will you cite a secondary source in writing a memorandum or brief. Some sources, such as indexes for finding periodicals, are not "authority" at all. Rather, they are authority-finding tools and should never be cited. Encyclopedias, ALR annotations, and CLE material should be cited only as a last resort. Even sources that carry some authority, including law review articles and treatises, should be cited infrequently. By citing secondary sources, you are admitting to your reader that you could not find any primary authority supporting your arguments, thereby weakening those arguments substantially.

Three exceptions exist. First, sometimes you need to summarize the development of the law. If no case has provided a summary, citing a treatise or law review article that traces that development could be helpful to your reader. Next, citation to secondary authority is appropriate when there is no law on point for an argument you are making. This is likely to occur with new issues. It may also occur when you are arguing to expand or change the law. In these situations, your only support might come from a law review article. Finally, secondary authority may provide additional support for a point already cited to primary authority. For example, you can bolster an argument supported by a case, especially if it is from another jurisdiction, by also citing an article or treatise by a respected expert on the topic.

Whether or not you cite a secondary source in a document, you must decide the weight to give secondary authority in developing your own analysis. Consider the following criteria:

- *Who is the author?* The views of a respected scholar, an acknowledged expert, or a judge carry more weight than a student author or an anonymous editor.
- *When was the material published?* Especially for cutting-edge issues, a more recent article is likely to be more helpful. Even with more traditional issues, be sure that the material analyzes the current state of the law.
- *Where was the material published?* Treatises from leading publishers will always be more authoritative than an opinion expressed on a blog. For law review articles, those published in established law journals are generally granted the most respect. A school's prestige and the length of the journal's existence can influence how well established a journal is. Thus, a journal that has been published for a century at a top law school may carry more respect than a new journal at an unaccredited school. A publication specific to your jurisdiction or dedicated to a particular topic, however, could be more helpful than a publication from another state or one with a general focus.
- *What depth is provided?* The more focused and thorough the analysis, the more useful the material will be.
- *How relevant is it to your argument?* If the author is arguing your exact point, the material will be more persuasive than if the author's arguments are only tangential to yours.
- *Has this secondary source been cited previously by courts?* If a court has found a source persuasive in the past, it is likely to find it persuasive again. Remember that the text of a secondary source may become primary authority if it is adopted by a court or legislature.

Chapter 3

The Constitution

"We the people of the State of Oregon to the end that Justice be established, order maintained, and liberty perpetuated, do ordain this Constitution."[1]

The Oregon Constitution was written and approved by the people of the Oregon Territory in 1857. It became effective on February 14, 1859, when Oregon was admitted to the Union.[2]

The provisions of the Oregon Constitution parallel many of the most familiar provisions of the United States Constitution. Article I of Oregon's constitution ensures religious freedom, the right to a jury trial, and freedom from unreasonable search and seizure. Articles IV through VII provide for the legislative, executive, administrative, and judicial departments of the state government.

Like many state constitutions, the Oregon Constitution also covers some issues often thought of as being more statutory in nature. For example, in addition to the provisions mentioned above, Article I gives the state the power to permit the sale of liquor by the glass. Table 3-1 lists the articles of Oregon's constitution. Because of the breadth of issues covered by the Oregon Constitution, you should check to see whether a constitutional provision affects your research problem even when that possibility may seem unlikely.

I. Researching the Oregon Constitution

The Oregon Constitution is available on the Oregon Legislature's website,[3] on commercial sites, and in print. Each of these sources is discussed in this

---

1. *Preamble to the Oregon Constitution.*
2. For a fascinating introduction to these events, see David Schuman, *The Creation of the Oregon Constitution,* 74 Or L Rev 611, 640 (1995).
3. The address is www.oregonlegislature.gov/bills_laws/Pages/OrConst.aspx.

Table 3-1. Articles of the Constitution of Oregon

Article I	Bill of Rights
Article II	Suffrage and Elections
Article III	Distribution of Powers
Article IV	Legislative Department
Article V	Executive Department
Article VI	Administrative Department
Article VII	(Amended) Judicial Department
Article VII	(Original) The Judicial Department
Article VIII	Education and School Lands
Article IX	Finance
Article X	The Militia
Article XI	Corporations and Internal Improvements
Article XI-A	Farm and Home Loans to Veterans
Article XI-D	State Power Development
Article XI-E	State Reforestation
Article XI-F(1)	Higher Education Building Projects
Article XI-F(2)	Veterans' Bonus
Article XI-G	Higher Education Institutions and Activities; Community Colleges
Article XI-H	Pollution Control
Article XI-I(1)	Water Development Projects
Article XI-I(2)	Multifamily Housing for Elderly and Disabled
Article XI-J	Small Scale Local Energy Loans
Article XI-K	Guarantee of Bonded Indebtedness of Educational Districts
Article XI-L	Oregon Health and Science University
Article XI-M	Seismic Rehabilitation of Public Education Buildings
Article XI-N	Seismic Rehabilitation of Emergency Services Buildings
Article XI-O	Pension Liabilities
Article XII	State Printing
Article XIV	Seat of Government
Article XV	Miscellaneous
Article XVI	Boundaries
Article XVII	Amendments and Revisions
Article XVIII	Schedule

Note: Article XIII has been repealed. It set 1857 salaries for key government officials (e.g., the Governor earned $1500 annually).

part. The constitution is cited by article and section, for example, Or Const, Art IV, § 9.[4]

A. Free Online Sources for the Oregon Constitution

The full text of the constitution is available on the state legislature's website at www.oregonlegislature.gov. Click on "Bills and Laws" and then "Oregon Constitution" to review the text. To search for a particular term, use the ORS General Index, which includes references not only to statutes but also to constitutional provisions.

To find references to cases and other documents discussing the constitution, click on "Annotations," and scroll down to the box labeled "Annotations to the Oregon Constitution."[5] Under the caption for the constitutional article and section that you are researching, you will find the annotations. If there are many annotations for that article and section, you may also find a short outline of annotations that appears just before the annotations themselves. Otherwise, all the annotations for that section will be listed together. Each annotation contains a brief summary of the source referenced and its citation, which will enable you to locate the full source. You cannot rely on the short summary; reading the text of the source itself will allow you to analyze its relevance to your research.

Additionally, the *Oregon Blue Book* provides both a web version and a PDF version of the constitution.[6] The *Oregon Blue Book* is published in odd-numbered years by the Secretary of State's archives division. Like "Blue Books" in other states, it provides a wealth of factual information about the state's government.

---

4. As explained in Appendix B of this book, Oregon's appellate courts use a slightly different citation format than the national citation manuals. The citation in the text above follows the Oregon format, omitting periods and capitalizing the abbreviation for "article." Under the *Bluebook* or the *ALWD Guide*, the citation would appear as Or. Const., art. IV, § 9.

5. The "Notes of Decisions" include both judicial opinions and Attorney General opinions, which are explained in this book in Chapters 7 and 6 respectively. The ORS annotations also reference the state's law reviews: OLR is *Oregon Law Review*, WLR is *Willamette Law Review*, and EL is *Environmental Law* (published by Lewis & Clark Law School). Law review articles are covered in Chapter 2, Part III.

6. The online version is available from www.bluebook.state.or.us/state. Do not confuse the *Oregon Blue Book* with the citation manual entitled *The Bluebook: A Uniform System of Citation*.

B. The Oregon Constitution on Lexis and Westlaw

Often online services include constitutions in databases containing statutes, perhaps because historically constitutions were published in books along with statutes. Even when a separate database for the constitution exists, remembering this historical connection might help you locate the correct link.

To find the Oregon Constitution on Lexis, go to "Browse" and "Sources" and use the box provided to search for that term. You can begin research either in the database "LexisNexis Oregon Annotated Constitution" or in the constitution's table of contents. In the table of contents, you have several alternatives, including (a) searching the table of contents itself using the bar provided and (b) expanding to a list of articles and scrolling through to find sections that seem relevant. Another approach for beginning your search is to enter a search in the universal search bar, then limit your search to "Statutes and Legislation" and "Oregon."

An easy way to access the Oregon Constitution on Westlaw is to type that term into the universal search bar. Alternatively, browsing content tabs on Westlaw, you can find the Oregon Constitution by clicking on "State Materials," then "Oregon," and finally "Oregon Statutes & Courts Rules." The link for the constitution appears after the numbered titles of the statutes. Either approach will lead to a screen listing the articles of the constitution. From there, you can use the universal search bar to construct a search. You can limit the search to particular articles or sections using the boxes next to the title of each. Effective searches can be applied anywhere, including searching within a constitution. Keep in mind that a narrow search may not produce any results when searching within a constitution, so try to create broad searches around your issue. Another option is to scan the articles and sections listed, and open those that seem relevant so that you can browse their content. In a database with annotations, your research terms might appear just in the constitution, just in annotations, or in both. See Figure 3-1 for annotations related to Oregon's search and seizure provision, in Article 1, Section 9. The text of that provision is in Table 3-2, later in this chapter.

C. The Constitution in *Oregon Revised Statutes*

The Oregon Constitution is published in full every two years in *Oregon Revised Statutes* (ORS). Immediately following the Oregon Constitution, ORS provides an index specifically for the constitution. Currently, the constitution and its index are located in volume 17. ORS also contains a general index that provides references to the state constitution as well as to Oregon statutes.

Figure 3-1. Annotations to Oregon Constitutional Provision

§ 9. Unreasonable search or seizure
West's Oregon Revised Statutes Annotated Constitution of Oregon *(Approx. 2 pages)*

Notes of Decisions (4,058)

1.In general

The Fourth Amendment indicates with some precision the places and things encompassed by its protections: persons, houses, papers, and effects. Florida v. Jardines (2013) 133 S.Ct. 1409, 569 U.S. 1, 185 L.Ed.2d 495. Searches and Seizures 25.1

The unreasonable search and seizure provision of the Oregon Constitution imposes limits on searches and seizures in order to prevent arbitrary and oppressive interference by law enforcement officials with the privacy and personal security of individuals. State v. Keller (2017) 396 P.3d 917, 361 Or. 566. Searches and Seizures 12

State constitution does not protect against every search or seizure by the government, but only against those that are arbitrary, oppressive, or otherwise unreasonable. State v. Scott (2017) 388 P.3d 1148, 283 Or.App. 566. Sentencing And Punishment 1995

Source: Westlaw. Reprinted with permission of Thomson Reuters.

References to cases, Attorney General opinions, and law review articles that have discussed the state constitution are listed in the last volume of ORS, entitled "Annotations." The annotations for constitutional provisions are included near the end of the volume, after annotations for Oregon statutes. There is no table of contents for this volume; simply skim through it until you see headings that refer to article and section numbers.

The annotations volume of ORS is published annually and includes annotations to authority since 1971. To find annotations to earlier authority, use the Compiled Annotations published as part of the 1971 edition of ORS. The annotations listed in these sources do not represent every authority that may be relevant to your research. Another statutory compilation called *West's Oregon Revised Statutes Annotated* (WORSA), described next, also contains the state constitution and typically provides more annotations than ORS does.

D. The Constitution in *West's Oregon Revised Statutes Annotated* (WORSA)

The Oregon Constitution is published in the print series *West's Oregon Revised Statutes Annotated* (WORSA). The constitution is included with annotations in the last two volumes of the series, currently volumes 46 and 47. An index for just the constitution is included in volume 47. A general index for WORSA, published in soft-cover volumes, also includes references to constitutional provisions.

The research process is generally the same for ORS and WORSA. Research terms in an index will lead to relevant provisions of the constitution. Unlike

ORS, however, the West series includes annotations immediately following the text of each article rather than in a separate annotations volume. Typically, WORSA contains more types of annotations and more case annotations than ORS does. In addition to references to cases, Attorney General opinions, and law review articles, WORSA provides cross references to other Oregon statutes and administrative regulations as well as to other resources published by West. Another important difference is that WORSA is kept current through pocket parts, additional pages that are inserted into the back cover of each volume.

II. Interpreting the Oregon Constitution

How a provision of the Oregon Constitution is interpreted by Oregon courts depends on whether the provision was part of the original constitution in 1859 or was added later by referral to the voters from the legislature or through the initiative process.

A. The *Priest* Framework

The Oregon Supreme Court has provided a framework for interpreting original provisions of the state's constitution. "There are three levels on which that constitutional provision must be addressed: Its specific wording, the case law surrounding it, and the historical circumstances that led to its creation."[7]

1. Text and Case Law

Begin by reading the words of the constitutional provision carefully. If it is a lengthy provision, outlining it may help you understand it. Then read cases that address that provision. Reading the cases cited in those cases may provide important context.

Do not assume that cases interpreting the federal constitution also interpret Oregon's constitution. State constitutions can grant citizens *more* protection than is provided by the federal constitution, and Oregon's constitution does so. Even when the text of the Oregon Constitution is almost identical to the text of the United States Constitution, the Oregon Supreme Court may have interpreted it differently. For example, Article I, Section 9 of the Oregon Constitution contains almost the same text as the Fourth Amendment to the United States Constitution (see Table 3-2), but Oregon's Supreme Court has interpreted

---

7. *Priest v. Pearce*, 314 Or 411, 415–16 (1992).

Table 3-2. Comparison of Constitutional Wording Regarding Unreasonable Search and Seizure

---

Oregon Constitution
Article I, Section 9

No law shall violate the right of the people to be secure in their persons, houses, papers, and effects, against unreasonable search, or seizure; and no warrant shall issue but upon probable cause, supported by oath, or affirmation, and particularly describing the place to be searched, and the person or thing to be seized.

United States Constitution
Fourth Amendment

The right of the people to be secure in their persons, houses, papers, and effects, against unreasonable searches and seizures, shall not be violated, and no Warrants shall issue, but upon probable cause, supported by Oath or affirmation, and particularly describing the place to be searched, and the persons or things to be seized.

---

the state constitution to provide more protection in this area than the federal constitution does.[8]

2. Historical Circumstances

For frugality reasons, the drafters of the Oregon Constitution decided against retaining an official reporter despite the significance of this historical event.[9] The *Journal of the Constitutional Convention* contains only a record of the official actions of the delegates, so it is of limited value. In 1926, long after the Oregon Constitution was adopted, Charles H. Carey collected the various newspaper accounts from the convention and combined them with entries from the *Journal*. The resulting book, *The Oregon Constitution and Proceedings and Debates of the Constitutional Convention of 1857*,[10] is an invaluable resource for understanding the historical circumstances surrounding Oregon's consti-

---

8. *E.g., State v. Caraher*, 293 Or 741, 750–51 (1982); *State v. Tanner*, 304 Or 312, 315 (1987).

9. David Schuman, *The Creation of the Oregon Constitution*, 74 Or L Rev 611, 619 (1995).

10. *The Oregon Constitution and Proceedings and Debates of the Constitutional Convention of 1857* (Charles H. Carey ed., State Printing Dept. 1926).

tution and is cited frequently by courts.[11] Both the *Journal* and the Carey book, as well as other historical materials, are available on a microfiche set called *State Constitutional Conventions*, published by Congressional Information Service.

Through the twentieth century, *The Oregon Constitution and Proceedings* compilation was the primary source of information regarding the drafting of the state's constitution. However, a three-part series of articles by Professor Claudia Burton entitled *A Legislative History of the Oregon Constitution of 1857* now provides indispensable insights into the drafters' intent.[12] In a box of materials discovered at the Oregon Historical Society, Professor Burton found a nearly intact set of documents for each article of the Oregon Constitution. Her articles compile and comment on these documents. Reviewing the information in her articles is critical to understanding the historical background of the state constitution.[13]

In examining the historical circumstances of Oregon's constitution, Oregon courts look to other material as well. The Magna Carta and English legal commentators are sometimes cited. Because the drafters modeled the Oregon Constitution after the Indiana Constitution's Bill of Rights, that document has been persuasive. A chart by W.C. Palmer entitled *The Sources of the Oregon Constitution* compares sections of Oregon's constitution to the constitutions of Indiana and other states.[14] A survey of cases found that the Oregon Supreme Court referred in its opinions more often to Indiana's constitution than to any other state's, with neighboring California as a close second.[15]

---

11. Caution should be used when referencing the articles in this book, however, since major newspaper editors were also delegates at the convention. Schuman, *supra* n. 9, at 622.

12. Claudia Burton & Andrew Grade, *A Legislative History of the Oregon Constitution of 1857 — Part I (Articles I & II)*, 37 Willamette L Rev 469 (2001); Claudia Burton, *A Legislative History of the Oregon Constitution of 1857 — Part II (Frame of Government: Articles III–VII)*, 39 Willamette L Rev 245 (2003); Claudia Burton, *A Legislative History of the Oregon Constitution of 1857 — Part III (Mostly Miscellaneous: Articles VIII–XVIII)*, 40 Willamette L Rev 225 (2004).

13. As constitutional scholar and former judge David Schuman observed, "[A]ny attorney who writes a memorandum or brief ... [on] the Oregon Constitution without first having consulted Professor Burton's article[s] is risking malpractice." David Schuman, Lecture, *Back to the Future, Forward to the Past: The Oregon Supreme Court's New History Fetish* (Univ. Or. Sch. Law, Oct. 19, 2001) (CLE handout on file with author).

14. 5 Or L Rev 200 (1925–1926).

15. Patrick Baude, *Interstate Dialogue in State Constitutional Law*, 28 Rutgers LJ 835, 838, 859 (1997).

B. Interpreting Other Constitutional Provisions and Amendments

The Oregon Supreme Court uses a different methodology for interpreting provisions and amendments of the constitution that were adopted after 1859. The Oregon Constitution can be amended in two ways. In the traditional method, the legislature passes an amendment that is voted on by the voters of the state.[16] The second method is the initiative process.[17]

The initiative process was adopted in 1902 in response to legislative corruption.[18] The initiative process allows voters to propose amendments to the state constitution by placing measures on the election ballot. Voters begin the process by submitting a petition with at least a certain number of signatures of qualified voters; this number is equal to eight percent of the votes cast for Governor in the preceding election. The initiative petition must clear other procedural hurdles before being presented to the voters in the next election.[19]

In interpreting amendments to the Oregon Constitution, the Court's goal is to determine the intent of the voters. "The best evidence of the voters' intent is the text of the provision itself. The context of the language of the ballot measure may also be considered; however, if the intent is clear based on the text and context of the constitutional provision, the court does not look further."[20] If the voters' intent is not clear from the text and context of the provision, the court examines the history of the provision.[21] This history includes "the ballot title and arguments for and against the measure included in the voters' pamphlet, and contemporaneous news reports and editorial com-

---

16. Or Const, Art XVII.

17. Or Const, Art IV, § 1; *see also State Initiative and Referendum Manual,* Or. Sec. of St. (available at sos.oregon.gov/elections under "Election Laws, Rules and Publications" and "Manuals and Tutorials").

18. *See* David Schuman, *The Origin of State Constitutional Direct Democracy: William Simon U'Ren and "The Oregon System,"* 67 Temp L Rev 947, 948–49 (1994).

19. A useful resource in understanding these processes is the *State Initiative and Referendum Manual,* which is provided by the Oregon Secretary of State. The address is sos.oregon.gov/elections/Documents/stateIR.pdf. The manual provides descriptions of the overall process as well as step-by-step instructions and examples of required forms.

20. *Roseburg Sch. Dist. v. City of Roseburg,* 316 Or 374, 378 (1993); *see also Stranahan v. Fred Meyer, Inc.,* 331 Or 38, 58 n. 13 (2000) (stating the Supreme Court's intention to apply this methodology to "constitutional provisions and amendments adopted by legislative referral").

21. *Ecumenical Ministries of Oregon v. Oregon St. Lottery,* 318 Or 551, 559 (1994).

ment on the measure."[22] Voters' pamphlets are available from the State Library website.[23]

Additionally, the *Oregon Blue Book* contains a comprehensive listing of initiatives and referenda providing election dates, measure numbers, ballot titles, and the resulting tally of "Yes" and "No" votes. An electronic version of the *Oregon Blue Book* is available online[24] and is linked to the Secretary of State's website.

Although the initiative process remains an integral part of Oregon law, criticism of problems inherent with this system exists. One criticism is that voters vote to decrease taxes and increase spending at the same time.[25] Additionally, the ease by which the state constitution may be amended raises concerns that the Oregon Constitution will become a "museum of unrelated laws enshrining the temporary political preoccupations of ... [the] times."[26] However, the initiative system also enables Oregon voters themselves to improve the process, as happened when they voted to prohibit payment based on the number of signatures obtained on initiative petitions.[27]

---

22. *Id.* at 559 n. 8.

23. The address is library.state.or.us/databases/subjects/Voters_Pamphlet.php.

24. A summary of elections history is available at www.bluebook.state.or.us/state/elections/elections06.htm.

25. Hans A. Linde, *On Reconstituting "Republican Government,"* 19 Okla City U L Rev 193, 204 (1994).

26. David B. Frohnmayer & Hans A. Linde, *Appendix: Initiating "Laws" in the Form of "Constitutional Amendments": An Amicus Curiae Brief,* 34 Willamette L Rev 749, 773 (1998). As Justice Gillette stated, "Constitutional amendments should be made of sterner stuff." Michael Gillette, *The Legislative Function: Initiative and Referendum,* 67 Or L Rev 55, 62 (1988).

27. *See* November 5, 2002 Election Date, Measure 26: Amends Constitution: Prohibits Payment, Receipt of Payment Based on the Number of Initiative, Referendum Petition Signatures Obtained (available at www.bluebook.state.or.us/state/elections/elections22a.htm).

Chapter 4

Oregon Statutes

Statutes affect a multitude of legal issues. Often, a statute defines a client's rights or responsibilities. A statute may set penalties for failure to comply with the statutory mandate. Some statutes address new issues that are not dealt with at common law; for example, the use of electronic signatures was a new statutory area when that technology first became available. Other statutes may codify or alter the common law, for example, making embezzlement a felony. Still other statutes are driven by policy concerns. For instance, in Oregon, the host of a party who serves alcohol to someone visibly drunk may be liable for off-premise damages caused by that person. Even when no statute affects the substance of a claim, a statute of limitations may prescribe the period during which the claim may be brought.

This chapter explains the fundamentals of statutory research.[1] It covers the official *Oregon Revised Statutes* and the state legislature's website, West's unofficial publication of Oregon statutes in print and online, and Oregon statutes on Lexis. After explaining how to conduct research to identify relevant statutes, this chapter discusses the Oregon courts' methodology for interpreting statutes. This chapter concludes with an introduction to court rules, which are often grouped with statutes in research sources.

I. Oregon Statutory Research

Oregon statutes originate as bills in the legislature. When a bill is enacted, it becomes a session law. Then session laws are *codified* as statutes, meaning

---

1. This chapter explains how to research Oregon state statutes, but not law enacted by county or city governments that might be relevant for an issue arising in Oregon. County and city codes are increasingly available online. The *Oregon Blue Book* website at www.bluebook.state.or.us connects to county and city information under the "Local" link. Some county and city codes are also available on Lexis and Westlaw.

Figure 4-1. Publication of a Statute

that they are grouped according to subject matter. Figure 4-1 illustrates this process for a recent statute allowing property owners to sue anyone flying drones over that property.[2]

The current codification of Oregon statutes is called Oregon Revised Statutes (ORS). ORS is divided into sixty-two *titles*, each on a particular subject. Each title is subdivided into *chapters* that address specific topics within each subject area. Each new statute that is enacted will be added to a title and chapter containing other statutes on the same or similar subject. The statute will be assigned a *section number* that places it sequentially within a chapter. For example, title 16 of ORS includes statutes on Crimes and Punishments. Under chapter 164, Offenses Against Property, are statutes for theft, burglary, robbery, and similar crimes. One section, ORS 164.225, addresses first-degree burglary. Note that the title number is not part of the citation; simply use the abbreviation ORS and the statute's chapter and section number, separated by a period.[3]

Many types of resources are available for researching statutes: print codes, free government websites, and commercial databases. The details of using each of these methods are different, but the fundamental steps of the research process are similar, as shown in Table 4-1.

A. Researching *Oregon Revised Statutes*

The official source for Oregon statutory law is also called *Oregon Revised Statutes* (ORS). Thus, "ORS" refers both to the official codification of Oregon statutes and to the official set of books containing those statutes. The statutes and research aids discussed below are available both in print and on the legislature's website (though only the print version is official). Some attorneys

---

2. Chapter 5 begins with a more detailed overview of the legislative process through which statutes are enacted; some readers might want to review that portion of Chapter 5 now for background.

3. National citation systems use the abbreviation "Or. Rev. Stat." rather than ORS. Citation is covered in Appendix B of this book.

Table 4-1. Overview of Statutory Research Process

---

1. Find the statute

    Look up the statute by citation, if available

    Use an index or Popular Name Table

    Browse a table of contents

    Conduct an online search

2. Read the statute

    Read the text thoroughly

    Look at surrounding sections

    Outline the statute, if it is long or complex

3. Use the statute to find other information

    Look at annotations, including Notes of Decisions

    Use a citator such as KeyCite or Shepard's

    Look at source notes for historical information

4. Apply and interpret the statute

    Examine the text and context of the statute

    Look at legislative history

    Use rules of statutory construction

---

find that beginning to research statutes in print is more efficient than beginning online. Even if you plan to conduct your research online, the following explanation of the print version provides a helpful foundation for locating and understanding Oregon statutes and for finding cases related to those statutes.

1. *Oregon Revised Statutes* in Print

ORS is published in print by the State of Oregon Legislative Counsel Committee in odd-numbered years (e.g., 2015, 2017). A complete list of all titles and chapters in ORS is included at the beginning of volume 1. See Table 4-2 for an example of chapters under one title.

a. Finding Statutes

If you have a statute number, review the spines of ORS volumes to find the one that contains the chapter for that statute; then look through that volume numerically to find the statute. Statute numbers are included on the top, outside corner of each page.

Table 4-2. Chapters in Title 16, Crimes and Punishments

161.	General Provisions
162.	Offenses Against the State and Public Justice
163.	Offenses Against Persons
164.	Offenses Against Property
165.	Offenses Involving Fraud or Deception
166.	Offenses Against Public Order; Firearms and Other Weapons; Racketeering
167.	Offenses Against Public Health, Decency and Animals
169.	Local and Regional Correctional Facilities; Prisoners; Juvenile Facilities

Source: *Oregon Revised Statutes*, volume 4, page 441 (2017).

If you know only the client's facts and the legal issue, begin by searching for your research terms in the two index volumes that are shelved at the end of ORS. As you find the terms in the index volumes, write down any statutory references given. Do not stop reviewing the index after finding just one statute's reference; several statutes may address your issue. Note that "*et seq.*" refers to the statute listed and the sections that follow it. Sometimes a term in the index will be followed by a cross reference to another index term. Referring to that term may lead you to relevant statutes.

b. Understanding Statutes

As you find each statute in the ORS volumes, be sure to read the statutory language very carefully. Too many researchers fail to take the time necessary to read the language of the statute and consider all its implications before deciding whether it is relevant to the research problem. And because few statutes are so clear that they can be understood on one reading, careful research often requires you to read a statute several times to understand its meaning and relevance.

To understand a single statute you may have to read other, related statutes. One statute may contain general provisions while another contains definitions. Yet another statute may contain exceptions to the general rule. In the example in Table 4-3, the statute ORS 164.215 refers to another statute, ORS 164.255, on criminal trespass in the first degree. Additionally, under the definitions section of ORS 164.205, the term "building" includes not only the common meaning of building but also a booth, vehicle, boat, and aircraft.

Table 4-3. Example Oregon Statute

164.215 Burglary in the second degree.

(1) Except as otherwise provided in ORS 164.255, a person commits the crime of burglary in the second degree if the person enters or remains unlawfully in a building with intent to commit a crime therein.

(2) Burglary in the second degree is a Class C felony.

Source: *Oregon Revised Statutes*, volume 4, page 577 (2017).

To guarantee that you understand the statute, break it into elements. Using bullet points or an outline format is helpful for identifying key ideas. Connecting words and punctuation provide guidance for the relationships between the different requirements of the statute. Small words like "and" and "or" can drastically change the meaning of the statute. With "and" all statutory requirements must be present for the statute to apply, while with "or" only one part is needed. Note, too, the difference between "shall," which requires action, and "may," which is permissive. In Table 4-4, ORS 164.215 is broken into its elements.

c. Finding Cases that Interpret or Apply Statutes

It is rare to locate a relevant statute and apply it immediately to a client's facts without having first to research case law. Legislatures write statutes generally to apply to a wide array of circumstances. To be able to predict how a court may apply a statute to a client's specific facts, you must know how the courts have interpreted the statute and applied it in the past.

Table 4-4. Requirements for Second-Degree Burglary

- a person
  - enters or
  - remains unlawfully
- in a building
- with intent to commit a crime therein.

The last volume of ORS is entitled "Annotations"; it contains references to (1) cases, (2) opinions of the Oregon Attorney General, and (3) articles from the law reviews of Oregon's three law schools that deal with Oregon statutes. Indexed under each statutory number are lists of annotations, divided into three categories: *Notes of Decisions, Atty. Gen. Opinions,* and *Law Review Citations.* The Annotations volume is published yearly and is cumulative from 1971. Annotations to earlier authority can be located in the Compiled Annotations volume of the 1971 edition of ORS.

Listed under *Notes of Decisions* are short summaries of cases that have interpreted and applied that statute. Oregon cases are listed first, followed by federal cases. Each summary concludes with the name of the case, followed by a citation. The citation indicates which court decided the case and where it can be found. You must record the citation information accurately to enable you to find the cases in the reporters or online. In most instances, there is no need to record at this initial stage of research whether the Oregon Supreme Court denied a petition for review, although that information is given in the Annotations volume.

The Annotations volume also includes references to Attorney General opinions and law review articles. Though the list of entries in the annotations for each statute is not necessarily complete or current, it does provide a helpful starting point for research. Conducting additional research as explained below will likely lead to additional authority that is relevant to the statute.

d. Other Helpful Features of ORS

To make ORS more helpful to researchers, the following information is also included.

After the text of some statutes, ORS includes *source notes* in brackets. In general, these notes state when the statute was enacted, amended, or repealed. (The source notes are also called *history notes* or *credits*.) When working for a new supervisor, you may want to point out that a separate statute has been repealed or that a related statute exists but is not on point. In other situations, simply omit any reference to a statute that is no longer in force or does not apply to your facts. For statutes that have been renumbered, ORS has a placeholder for the old number with a cross reference to the new number.[4] A note may also indicate when the statute became effective.

---

4. In 2015, for example, a statute regarding immunity of a witness from arrest or service of process was moved to ORS 136.633. Under the old number, ORS 139.240, there is a reference in brackets to the new number, and vice versa.

ORS volume 1 reprints the Oregon Rules of Civil Procedure just after chapter 10. These rules are important for lawyers practicing in Oregon courts. The Oregon and United States constitutions are reprinted in volume 17. Each constitution is followed by an index to help locate relevant sections.

At the beginning of the first index volume is a "Quick Search" index. This index includes the following:

- Popular names of statutes (for example, "Adopt-a-Highway Program" and "Adult Literacy Act"),
- Terms defined by statute (for example, "adverse possession"), and
- Subjects that are frequently searched.

Reviewing this index may lead quickly to several statutes that are on point for your research issue. For example, the entry "adverse possession" refers you to ORS 105.620, where the requirements for adverse possession are found. It is a good idea to skim the text of statutes just before and after the ones referenced in the index. The index reference for "Adult Literacy Act" is ORS 344.770, but that statute contains only the short title of the act. The operative provisions are in preceding statutes.

2. Researching ORS on the State Legislature's Website

The Oregon State Legislature maintains a very helpful website at www.oregonlegislature.gov. The site provides a link under the tab "Bills and Laws" to an online version of *Oregon Revised Statutes* that mirrors the print version. This online version of ORS is not official, even though it is maintained by the state. In any discrepancy, rely on the print version of ORS.

If you know the statute's number, open the current ORS, click on the correct volume (noting the chapter ranges given for each volume), and then click on the statute's chapter. All of the statutes in that chapter will be listed. To go directly to a particular statute, use the "Find" feature on your computer. To locate annotations, open the separate database "Annotations" from the "Bills and Laws" tab. See Figure 4-2, where the "Bills and Laws" tab has been opened and the drop-down menu is shown.

The site has a rudimentary search engine. Look for the "Search the ORS" box and be sure to use the site's unique Boolean connectors (e.g., "AND" must be capitalized). Search results include anything you may encounter in the print version of ORS: statutory language, historical notes, case annotations, references to law review articles and Attorney General opinions, and court rules.

Another way to search for a statute when you do not have its number is to use the online index, which is the same as the print index in ORS volumes.

Figure 4-2. Bills and Laws on Oregon Legislature Website

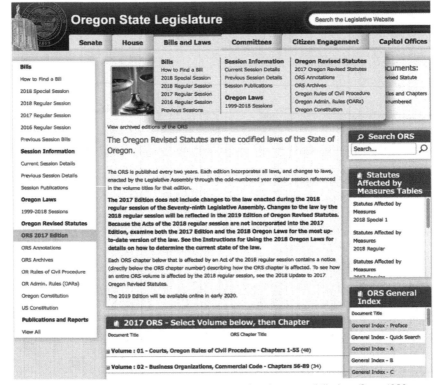

Source: Oregon State Legislature at http://www.oregonlegislature.gov/bills_laws/Pages/ORS.aspx.

From the ORS page, scroll down to the link "ORS General Index," shown at the bottom right in Figure 4-2. You can do a "Quick Search" of the mini-index or go to a particular letter and search the index for entries beginning with that letter. Then either scroll through the index pages or use the "Find" feature to locate your research terms in the index.

B. Searching West Resources

1. *West's Oregon Revised Statutes Annotated*

In 2003, West began publishing *West's Oregon Revised Statutes Annotated* (WORSA). This series is not only a valuable source for print research, but also the foundation for Oregon statutes on Westlaw. Although WORSA is an unofficial publication, it uses the same statutory numbering as ORS and the text of statutes in WORSA should be the same as in ORS. If there is ever a discrepancy, ORS is the official version.

WORSA in print differs from ORS in organization, annotations, and updating. First, regarding organization, the main volumes of WORSA include not only the text of each statute, but also the annotations that interpret or apply the statute. The annotations are not segregated in a separate volume. Second, the annotations provided by West are much more extensive than those found in ORS. Some researchers find these extensive annotations make WORSA a more effective research tool, while others note that the additional annotations may be only tangentially related to the statute. Third, WORSA is updated periodically with pocket parts—updates inserted into a slot in the back cover of a volume—while ORS is reprinted in full every two years.

To use WORSA in print, skim the soft-cover index volumes for each of your research terms, recording the statutory references. Turn to the bound volumes and read the statutory language carefully. Historical information and notes on each statute follow the statutory language. Next are cross references to related statutes and library references, including West's Topics and Key Numbers (which can be used in West's digests and on Westlaw, as explained in Chapter 7), citations to *American Law Reports*, and references to legal encyclopedias, treatises, practice aids, and forms. Following the library references are "Notes of Decisions," listing cases and opinions of the Oregon Attorney General that apply the statute.

2. Oregon Statutes on Westlaw

a. Beginning with a Citation

When you know the statute's number, go to the universal search bar and enter "ORS" followed by the number, for example, *ORS 164.215.* Westlaw also recognizes the abbreviation "Or St," so a search for *Or St 164.215* would be successful. See Figure 4-3 for an example of this statute on Westlaw.

The text of the statute is followed by the source note for the statute, called "Credits." An index of specific subjects covered by cases in "Notes of Decisions" appears on the right side of the screen. Clicking on a subject will lead to headnotes of relevant cases. For example, clicking on "Buildings" leads to headnotes of cases where courts decided whether certain structures (e.g., a detached tractor trailer) were buildings. You can also access all of the Notes of Decisions by opening the tab at the top left of the screen and by clicking on a link that appears just below "Credits" (not shown in Figure 4-3).

Figure 4-3. ORS 164.215 on Westlaw

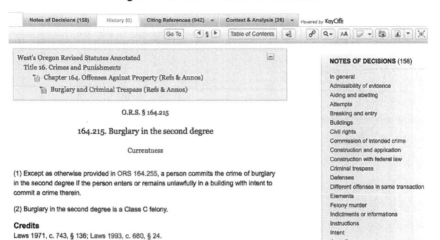

Source: Westlaw. Reprinted with permission of Thomson Reuters.

Near the top of the screen are green arrows that allow you to flip between sequential sections of this portion of the Oregon code. A "Table of Contents" link gives the context for the statute you are viewing. At the top of the screen are tabs for "Notes of Decisions," "History," "Citing References," and "Content and Analysis." The first and last mirror the annotations in WORSA (i.e., "Notes of Decisions" are references to cases that discuss the statute, and "Content and Analysis" provides other research cross references). "History" allows you to explore the validity of a statute by reading cases and legislation (enacted or proposed) that might have a negative impact; to review legislative history, including prior drafts of the bill and reports; and to read notes by West editors and state revisors.[5] "Citing References" lists all of the documents in Westlaw that refer to the statute. While "Citing References" overlaps some with "Notes of Decisions," you should consider checking both.

---

5. For a detailed explanation of this tab, hold your cursor over the tab and click on "General Overview." There is no history for the statute shown in Figure 4-3, but a wealth of information is sometimes available. Open ORS 164.225 for an example of a statute with extensive history. See Chapter 5 for a discussion of Oregon legislative history materials.

Figure 4-4. Oregon Statutory Titles

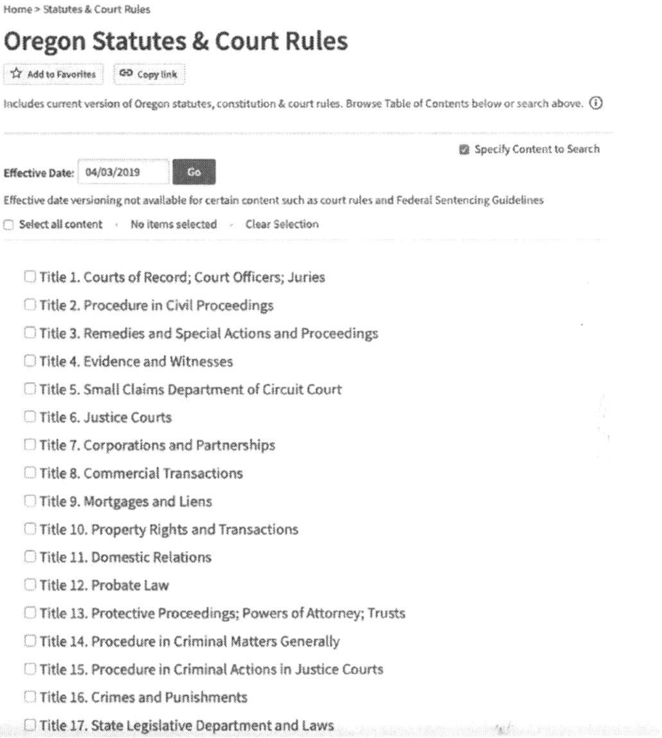

Home > Statutes & Court Rules

Oregon Statutes & Court Rules

☆ Add to Favorites   ⊖ Copy link

Includes current version of Oregon statutes, constitution & court rules. Browse Table of Contents below or search above. ⓘ

☑ Specify Content to Search

Effective Date: 04/03/2019   Go

Effective date versioning not available for certain content such as court rules and Federal Sentencing Guidelines

☐ Select all content · No items selected · Clear Selection

☐ Title 1. Courts of Record; Court Officers; Juries

☐ Title 2. Procedure in Civil Proceedings

☐ Title 3. Remedies and Special Actions and Proceedings

☐ Title 4. Evidence and Witnesses

☐ Title 5. Small Claims Department of Circuit Court

☐ Title 6. Justice Courts

☐ Title 7. Corporations and Partnerships

☐ Title 8. Commercial Transactions

☐ Title 9. Mortgages and Liens

☐ Title 10. Property Rights and Transactions

☐ Title 11. Domestic Relations

☐ Title 12. Probate Law

☐ Title 13. Protective Proceedings; Powers of Attorney; Trusts

☐ Title 14. Procedure in Criminal Matters Generally

☐ Title 15. Procedure in Criminal Actions in Justice Courts

☐ Title 16. Crimes and Punishments

☐ Title 17. State Legislative Department and Laws

Source: Westlaw. Reprinted with permission of Thomson Reuters.

b. Beginning without a Citation

If you do not know the citations of any relevant statutes, you can conduct research on Westlaw by going through any of the following steps.

1. Beginning with "Content types" or "State Materials"

From the home page "Content types," click on the "Statutes and Court Rules" link and then on "Oregon." The next screen lists all titles of the Oregon code. You can reach the same screen from the Westlaw home page by clicking first on "State Materials," then the "Oregon" link, and finally the "Statutes and Court Rules" link. The resulting screen is shown in Figure 4-4. Clicking the "i" icon at the top of the page opens an explanation of the content of the database.

From the screen displaying the titles of the Oregon code, you can enter terms in the search bar at the top of the page to search the statutory database. Alternatively, you can check specific titles to search. When conducting research on burglary, restricting the search to "Title 16, Crimes and Punishments" might be more effective than running a general search of all Oregon statutes. See Fig-

Figure 4-5. Results for Statutory Search for *Burglary*

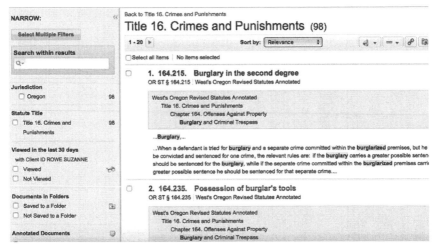

Source: Westlaw. Reprinted with permission of Thomson Reuters.

ure 4-4. Note that this search will capture everything in the database that contains your terms: statutes, annotations, notes of decisions, etc.

The results page of a search for the term *burglary* in title 16 is shown in Figure 4-5. From the results page, you can sort documents by relevance, most cited, or table of contents. Using the left frame, you can narrow results by term and other filters. After opening a statute from your results list, use the green arrows at the top of the page to go directly to each point where your search terms appear.

2. Using "Tools"

Westlaw provides a number of "Tools and Resources" for searching Oregon statutes, including the "Oregon Statutes Index" and the "Oregon Statutes Popular Name Table." (These links would appear on the right side of the screen shown in Figure 4-4.) In the index, you can search by term, click on a particular letter to browse, or browse through the entire index. Blue entries open to reveal subentries. The popular name table allows you to search for a statute by its common name, for example, the "Adult Literacy Act," which is codified in ORS 344.760 and following statutes.

Another useful tool is "Oregon Statutes Annotated—Historical." Opening that link and then clicking on one of the years listed opens a database with Oregon statutes in effect in that year. You will need to research statutes from prior years when a client is involved in litigation concerning a statute that has

Figure 4-6. Database Options on Westlaw

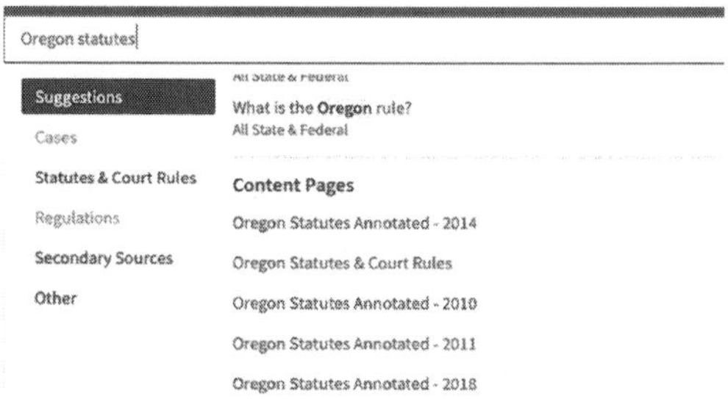

Source: Westlaw. Reprinted with permission of Thomson Reuters.

changed since the incident took place.[6] Yet another database listed under "Tools and Resources" is "Oregon Statutes — Unannotated." You may decide to search the unannotated code if your search terms are appearing only in annotations, making you wonder whether any statute is on point.

3. Beginning with an Oregon Statutes Database

To go directly to a database containing Oregon statutes, begin typing *Oregon statutes* into the universal search bar. West will suggest various database options, allowing you to select the year of the statutes you need to research and whether you want annotations, as shown in Figure 4-6.[7] Scroll down to the database you want and click on it. (If instead you hit "enter," Westlaw will run a search for *Oregon* or *statutes*.) Typing *Oregon index* into the universal search bar will lead to an index, where you can either type terms into a search box or scroll through a portion of the alphabetical index. Links lead to statutory citations or to other terms cross referenced in the index.

After selecting one of these database options, be sure to click the small "i" icon for information about what is included in the database. (Figure 4-4 contains this icon at the end of the brief explanation just below "Oregon Statutes and Court Rules.")

The "advanced" search button allows you to exercise more control over the results by using Boolean terms and connectors. A reminder of the Boolean commands (both the connectors and the expanders) is provided on the right side of the screen. Chapter 1 contains a list of these commands in Table 1-3. Sometimes, selecting a particular database will take you to an "Advanced Search"

---

6. Recognize that the name of a statute might have changed in the interim; be persistent if you don't find the same statute immediately.

7. Explanations about when to use statutory databases for particular years or the unannotated code are included earlier in this chapter under *2. Using "Tools."*

Figure 4-7. Advanced Statutory Search Page on Westlaw

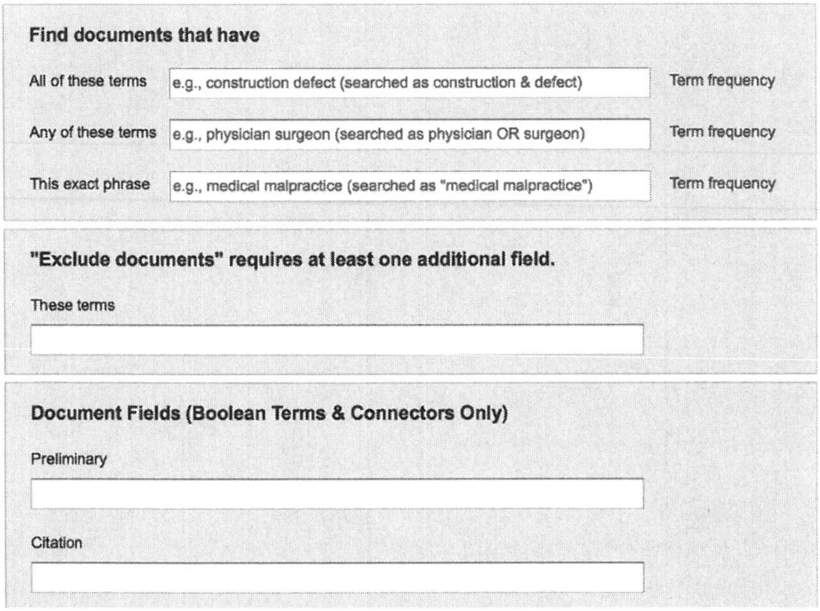

Find documents that have

All of these terms | e.g., construction defect (searched as construction & defect) | Term frequency

Any of these terms | e.g., physician surgeon (searched as physician OR surgeon) | Term frequency

This exact phrase | e.g., medical malpractice (searched as "medical malpractice") | Term frequency

"Exclude documents" requires at least one additional field.

These terms

Document Fields (Boolean Terms & Connectors Only)

Preliminary

Citation

Source: Westlaw. Reprinted with permission of Thomson Reuters.

page, as shown in Figure 4-7 (note that the image is cropped, so the list of Boolean commands is not shown). Of course, you can always run a terms and connectors search using the universal search bar; going to the "Advanced Search" page makes that a bit easier because of the prompts provided.

4. Running an Open Search

As explained in Chapter 1, you can simply run a word search from the universal search bar, selecting Oregon as the jurisdiction. Figure 4-8 demonstrates, however, that search can result in hundreds of statutes and thousands of cases that you then have to cull. One of the other approaches is likely to be more efficient.

Figure 4-8. Results of Open Search for *Burglary*

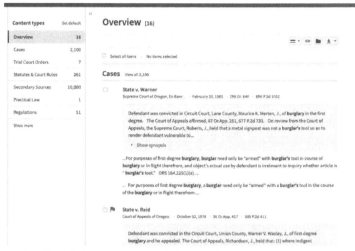

Source: Westlaw. Reprinted with permission of Thomson Reuters.

C. Oregon Statutes on Lexis

There is no print version of Oregon statutes published by Lexis. The following explanation is for Lexis Advance, the online product currently available from LexisNexis.

1. Beginning with a Citation

You can search for a statute by citation from the universal search bar. Enter "ORS" and the number, for example, *ORS 164.235*. See Figure 4-9.

At the top left and right corners of the document are arrows with the words "Previous" and "Next," which allow you to view sequential sections of this portion of the Oregon code. The "Table of Contents" link on the left of the screen places this statute in context. That link also allows you to view the full table of contents and to search it as well as the statutory text.

Following the text of the statute is its history, then its annotations. The first annotations are "Case Notes." An index of specific subjects covered by cases appears first; clicking on one of the subjects will link you farther down the page to those cases. For example, clicking on "Criminal Law and Procedures: Criminal Offenses: Property Crimes: Burglary & Criminal Trespass: General Overview" will take you to cases indexed under that heading. Following the Case Notes are any other annotations, including references to related law review articles.

Figure 4-9. Statute on Lexis

Document: ORS § 164.235

164.235 Possession of a burglary tool or theft device.

(1) A person commits the crime of possession of a burglary tool or theft device if the person possesses a burglary tool or theft device and the person:

(a) Intends to use the tool or device to commit or facilitate a forcible entry into premises or a theft by a physical taking; or

(b) Knows that another person intends to use the tool or device to commit or facilitate a forcible entry into premises or a theft by a physical taking.

(2) For purposes of this section, "burglary tool or theft device" means an acetylene torch, electric arc, burning bar, thermal lance, oxygen lance or other similar device capable of burning through steel, concrete or other solid material, or nitroglycerine, dynamite, gunpowder or any other explosive, tool, instrument or other article adapted or designed for committing or facilitating a forcible entry into premises or theft by a physical taking.

(3) Possession of a burglary tool or theft device is a Class A misdemeanor.

History

1971 c.743 § 138; 1999 c.1040 § 13; 2003 c.577 § 9.

▼ Annotations

Source: Lexis Advance. Reprinted with the permission of LexisNexis. All rights reserved.

2. Searching without a Citation

a. Running an Open Search

You can enter terms in the universal search bar on the main page. Lexis will suggest additional searches as you type, as shown in Figure 4-10. Lexis also allows you to filter results after conducting the search using links on the left side of the screen See Figure 4-11.

b. Browsing Sources

On Lexis, you can browse sources by clicking on the "Browse" drop down menu above the universal search bar. There are a variety of search techniques available, illustrated in Figure 4-12.

- Select "Sources" from the browse options. Either enter *Oregon statutes* into the search box at the top of the left margin or click through various

Figure 4-10. Lexis Search Term Suggestions

Lexis Advance®

Advanced Search | Tips

burgla		Search:
Legal Phrases	aggravated **burglary**	
	burglary conviction	
	first degree **burglary**	
	residential **burglary**	Inter
	second degree **burglary**	
	attempted **burglary**	
	burglary charge	

Figure 4-11. Lexis Filters

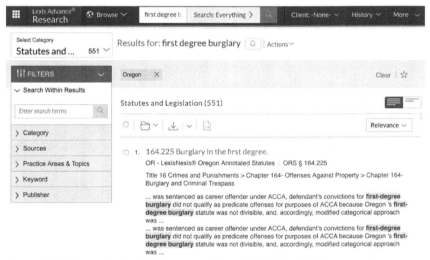

Figure 4-12. Lexis "Browse Sources"

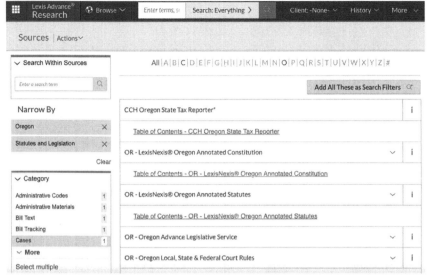

source options (e.g., By Jurisdiction and By Category). Use the "Narrow by" option in the left margin to restrict further. By selecting "Oregon" and "Statutes and Legislation," one of the results will be "LexisNexis Oregon Annotated Statutes." A pop-up box lets you get source documents (in this instance, all statutes), provides information about that source, or allows you to add the source to your search. Adding the source to your search will restrict the results to documents found in that source.

- A separate link just under the statutes link will open the table of contents, where you can search by term throughout the statutory text or scroll through the list of titles.
- You can use the letters at the top of the screen to search for the source alphabetically.

After selecting the source and entering your search query, you will see a list of search results. Identify and click on a relevant statute from those results, and the screen will be similar to that shown in Figure 4-9, but will include additional navigational tools. For example, you will be able to skip to your highlighted search terms using arrows next to your search term in a box near the top of the screen. You can also "Go to" other parts of the annotated code document, such as "Case Notes" or "Research References" (where your search terms will also be highlighted or in bold print). In addition to using these navigational tools, you can scroll down from the text of the statute to find "History" and "Annotations" that include "Case Notes." If a statute has been cited by many cases, there might be an index listing different headings.

II. Applying and Interpreting Oregon Statutes

Most often in legal work, applying a statute will mean reading its words carefully, referring to related statutes, analyzing cases that involve those statutes, and applying the law to the facts of your client's situation.

In litigation, the role of an Oregon court in construing a statute is to determine the intent of the legislature in enacting the statute.[8] The Oregon Supreme Court has provided a three-part template for statutory interpretation, first in the 1993 *PGE* case, which was modified in 2009 by the *Gaines* case.[9]

1. Examine the text and context of the statute.
2. Review the legislative history of the statute.
3. Consider general maxims of statutory construction.

The first level of analysis consists of two steps: reading the text of the statute, then understanding the context of the statute. In reading the text of any statute, the court follows rules of construction set by Oregon law. For example, words are given their "plain meaning,"[10] and the court reads the statute exactly as written, without adding or deleting anything.[11]

The context of the statute includes other sections and subsections of the same statute as well as other related statutes. In the burglary example used earlier in this chapter, understanding "burglary in the second degree" in ORS

---

8. ORS 174.020.

9. *PGE v. Bureau of Lab. and Indus.*, 317 Or 606, 610–12 (1993); *State v. Gaines*, 346 Or 160, 171–72 (2009) (modifying *PGE* to delete the requirement that a statute be ambiguous before a court could consider legislative history). Two helpful articles that analyze statutory construction in Oregon are Jack Landau, *Some Observations About Statutory Construction in Oregon*, 32 Willamette L Rev 1 (1996), and Steven J. Johansen, *What Does Ambiguous Mean? Making Sense of Statutory Analysis in Oregon*, 34 Willamette L Rev 219 (1998).

10. *PGE*, 317 Or at 611.

11. ORS 174.010.

164.215 required reference to the definition of "building" in ORS 164.205. The context of a statute also includes cases that have previously interpreted the same statute. In examining the context of the statute, the court follows additional rules of construction. For example, if a statute suggests two intents—one particular and one general—the particular intent controls.[12] If the first step proves that the text of the statute has only one meaning, the inquiry stops.[13]

The second level of analysis refers to the legislative history of the statute, which includes the deliberations of the House and Senate as well as the committees that considered the bill that was enacted as this statute.[14] Legislative history research is covered in Chapter 5.

If the meaning of the statute remains unclear, a court will reach the third part of the *PGE* template, where it may follow still other rules of construction. The *PGE* opinion refers to these as "general maxims of statutory construction"[15] and gives two examples: First, ORS 174.030 expresses a preference for "natural rights" over others. Second, from case law, there is a maxim that the court will try to divine legislative intent even when there is no legislative history.[16]

An invaluable tool in statutory construction is the multi-volume treatise *Statutes and Statutory Construction.*[17]

Writing about statutory analysis often will be the last step in statutory interpretation and application. As you locate relevant statutes, begin to under-

---

12. ORS 174.020(b).

13. "When the text of a statute is truly capable of having only one meaning, no weight can be given to legislative history that suggests—or even confirms—that legislators intended something different." *Gaines*, 346 Or at 173.

14. In response to *PGE*'s statement that legislative history could be considered only if the statute was ambiguous, the legislature amended ORS 174.020 to allow parties to offer legislative history to assist courts in construing the text of statutes. The Oregon Supreme Court determined the impact of this statute in *Gaines*, 346 Or at 171–72. Parties are allowed to present legislative history and the court will consult it, but the court remains free to determine the weight the legislative history receives. *Id.*

15. *PGE*, 317 Or at 612.

16. *Id.* A classic article summarizing and commenting on numerous canons of construction is Karl N. Llewellyn, *Remarks on the Theory of Appellate Decision and the Rules or Canons About How Statutes Are to Be Construed*, 3 Vand L Rev 395 (1950).

17. The authors of the recent editions are Norman J. Singer and J.D. Shambie Singer, but the work is still known as *Sutherland Statutory Construction.*

stand them, and develop your analysis, follow these guidelines in drafting your document:

- Quote only the relevant portion of the statute. Include just enough context to orient but not overwhelm the reader.
- Omit parts of the statute that clearly do not apply to your facts.
- Paraphrase parts of the statute that are difficult for the reader to understand and not critical to your analysis. If quoting requires you to use many ellipses to indicate omissions, it may be better to paraphrase.

III. Court Rules

Court rules govern litigation practice from the filing of initial pleadings through the final appeal. Rules dictate litigation details ranging from the correct caption for pleadings to the standard for summary judgment. Court rules like the Oregon Rules of Civil Procedure and the Uniform Trial Court Rules are primary authority even when the court or legislature responsible for them has delegated rulemaking power to a council, committee, or other body. Success in litigation may depend as much on compliance with these rules as with the merit of the claim.

The website of the Oregon courts, at courts.oregon.gov, links to court rules: click on the "Forms/Rules/Fees," at the top of the page and then "Rules Center." The resulting page includes links to most of the rules listed above as well to Supplementary Local Rules (SLR) adopted by an Oregon trial court. These rules might also appear on the individual court's website. As an example, the Third Judicial Circuit (Marion County, where Salem is located) sets out in its SLR the hours the court is open, the requirements for being approved by the court as a mediator, and many other details. Use the index or table of contents provided with each set of rules to locate particular rules that affect your work.

In addition to the Oregon courts website, rules are available through a number of other sources, some of which are described below. Be sure that you are working with the current rule, whether working with print or online sources.

Court rules are frequently published in statutory codifications, both in print and in online resources.

A print compilation of rules is sometimes referred to as a *deskbook*. The following rules are among those published in *Oregon Rules of Court: State*, published annually by West:

Oregon Rules of Civil Procedure

Evidence Code[18]

Oregon Rules of Appellate Procedure

Uniform Trial Court Rules

Rules of the Oregon Tax Court

Lexis provides a database that contains Oregon local, state, and federal rules. Westlaw includes court rules in databases with state statutes. Open the table of contents for that database and check the appropriate box to search only the set of rules that is relevant to your project (see Figure 4-13). Westlaw also has databases solely containing Oregon Rules of Civil Procedure and the Evidence Code.

Figure 4-13. Court Rules Databases on Westlaw

☐	Oregon Rules of Appellate Procedure
☐	Uniform Trial Court Rules
☐	Rules of the Oregon Tax Court Regular Division
☐	Rules of the Oregon Tax Court Magistrate Division
☐	Administrative Rules of the Land Use Board of Appeals [Oregon Administrative Rules, Chapter 661, Divisions 1 and 10]
☐	Oregon Code of Judicial Conduct
☐	Oregon Rules of Professional Conduct
☐	Oregon State Bar Rules of Procedure
☐	Client Security Fund Rules
☐	Rules for Admission of Attorneys
☐	New Lawyer Mentoring Program Rule
☐	Oregon State Bar Minimum Continuing Legal Education Rules, Regulations and Forms
☐	Qualification Standards for Court-Appointed Counsel to Represent Financially Eligible Persons at State Expense
☐	Public Defense Payment Policies and Procedures
☐	Court-Connected Mediator Qualifications Rules
☐	Baker County Local Rules

Source: Westlaw. Reprinted with permission of Thomson Reuters.

---

18. Rules 100 to 1008 are codified in chapter 40 of *Oregon Revised Statutes.*

Rules are written in outline form like statutes, and they should be read like statutes. Read each word carefully, refer to cross-referenced rules, and scan other rules nearby to see whether they are related.

After locating a rule on point, find cases that apply the rule by searching annotations published with the rule or by searching a topical index. Never assume that an Oregon rule mirrors its federal counterpart or that cases applying a federal rule will be relevant to application of an Oregon rule.

The text of some rules is accompanied by commentary by the committee charged with drafting or modifying the rules. The commentary is persuasive authority.

Chapter 5

Legislative History

This chapter begins with an overview of the legislative process in Oregon; through that process, the statutory laws of Oregon are enacted and changed. The chapter then describes the process of *bill tracking*, monitoring the status of a current bill that may or may not ultimately be enacted. Lawyers track bills that may affect a client's interests when they are acting in an advisory role.

Next, the chapter explains how to research the *legislative history* of a statute that has already been enacted. Legislative history research is most often relevant in litigation, when a lawyer needs to convince a court to interpret an ambiguous statute in a way that is favorable to the client's position. Understanding the legislative process is important here because that process produces documents that may help determine the legislature's intent in passing a statute, which is a key to statutory interpretation. This chapter also includes a brief introduction to Oregon's initiative and referendum processes, which also affect state legislation.

Researchers who frequently turn first to commercial services like Lexis or Westlaw should realize that Oregon state websites have valuable information — for free — that is not available on the commercial sites. Thus, even researchers who begin their Oregon legislative history research on Lexis or Westlaw will need to refer to the state websites. The most important state websites for Oregon legislative history research are listed below:

- Oregon State Legislature
- Oregon Legislation Information Service (OLIS)
- Oregon Secretary of State

I. The Legislative Process

The Oregon Legislative Assembly consists of a Senate, with thirty members, and a House of Representatives, with sixty members. The Assembly meets annually, though the regular sessions in odd-numbered years are much longer than those in even-numbered years.[1] The general process of enacting or amending laws in Oregon is similar to that in other states and in the United States Congress. Figure 5-1 shows the basic progression of an idea from bill to statute.

II. Oregon Bill Tracking

Of the many bills that are introduced in each legislative session, some may affect the rights of a client by proposing new laws or amending existing laws. In advising a client, an attorney needs to learn of any bills on topics relevant to the client's interest and follow their progress through the process outlined below. Note that regular bills introduced in the Oregon House of Representatives begin with HB (for "House bill") while bills introduced in the Senate begin with SB (for "Senate bill").

Bill Tracking Overview

1. Search a specific bill number
2. Search for a pending bill with terms or by Oregon Revised Statute number
3. Learn if a bill has been enacted

A. Searching with a Bill Number

If you know the number of a bill that you need to track, you can do so easily on the Oregon Legislature Information System (OLIS) website at no charge. Go to that website, and first click on the "Session" icon at the top right of the OLIS page so that you can select the current session. Then click on the "Bills" icon at the top right of the OLIS page, and enter the bill's number (e.g., 4110). The resulting page will begin with an overview of the bill. You can use various tabs and links on that page to view the bill's text, read staff analysis of the bill, review amendments, track its history thus far, see its current status and scheduled events, etc. See Figure 5-2 for an example from the 2018 Regular Session.

---

1. The Oregon State Legislature's website at www.oregonlegislature.gov contains more detailed information about the Assembly and its processes under the link for "Citizen Engagement."

Figure 5-1. Bill to Law Process

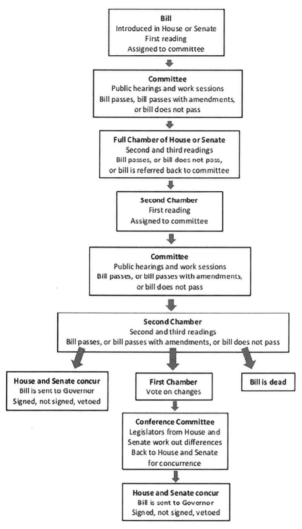

Source: Based on "How an Idea Becomes Law" on the Oregon Legislature's website under "Citizen Engagement."

You can also begin bill tracking on the Oregon State Legislature's website (see Figure 4-2 in the last chapter), but links on that website frequently take you to OLIS. For example, if you open the "Bills and Laws" page on the legislature's website and enter the bill number in the search box for "Search Bills," clicking on any of the results will take you to OLIS. Similarly, if you open the

Figure 5-2. Oregon Bill Overview

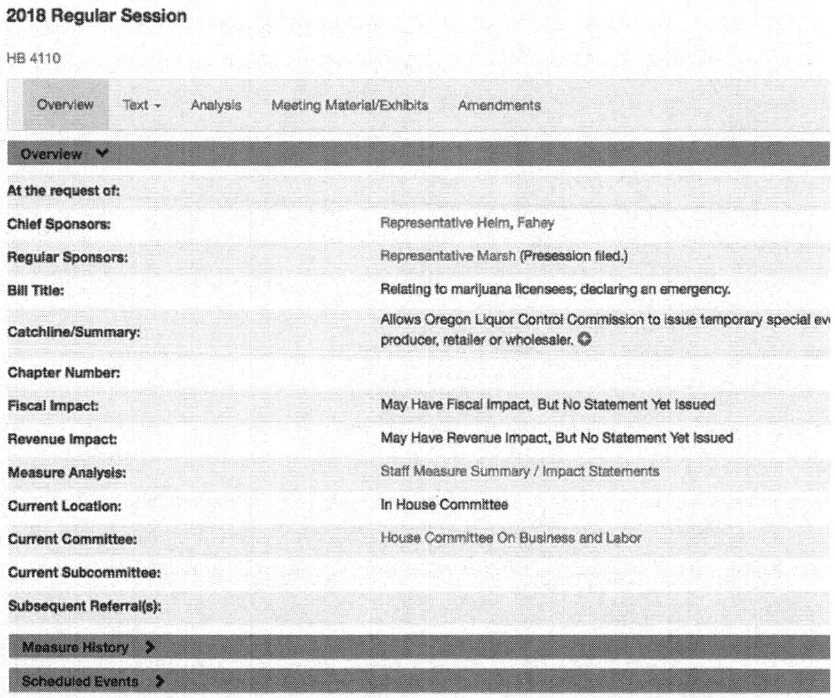

2018 Regular Session

HB 4110

| Overview | Text ▾ | Analysis | Meeting Material/Exhibits | Amendments |

Overview ∨

At the request of:	
Chief Sponsors:	Representative Helm, Fahey
Regular Sponsors:	Representative Marsh (Presession filed.)
Bill Title:	Relating to marijuana licensees; declaring an emergency.
Catchline/Summary:	Allows Oregon Liquor Control Commission to issue temporary special ev producer, retailer or wholesaler. ⊕
Chapter Number:	
Fiscal Impact:	May Have Fiscal Impact, But No Statement Yet Issued
Revenue Impact:	May Have Revenue Impact, But No Statement Yet Issued
Measure Analysis:	Staff Measure Summary / Impact Statements
Current Location:	In House Committee
Current Committee:	House Committee On Business and Labor
Current Subcommittee:	
Subsequent Referral(s):	

Measure History ＞

Scheduled Events ＞

Source: Oregon Legislative Information System, https://olis.leg.state.or.us/liz/2018R1/Measures/Overview/HB4110.

"Bills and Laws" tab, look under "Bills," and click on the "Current Session Details" link, you will be redirected to OLIS.

Bill tracking is available on both Lexis and Westlaw. The following are examples of searches that will lead to information related to the bill described in Figure 5-2. On Lexis, type *bill 4110* into the universal search bar, then select "Statutes and Legislation" for content type and "Oregon" as the jurisdiction. On Westlaw, type *Oregon House Bill 4110* into the universal search bar.

The Oregonian newspaper provides a unique bill tracking service from gov. oregonlive.com/bill. For each bill, the site lists sponsors, measure activity, votes of individual assembly members, and links to relevant news articles. It also provides a link to the OLIS site for the bill.

Figure 5-3. OLIS "Bill Text" Search

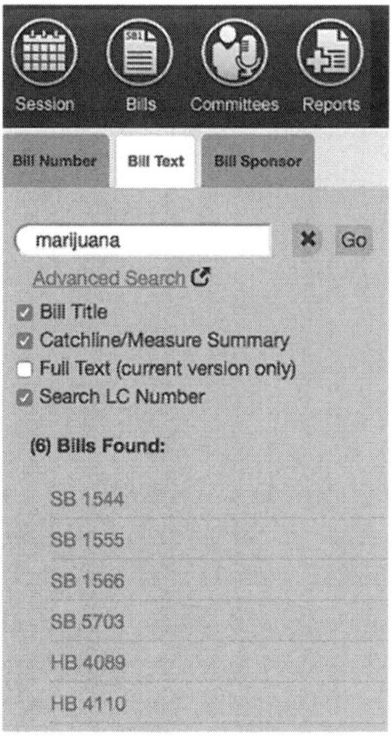

Source: Oregon Legislative Information System.

B. Learning about Pending Bills

1. Searching with Terms

If you do not know the bill number, or if you need to learn whether there even is pending legislation that affects your work, you can begin with the OLIS "Bills" icon (after selecting the current session, of course). Under the "Bill Text" tab, enter search terms as shown in Figure 5-3, and you will receive a list of bills with those terms. Clicking one of the resulting links (e.g., "HB 4110"), takes you to the OLIS Overview of the bill, which is shown in Figure 5-2.

You can conduct a similar search from the Oregon Legislature's website. Enter search terms into the "Search Bills" box on the home page, select the current session on the left side of the results page, and select one of the bill results. You will be redirected to an OLIS page with the text of that bill. You can then select the "Overview" tab for general information about the bill.

Lexis and Westlaw allow you to search by keywords to find information about bills that might affect your client's situation. On Lexis, consider one of these four databases:

OR Bill Tracking Reports	bill summary as well as legislative events related to each bill in the current session
OR Full-Text Bills	text of all pending legislation
Oregon Advance Legislative Service	text of all enacted laws during the session
Oregon Legislative Bill History — from 2006 through current	revenue and fiscal impact statements, staff measure summaries, and Governor's messages

All are easily located using "Browse," "Sources," and "All Sources," and searching under the "O" link. The "Bill Tracking" database is the most current, with information provided within two days of publication.

On Westlaw, similar material is included in the database "Oregon Proposed Legislation (Bills)." You can access it by typing the name of the database in the universal search bar or by browsing under "Content types" for the "Proposed and Enacted Legislation" link. Westlaw tabs for each bill provide the original bill text, bill tracking (a chronology of events), bill activity (including the latest version of the bill), and a graphical display of the bill's progress (with links to various versions of the bill).

2. Searching by ORS Number

When you know a particular section of Oregon Revised Statutes (ORS) that affects your client, but not the number of any relevant bills, you can review a table that shows whether existing statutes would be "amended, repealed, or added to" if the legislature were to act on various bills introduced in the current session. The following three approaches lead to that table:

- Go to the OLIS website.
    Use the "Session" icon, and select the current session.
        Click on the "Reports" icon for a drop-down menu.
            Select "Daily and Cumulative Session Publications."
                Click the arrow next to the "Cumulative Session Publications" link.
                Click on "Statutes Affected by Measures."

- An alternate path begins on the legislature's website, opening "Bills and Laws" and then "Oregon Laws," and next looking in the left frame under "Session Information" for "Session Publications." Finally, click on "Statutes Affected by Measures."
- Use your search engine to search for *Oregon statutes affected by measures tables*. One of the first results should be a link to a page on the Oregon State Legislature's website. In the right margin, look for the heading "Statutes Affected by Measures Tables" and select the current session.

Lexis and Westlaw inform you when a bill would affect a statute you know is relevant to your client's interests. When you are viewing a relevant statute on Lexis, a yellow triangle with an exclamation point indicates pending legislation. Clicking that icon will take you to the bill and related tracking information. On Westlaw, a KeyCite flag appears at the top of the screen if there is legislation affecting the statute. Clicking on the flag will lead you to the bill and allow you to track its activity. As an example, a yellow flag will appear if a bill has been introduced to amend the statute you are viewing.

C. Learning Whether a Bill Has Been Enacted

Once you know of a bill that you need to track, you can learn whether it has been enacted by searching the OLIS website. Follow the paths in one of the first two bullets in Section B.2. above, but select "Senate and House Bills Enacted" for a table listing the enacted bills, the chapter of ORS they affect, and their effective dates. From the same paths, "Senate Measure History" and "House Measure History" provide the history of each bill as it worked its way through the legislature, including whether it was left in committee at the end of the session or it was enacted.

D. Searching in Print

For researchers without online access, some libraries maintain bill compilations during the legislative session. These are simply copies of the bills that have been introduced, in their original, engrossed, or enrolled form.[2] Cumulative indexes are issued periodically for these compilations, providing indexing both by subject and by ORS sections "amended, repealed, or added to." Cu-

---

2. An "engrossed" bill is one that has been amended; the "enrolled" bill is the final version that is sent to the Governor.

mulative status reports are also issued, which allow tracking of legislative activity concerning the bills.

III. Oregon Legislative History Research

Legislative history research is needed when the meaning of a statute is not clear or when the meaning is at issue in litigation. It is especially useful for new legislation, which has not yet been interpreted by the courts. When a statute is ambiguous, reviewing the legislative history assists in the effort to determine the legislature's intent in enacting the statute.[3] When you are involved in litigation where the meaning of a statute is unclear, first see whether other statutes, cases, or administrative agency regulations have addressed the ambiguity. If not, you will need to find the available legislative history and refer to it in your briefs to the court.

Legislative history research is the reverse of bill tracking. Bill tracking follows the legislative process forward, from the introduction of a bill to its possible enactment. In contrast, legislative history research works backwards, beginning with an enacted statute. From the codified statute, you will find the session law chapter number, then the bill number, and finally the documents produced by the legislative process.[4] Table 5-1 explains the legislative process and notes the documents that are important in legislative history research. The following pages explain the sources of legislative history in Oregon and how to conduct legislative history research. Much recent information is available online; additional information is provided at libraries around the state in print, microfilm, and audio tapes. Sometimes, however, a trip to the Oregon State Archives is necessary.[5]

---

3. *See* ORS 174.020 (instructing courts to "pursue the intention of the legislature if possible" in construing statutes); *see also PGE v. Bureau of Lab. and Indus.*, 317 Or 606, 611–12 (1993); Steven J. Johansen, *What Does Ambiguous Mean? Making Sense of Statutory Analysis in Oregon*, 34 Willamette L Rev 219 (1998).

4. Most often you will be researching the history of bills that were enacted. Sometimes you may also research bills that did not become law; learning the text that was rejected earlier may provide insight into a subsequent bill that was passed.

5. The Archives building is located at 800 Summer Street N.E., Salem, Oregon. The telephone number for the reference room is (503) 373-0701, extension 1. The e-mail address is reference.archives@state.or.us.

A. Sources of Oregon Legislative History

Much of Oregon's legislative work takes place in committees. This means that legislative history research focuses on the documents and audio or video recordings produced by the committees that considered a bill. In Oregon legislative history research, you are primarily searching for the following:

(1) committee minutes (until 2005) or audio and video logs (since 2007) for the hearings and work sessions of committees that considered the bill;

(2) audio or video recordings of the actual hearings and work sessions at which the bill was discussed;

(3) any exhibits that were introduced and preserved;

(4) the original bill file for a particular bill;

(5) chamber debates, audio or video recordings of proceedings on the floor of each chamber; and

(6) journals that show votes recorded in the House and Senate.

Table 5-1. Legislative Process and Documents Produced

Legislative Action	Documents Produced
An idea for legislation is suggested by a citizen, group, or legislator. A legislator or legislative committee sponsors the bill, and the legislative counsel drafts the language.	The text of a **bill** is obviously important; if enacted, the bill's requirements or prohibitions may affect a client's interests. Even if a modified version is passed, comparing the original to the final version can help determine the legislature's intent.
The bill is introduced in either the House or Senate. It is read for the first time and assigned to a committee.	
The committee holds public hearings and work sessions and acts to pass the bill, pass the bill with amendments, or not pass the bill.	In Oregon, the **minutes and logs**, along with **the recordings** of hearings and work sessions, form the largest part of the legislative history. In addition, the **original bill file** contains a **staff analysis**, explaining the need for and goals of the legislation. A bill passed with amendments is called an **A-engrossed bill** (abbreviated A-Eng.).

Table 5-1. Legislative Process and Documents Produced, *continued*

Legislative Action	Documents Produced
If the bill is passed by the committee, it goes back to the full chamber (House or Senate) for a second and third reading. That chamber votes to pass, not pass, or refer the bill back to committee. If the bill is not passed, it dies.	**Recordings** of floor proceedings are available from the state archives. Votes are available in the **journals** of the House and Senate.
If the bill is passed by this chamber, it goes to the second chamber for the first reading, and then it is assigned to a committee. The committee holds public hearings and work sessions and acts to pass the bill, pass the bill with amendments, or not pass the bill. If the bill is not passed, it dies.	Additional legislative history, of the type described above, is produced in the second chamber. If the bill is amended for a second time, it is reprinted as a **B-engrossed bill**.
If the second chamber passes the bill in the same form as the first chamber, it is enrolled and sent to the Governor. If the bill is passed with amendments, it goes back to the first chamber for a vote on the changes. If needed, a conference committee is appointed with legislators from both chambers, who work out the differences. When the two chambers concur on the final bill, it is sent to the Governor. If the bill is not passed, it dies.	The final version of the bill that is sent to the Governor is the **enrolled bill**.
If the Governor signs the bill, it becomes law. If the Governor does not sign the bill within a certain period, it becomes law without signature. If the Governor vetos the bill, a two-thirds vote in both chambers will override the veto.	Some **veto statements** of Governors are published in the journals of the House and Senate.
The enacted bill is assigned a *session* law number; in Oregon this is called a *chapter number*. This is a chronological number based on when the bill was passed in that session of the legislature.	**Session laws** are published in numerical order in *Oregon Laws*.
The law is *codified*, meaning that it is assigned a number that places it with other laws on similar topics.	Oregon **statutes** are codified in *Oregon Revised Statutes*.

Source: Based on "How an Idea Becomes Law" on the Oregon Legislature's website under "Citizen Engagement."

Because legislative history can be confusing in the abstract, the appendix of this chapter provides examples of some of the print documents described below. The links in Table 5-2, later in this chapter, lead to examples of documents and recordings available online.

1. Legislative Minutes and Audio and Video Logs

The legislature provides either committee minutes or audio and video logs for public hearings and committee work sessions where a bill was discussed. The legislative *committee minutes* are not verbatim transcripts, but summaries noting each person who spoke and the substance of the person's remarks. (See the chapter appendix for an example.) Minutes are kept in three-ring binders at the Archives building; some are available online. Since 2007, *audio logs* have been provided instead of minutes; the logs simply list the speakers, without summaries. Since July, 2014, recording logs associated with video have been provided. Be careful not to confuse the logs with the recordings of hearings and work sessions.

Minutes and logs from 1991 forward are available at the Oregon Secretary of State's Archival Records website. Minutes from 1926 through the mid-1990s are available in microfilm format at some university law libraries, including the University of Oregon and Lewis & Clark College, as well as at some county law libraries.

2. Committee Audio and Video Recordings

Audio recordings of committee hearings and work sessions have been available since 1957. Currently, the state uses digital audio recordings. From 1981 to 2007, cassettes were used; in prior years, reel-to-reel tapes and dictation tapes were used. Whatever the media, these are verbatim recordings of the meetings as they occurred. They are often cited by Oregon courts in determining the legislature's intent in enacting a particular statute.

Accessing the audio recordings requires the date and time the bill was discussed by a particular committee. This information is found in the committee minutes or the audio logs. A key difficulty in using the audio recordings is distinguishing between speakers. Listening to the recordings while following along with the minutes or logs may be helpful.

Audio tapes are available at the State Archives in Salem; copies can be obtained for a small fee. Some audio tapes were digitized and are available online, but coverage varies.[6]

Recent digital audio recordings are available from OLIS. Select the session year using the "Session" icon, then click on the "Committees" icon. Clicking on "House," "Senate," or "Joint" will produce a list of committees. Select the appropriate committee, and scroll down to the date on which the hearing or work session was held. You may find an agenda, meeting materials, or a log. Clicking on the arrow to the right of the date will begin the audio recording. You can also access audio recordings when you are looking at the Measure History for a particular bill by linking to the public hearing or work session.

Since July of 2014, video recordings of legislative committees and Senate and House Chamber sessions are available from OLIS. The process for accessing video recordings is similar to accessing audio recordings. The Oregon Legislature's website also provides access to news conference video and non-legislative video, using the citizen engagement tab and then selecting the audio and video section.

3. Exhibits

Exhibits may include proposed amendments to a bill, written testimony submitted during consideration of the bill, reports related to the bill, and even letters from interested parties. These exhibits may have been submitted by legislators; by committee staff; or by experts, citizens, or organizations who appeared as witnesses. Exhibits may also include reports prepared by interim committees that met between regular sessions of the legislature.

In the Archives building, exhibits are generally stored in three-ring binders. In libraries, exhibits are available on microfilm through the mid-1990s. At that time, the state became dissatisfied with the quality of microfilm available and ceased making exhibits available in that form. Exhibits for recent years are sometimes included under the OLIS tab "Meeting Materials/Exhibits," but the Archives building remains the most comprehensive site for exhibits.

---

6. On the citizen engagement page of the Oregon Legislature's website, scroll down to the bottom and select the "Meeting Archives" box to find links to recordings back to 1999. The link is https://www.oregonlegislature.gov/citizen_engagement/Pages/Legislative-Video.aspx.

4. Original Bill Files

The *original bill file* is a manila file that contains the original text of the bill as well as any engrossed or enrolled copies. The cut-and-paste version of a bill that resulted from committee action may be included, with words scratched out and inserted text taped over old text. Because some of these versions may also be included as exhibits, there is some overlap between the contents of the exhibits binders and the original bill files.

The original bill file may also contain a *staff analysis*, now called a *staff measure summary*. (See the chapter appendix for an example.) This document describes the problem the bill is intended to address, states the purpose of the bill, and explains any committee amendments. Because bills are written in outline form and often include lists of statutory language to be modified or deleted, it may be difficult to grasp the key ideas by skimming the bill's text. The staff analysis is a helpful tool because it explains the bill in clear, concise language.

Additionally, the file may contain a *committee report*. This is simply a form for recording committee action, for example, recommending that the bill be passed or not. The file may also contain financial impact statements and tallies of votes on the floor of each chamber.

The original bill files are kept at the Oregon State Archives. For legislative sessions in 2007 onward, OLIS has put some of the material from the original bill files online. The text of bills is provided under the "Text" tab. The "Analysis" tab links to the staff measure summaries, revenue impact statements, fiscal impact statements, and any budget reports. Additional information may be available under the tabs for "Meeting Material/Exhibit" or "Amendments." Sometimes information from original bill files is cited by courts, so it is worth the effort to locate the files either in print or online.

5. Chamber Debate

Audio recordings of debate on the floor of each chamber are available, beginning in 1963 for the House and in 1973 for the Senate. For sessions from 1999 onward, audio or video recordings of chamber debates are available on the Oregon Legislature's website on the citizen engagement page, using the links in the meeting archives box. Audio tapes for prior sessions are kept at the Oregon State Archives. Also on the citizen engagement page, you can find links to live video for legislative events.

Table 5-2. Oregon Legislative History Research Online

Research Process	Example
Step 1: Find the statute in ORS online and review the source note to find the session law.	Go to the Oregon State Legislature's website at www.oregonleg-islature.gov, then hold your cursor over "Bills and Laws."
	In the drop-down menu, click on the current ORS (e.g., 2017 Oregon Revised Statutes).
	Scroll down to the volume that contains your statute (e.g., volume 6, Local Government, Public Employees, Elections, contains ORS chapter 250). Open that volume, and scroll down to your chapter (e.g., 250) or use the "Find" function. Open that chapter.
	Scroll through to the text of ORS 250.045 (or use the "Find" function). Note that the first time you see your statute's number, it will be in a table of contents format; continue scrolling to get to the text.
	At the end of the statute's text, the following information in brackets shows that the statute was last updated in 2009: [... 2009 c.533 § 1].
Step 2: Use the session law number to find the bill number.	Go back to the "Bills and Laws" page to open "Oregon Laws" (currently available for 1999 through 2018). Either use the drop-down menu, or click on "Bills and Laws" and use the list of links in the left margin.
	Scroll down to the 2009 regular session, and click the symbol to list the chapters. Scroll down to Chapter 533 and open it.
	You learn that this act was House Bill 2005. This screen shows additions to the existing law in bold type and deletions in bracketed italics. At the end of the statutory language, the date of approval by the Governor and the effective date are given.
Step 3: Use the bill number to find the measure history, legislative committee assignments, exhibits, and audio/video recordings of public hearings and work sessions.	On the Oregon legislature's website Bills and Laws tab, under Bills, select Previous Sessions. Select the 2009 Regular Session link. Note that this takes you to the OLIS website. Click on the House Bills drop-down menu to find the range of bill numbers that contains your bill, HB 2005. Expand that number range, and then click on the HB 2005 link. You can also go directly to the OLIS website at olis.leg.state.or.us/. Using the "Session" icon at the top right of the page, select the 2009 regular session.
	On OLIS, using the "Bills" icon and the "Bill Number" tab, enter HB 2005. The first screen you see gives an overview of the bill. Scroll down to the bar for "Measure History" and click on it for a list of the dates and actions taken on this bill, from when it was introduced until it was enacted. Review the list for public hearings and work sessions. For example, the House Rules Committee held hearings on March 25 and 27 and a work session on May 4.

Table 5-2. Oregon Legislative History Research Online, *continued*

Research Process	Example
Step 4: Locate recordings of the proceedings (if any).	Click on the link for any one of these dates for "Measure Details," summarizing that day's action. Then, in the right margin, scan the list of that committee's recordings for the same dates. These recordings will contain the substance of each hearing and work session.
Step 5: Listen to the recording.	You can link to recordings from OLIS. From the page you used in Step 4, just click the "play" button next to the date of the meeting you want to hear.*
Step 6: From the OLIS site, on the page for the bill, review other documents.	* From the "Text" tab, compare versions of the bill as it was introduced to later versions (i.e., engrossed, enrolled).
	* Under "Analysis," read the staff measure summaries, revenue impact statements, fiscal statements, or budget reports.
	* Check "Meeting Material/Exhibits" and "Amendments" for documents that might be available.

* The Secretary of State Archives website, sos.oregon.gov/archives, may have audio or video logs for specific bills; the logs include a detailed list of the times when testimonies begin. On the website, Click on "Archival Records" and "Legislative Committee Minutes, Audio Logs and Recordings" and then scroll down to "2009 Regular Session." From that link, select "House," then "Rules" for the committee. Scroll down to 3/25/2009 and the other dates noted in the "Measure History"; clicking on that link will open the audio log that accompanies the audio proceedings. You can also listen to the recording by clicking the "Audio" link to the right of the date that provided the audio log. Note that accessing materials in the Archives on the Secretary of State website may involve technical glitches depending on the browser you are using.

6. Journals

The journals of the House and Senate record the actions of each chamber when it is in session. Included in these journals are votes on bills and other measures, explanations of votes by representatives, and messages from the Governor. The journals are available in print and, in recent years, online. Senate journals are linked to the website of the Secretary of the Senate. House journals are linked to the website of the Chief Clerk of the House in the "House Journals" box.

Table 5-3. Oregon Legislative History Research in Print

Research Process	Example
Step 1: Find the statute in ORS or WORSA; refer to the history note to find the session law date of enactment.	Figure 5-4 contains numerous amendments that the researcher would need to check; the most relevant amendment for our example is chapter 713, section 3 of *Oregon Laws 1987*, which appears in the fourth line of the source note.
Step 2: Look up the session law in *Oregon Laws* to find the bill number.	Figure 5-5 shows the bill number is House Bill 2271.
Step 3: Go to *Final Status Report for Legislative Measures* to find the committee assignments and dates of consideration of the bill. (Note that, prior to 1997, this series was called *Final Legislative Calendar*.)	Figure 5-6 shows that the bill was considered by the House Labor Committee on March 6 and 25; then it was considered by the Senate Labor Committee on April 23 and 30 and June 8. Note: Appendix C of this chapter contains the Legislative Tracing for this bill. If you found this tracing early enough in your research, you could skip Step 3.
Step 4: Review the existing legislative history, including microfilm, audio tapes, exhibits, original bill files, and journals.	Appendix A of this chapter reproduces the staff analysis prepared for the Senate Labor Committee; this document is available in the original bill file in Salem. Appendix B of this chapter reproduces the minutes of the Senate Labor Committee of April 23, 1987; these minutes are not available on the Archives' website, though minutes from later years are. The researcher would have to go to the Archives in Salem or pay the Archives' staff to retrieve and photocopy these minutes. Similarly, to listen to the audio tapes, the researcher would have to go to the Archives or order a copy of the relevant tapes.

B. Legislative Tracing

Before conducting Oregon legislative history research on your own, first see whether the material you need has already been compiled. Whenever someone contacts the State Archives to request legislative materials, the reference staff compiles a *tracing*, meaning the staff determines which committees considered the bill and locates the minutes or logs from when the bill was discussed, including dates and page numbers. The staff also lists or summarizes related exhibits and compiles a list of committee audio recordings. This information is saved and made available to future researchers. (See the chapter appendix for an example.)

Legislative tracings are available for selected bills from the 1930s forward, with more tracings available for more recent legislative sessions. Currently, tracings are available online from the Secretary of State's E-files Document Center for selected bills from 1981 forward; a few older tracings are included as well.

If no tracing is available, the charges for the Archives staff to prepare one are reasonable. Alternatively, you can do the research yourself, as explained below. Legislative history prior to 1991 is available only in print, microfilm, and audio tapes. More recent legislative history research can be performed on the state's websites, though coverage changes as the state's websites are updated (and sometimes content disappears). Lexis and Westlaw provide many of the documents needed for Oregon legislative history research, in the databases listed above for bill tracking, but not the audio or video recordings.

C. Free Online Research

State websites contain much of the legislative history material explained above in Section A, but only for recent years. Currently, OLIS contains legislative material from the 2007 regular session forward.[7] The Secretary of State's website has legislative committee minutes from 1991 to 2005 and audio logs from 2007 forward.[8] The Oregon State Legislature's website provides *Oregon Laws* and ORS from 1999 forward.[9]

An outline for conducting legislative history research on these websites is provided in Table 5-2, using ORS 250.045 as an example. The example shows how the legislature amended the statute in 2009 to add rules regarding signature collection for Oregon's initiative and referendum processes. Those processes are discussed in Part IV of this chapter.

D. Oregon Legislative History on Lexis and Westlaw

Both Lexis and Westlaw provide some legislative history for recent years. Since coverage is limited both by date and content—significantly, neither service makes available audio recordings—using the state's free websites is often a better search strategy.

Some researchers prefer to find the measure history using one of the commercial providers, then pick up with Step 4 in Table 5-2. Using either Lexis or Westlaw, open the statute and scroll to the "History" or "Credits," where you will see the list of citations for *Oregon Laws*. Clicking one will take you to the session law and related information. Moreover, each service has databases containing bill analyses, reports, Governor's messages, etc.

---

7. The link is https://olis.leg.state.or.us/liz/sessions/.

8. The link is http://sos.oregon.gov/archives/Pages/records/legislative_minutes.aspx.

9. The link for *Oregon Laws* is https://www.oregonlegislature.gov/bills_laws/Pages/Oregon-Laws.aspx. The link for ORS Archives is https://www.oregonlegislature.gov/bills_laws/Pages/ORSarchive.aspx.

E. Print Research

Print research is required to compile legislative history for older statutes; while more recent legislative history research can be completed with print, online sources are much more effective.

To conduct print research, follow the steps in Table 5-3 to find the legislative documents and tapes that contain Oregon legislative history. That table includes examples from researching the legislative history of ORS 656.005(7)(b)(B) to determine whether a delivery man suffered a "compensable injury" when he broke his tooth on a piece of candy provided by his employer. Figures 6-4 to 6-6 provide excerpts from the legislative history in print.

Step 1: Before beginning legislative history research, you must know the codified number of the statute you need to research. (If you do not, review Chapter 4 on researching Oregon statutes.) At the end of the language of a statute is a source note that gives the statute's history; this note includes a reference to the session law that was codified as this statute and its date of enactment. For example, in Figure 5-4 the note [1975 c.556 §§ 2 to 19] means that ORS 656.005 was enacted by *Oregon Laws 1975*, chapter 556, sections 2 through 19.[10] The history notes in ORS provide information only as far back as 1953. If nothing appears in a history note, refer to *Prior Legislative History* to learn the derivation of the statute.[11]

Step 2: Session laws—the bills in the form in which they were enacted— are published in *Oregon Laws*.[12] The bills are organized by session law number, in chronological order based on the date of enactment. The bill number can be found after the words "An Act," following the chapter number. Senate bill numbers are preceded by "SB," and House bills are preceded by "HB."

---

10. Do not confuse the "chapters" in session laws with the "chapters" in ORS; the session law number provides purely chronological record keeping, while the ORS chapter places the enacted law in context with other statutes on similar topics.

11. *Prior Legislative History* was published with the 1953 edition of ORS. In the situation where you find nothing in the current ORS history note and have to refer to the *Prior Legislative History* volume for the source of the statute, you will likely find that there is no legislative history documentation because virtually none was produced.

12. *Oregon Laws* is published in bound volumes following the end of the legislative session in odd-numbered years. In even-numbered years, a paper supplement is published; that material is incorporated into the next bound set. Advance sheets are available earlier, while the legislature is in session. In addition, West publishes session laws in its *Oregon Legislative Service*.

Often a statute will be amended after it is enacted; the history note will give the session law number for subsequent amendments as well as the initial enactment. The example in Figure 5-4 shows numerous amendments. Reading each of them in *Oregon Laws* would reveal that in 1987 section 3 of chapter 713 amended the definition of "compensable injury," as shown in Figure 5-5.

Figure 5-4. Excerpt from *Oregon Revised Statutes* with History Notes

---

656.005 Definitions.

***

(7)(b) "Compensable injury" does not include:

***

(B) Injury incurred while engaging in or performing, or as the result of engaging in or performing, any recreational or social activities primarily for the worker's personal pleasure.

***

[1975 c.556 §§ 2 to 19 (enacted in lieu of 656.002); 1977 c.109 § 2; 1977 c.804 § 1; 1979 c.839 § 26; 1981 c.535 § 30; 1981 c.723 § 3; 1981 c.854 § 2; 1983 c.740 § 242; 1985 c.212 § 1; 1985 c.507 § 1; 1985 c.770 § 1; 1987 c.373 § 31; 1987 c.457 § 1; 1987 c.713 § 3; 1987 c.884 § 25; 1989 c.762 § 3; 1990 c.2 § 3; 1993 c.739 § 23; 1993 c.744 § 18; 1995 c.93 § 31; 1995 c.332 § 1; 1997 c.491 § 5; 2001 c.865 § 1 ...].

Source: *Oregon Revised Statutes*, volume 14, pages 309, 310 (2017).

Figure 5-5. Excerpt from *Oregon Laws 1987*

CHAPTER 713

AN ACT   HB 2271

Relating to workers' compensation; creating new provisions; amending ORS 656.005; and prescribing an effective date.

Whereas it is the desire of the Legislative Assembly to provide future guidance to the appellate courts of this state with respect to the interpretation of certain of the provisions of the Workers' Compensation Law included in this Act; now, therefore,

Be It Enacted by the People of the State of Oregon:

"Compensable injury" does not include: Injury incurred while engaging in or performing, or as the result of engaging in or performing, any recreational or social activities solely for the worker's personal pleasure.

Source: *Oregon Laws 1987*, pages 1402–03, excerpt from section 3(8)(a).

Step 3: To determine the committees to which the bill was assigned, refer to the series *Final Legislative Calendar*, renamed *Final Status Report for Legislative Measures* in 1997. This series is published after the legislative session ends. Each volume lists in separate sections Oregon Senate and House bills from a legislative session. The bills are listed in numerical order by bill number. For each bill, the series summarizes the legislative action taken, including which committees the bill was referred to. The excerpts in Figure 5-6 are for House Bill 2271, concerning the definition of "compensable injury," which was considered in 1987. The entries are in the House section, on pages H-55 and H-56. Each gives the date and the specific action taken.

Also included in *Final Legislative Calendar* or *Final Status Report for Legislative Measures* are lists of the members of the House and Senate for that session, committee assignments, executive appointments made, charts of which member introduced which bills, an index, and a table of sections of ORS that were amended, repealed, or added to during that session.

Figure 5-6. Example of *Final Legislative Calendar* Entries

HB 2271

1-15(H)	First reading. Referred to Speaker's desk.
	Referred to Labor.
3-6	Public Hearing and Work Session held.
3-25	Public Hearing and Work Session held.
3-30	Recommendation: Do pass with amendments, be printed A-Engrossed.
4-1	Second Reading.
4-2	Third reading. Carried by Shiprack. Passed.
4-3(S)	First reading. Referred to President's desk.
4-7	Referred to Labor.
4-23	Public Hearing held.
4-30	Public Hearing held.
6-8	Work Session held.
6-12	Recommendation: Do pass with amendments to the A-Eng. measure. Second reading.
6-15	Rules suspended. Third reading. Passed.
6-19(H)	House concurred in Senate amendments and repassed measure.
7-8	Speaker signed.
7-10(S)	President signed.
7-16(H)	Governor signed. (Chapter 713, 1987 Session Laws) Effective date, January 1, 1988.

Source: *Final Legislative Calendar 1987* (excerpts from pages H-55 and H-56).

Step 4: With a list of committees and dates, go to the microfilm to find the legislative history. The microfilm material is organized by committee, with committee names listed in alphabetical order. Under each committee, minutes are arranged by hearing date. The exhibits are contained on separate microfilms, arranged by committee and bill number.

Shortcuts: Cases may refer to the legislative history of a statute at issue, thus providing a shortcut in your research. Reading articles from newspapers, bar journals, law reviews, and websites can add to your understanding of the issue the legislature was concerned about, how the legislature intended to address it, and problems that may have resulted from the enacted statute.

F. Researching Older History

Searching for legislative history from the middle of the twentieth century and earlier is unlikely to produce results. Audio taping began on a selective basis in 1957, while minutes and other legislative materials have been deposited with the State Archives since 1961.[13] Finding legislative history before the 1950s will likely require the assistance of a law librarian or the Archives staff.

IV. Initiative and Referendum in Oregon

In addition to the traditional method of enacting laws, Oregon's initiative and referendum processes allow for direct legislation by the people of Oregon.[14] The initiative process enables voters to place a measure on the election ballot by collecting a certain number of signatures and meeting other procedural requirements. The number of signatures required is six percent of the votes cast for Governor in the preceding election.

Voters may also reject legislation adopted by the state legislature;[15] placing items on the ballot through this process requires signatures equal to four percent of the votes cast for Governor in the preceding election. Furthermore, Oregon voters may recall public officials by ballot.[16]

A useful resource in understanding these processes is the *State Initiative and Referendum Manual* provided by the Secretary of State. It may be downloaded in PDF at http://sos.oregon.gov/elections/Documents/stateIR.pdf. The manual

---

13. The statutes requiring record-keeping are ORS 171.415 and ORS 171.420.
14. Or Const, Art IV, § 1.
15. *Id.*
16. Or Const, Art II, § 18.

describes the overall processes and provides step-by-step instructions and examples of required forms.

The *Oregon Blue Book*, the official state directory that is compiled and published in odd-numbered years by the Secretary of State, contains a comprehensive listing of initiatives and referenda organized by election dates, measure numbers, ballot titles, and the resulting tally of "Yes" and "No" votes. An electronic version of the *Oregon Blue Book* is available online at www.bluebook. state.or.us.[17] Materials from initiative and referendum measures may be available from either the Elections Division or the State Archives.

Appendix

Examples of Oregon Legislative History

The following pages contain samples of the legislative history for the research example used in Section III.E. of this chapter. These documents are available through the Archives Division, Oregon Secretary of State. Errors in the originals have not been corrected.

---

17. The first electronic version of the *Oregon Blue Book* seems to have appeared with the 1997–1998 edition. *See* "Letter[s] to Oregonians" from Phil Keisling, Secretary of State, printed in the 1997–1998 and 1999–2000 editions of the *Oregon Blue Book*.

A. Staff Measure Analysis

OREGON STATE SENATE

LEGISLATIVE SESSION—1987

STAFF MEASURE ANALYSIS

Measure: HB 2271 B-Eng.

Title: Relating to workers' compensation; creating new provisions;amending ORS 656.005, 656.210, 656.307, 656.802 and 656.807; and prescribing an effective date.

Committee: Senate Labor

Hearing Dates: 4/23, 4/30, 6/8, 6/9

Explanation prepared by: Lynn-Marie Crider

PROBLEM ADDRESSED.

There is concern that the existing statutory definitions of occupational disease and injury do not adequately address micro-trauma or mental disorder problems; that the limitation period for filing an occupational disease claim is not realistic given the long latency period of some diseases; and that disease claimants may be undercompensated because temporary total disability benefits are calculated based on the wages the employee earned at the time of the last exposure—a time which may long precede the emergence of the disease.

FUNCTION AND PURPOSE OF MEASURE AS REPORTED OUT.

HB 2271 B-Eng. excludes from compensability injuries suffered while performing recreational activities solely for the worker's personal pleasure. It redefines occupational disease to specifically include certain mental disorders and conditions that arise out of a series of traumatic events. It limits compensability of mental disorders arising out of employment to disorders recognized as such by the medical and psychological communities and by requiring that, to be compensable, 1) there must be objective conditions in the workplace capable of stressing a worker; 2) those conditions must not be conditions to which workers are generally exposed; and 3) those conditions must not be reasonable disciplinary action. Furthermore, the worker must prove that the disorder arose out of employment by "clear and convincing" evidence.

The bill creates an arbitration procedure to decide which of two employers must pay a concededly compensable claim. The procedure permits only limited appeal from the arbitrator's decision.

The bill changes the time for filing an occupational disease claim from five years after the last injurious exposure to one year from the date the worker first learns of the disease, is disabled by the disease or is advised by a doctor that the worker is suffering from the disease, whichever is later.

It requires that temporary total disability benefits in occupational disease cases be calculated based on the wages earned by the worker in the worker's last regular employment rather than based on wages earned when last exposed to the disease—causing agent.

MAJOR ISSUES DISCUSSED.

The Committee reviewed the entire measure in considerable detail but with particular emphasis on none of the sections.

EFFECT OF COMMITTEE AMENDMENTS.

The Committee amended the bill to clarify that an injury is not compensable just because it occurred while the worker was enjoying his employment-related activities but only if it occurred while the worker was engaging in activity only for his own pleasure. The Committee also amended the occupational disease language to clarify that diseases arising from repeated trauma are compensable only if the traumas occur in the course of employment. The Committee deleted language denying compensability for mental disorders suffered by management employes if the disorder was caused by public controversy or job evaluations and substituted language excluding from compensability any disorder to any employee if it arose from reasonable disciplinary or corrective action or job evaluation. The Committee further amended the bill to allow full-scale appeals of arbitration decisions where the claimant's rights are affected and to limit the circumstances in which a claimant's attorney is entitled to fees for the attorney's participation in an arbitration proceeding.

Note: This analysis is intended for information only and has not been adopted or officially endorsed by action of the committee.

B. Minutes from Senate Committee

SENATE COMMITTEE ON LABOR

April 23, 1987   Hearing Room C
                                            3:00 pm. Salem, Oregon
                                                   Tapes 120—122

MEMBERS PRESENT: SEN. LARRY HILL, CHAIRMAN
                  SEN. GLENN OTTO, VICE-CHAIRMAN
                  SEN. BILL BRADBURY
                  SEN. LENN HANNON
                  SEN. C. T. "CUB" HOUCK
                  SEN. GRATTAN KERANS SEN. TONY MEEKER

STAFF PRESENT: LYNN-MARIE CRIDER, ADMINISTRATOR
                  CRAIG C. KUHN, ASSISTANT

WITNESSES: REPRESENTATIVE BOB SHIPRACK, DISTRICT 23
                  REPRESENTATIVE ELDON JOHNSON, DISTRICT 51
                  GROVER SIMMONS, NORTHWEST STEEL FABRICATORS
                    ASSOCIATION
                  DENNIS OLSON, MEDFORD CHAMBER OF COMMERCE
                  RANDY LUNDBERG, CASCADE WOOD PRODUCTS
                  SCOTT PLOUSE, ATTORNEY
                  JOE GILLIAM, CONTRACTORS FOR REFORM
                  STEVE SOCOTCH, AFL-CIO
                  DR. FRANK COLISTRO, OREGON PSYCHOLOGICAL
                    ASSOCIATION
                  CHUCK PALMER, FORMER PATIENT
                  ROGER SMITH, FORMER PATIENT
                  VINCENT LARSON, PATIENT
                  DR. DAVID WORTHINGTON, PSYCHOLOGIST
                  MARY BOTKIN, AMERICAN FEDERATION OF STATE,
                    COUNTY & MUNICIPAL EMPLOYES
                  DAVE HORN, OREGON WORKERS' COMPENSATION
                    DEFENSE ATTORNEYS ASSOCIATION
                  ED NIEBERT, TEKTRONICS

006   CHAIRMAN HILL called the meeting to order at 3:13 pm.

HB 2271 PUBLIC HEARING

015   REP. BOB SHIPRACK, District 23, said this was the only bill
      that came out of the Interim Task Force on Occupational
      Disease. The real issues in the bill are the definitions of
      "occupational diseases" and "mental disorders" associated
      with an individual's employment. Section 2 of the bill cod-
      ifies the current practice that the burden of proof in Work-
      ers' Compensation is on the worker. Section 3 codifies
      existing law with the addition of lines 18-19 on page two
      of the bill. Section 4 provides new definitions for "occupa-
      tional diseases", "mental disorders" and "micro-trauma". The
      intent is to ensure that the

Workers' Compensation system will be used for injured workers. Section 4 also defines what is not compensable.

098   REP. SHIPRACK said categorizing jobs according to stress was
       not the House intent for the direction of the bill. The
       bill is intended to provide better definitions for the
       courts. All occupations have inherent stress.

132   SEN. MEEKER said the bill needed more clarification regarding
       inherent pressure. REP. SHIPRACK said the most stress claims
       in Oregon come from office employees. The question is
       whether the job and not personal matters was responsible
       for the "breakdown". This bill tightens up the stress
       claims system.

175   SENATOR HOUCK spoke to the use of the words "clear and con-
       vincing" and asked how he felt about the term "real and ob-
       jective". REPRESENTATIVE SHIPRACK said they had discussed
       this in the House Labor committee. When the legislature at-
       tempts to define words that would only have meaning to the
       judge or jury, it is very difficult to ascertain specific
       definitions. He noted that, under the bill, to get into the
       Workers Compensation system with a stress claim, you have
       to prove by clear and convincing evidence that your dis-
       ability is work related; you're in the system and every-
       thing else must be proven by substantial evidence.

255   REPRESENTATIVE SHIPRACK noted that the last section of the
       bill repeals the statute of limitations for occupational
       disease claims and creates a new one. He said that many
       states are moving in this direction. There is a fear that
       people that are going to contract these occupational dis-
       eases may have a long latency period and not be able to be
       compensated through the Workers Compensation system.

314   REPRESENTATIVE JOHNSON, District 51, concurred with Repre-
       sentative Shiprack. He also reminded the committee that the
       bill passed the House 57-2 and passed unanimously in the
       House Labor committee.

330   REPRESENTATIVE SHIPRACK added that the bill also deals with
       cases where the issue is not whether the claim is compensa-
       ble but which employer or which insurer is responsible for
       the claim. The bill states that if the worker needs an at-
       torney present, then whoever is assigned the claim by the
       arbiter pays for the workers attorneys fees.

C. Legislative Tracing

Listing of Legislative records in
Oregon State Archives pertaining to: HOUSE BILL 2271, 1987
(At the request of
House Task Force on
Occupational Disease;
re. worker compen-
sation....)

HOUSE LABOR COMMITTEE MINUTES:

Mar 6: p. 1-6   (Also on Cassette 48, side A, ALL;
Cassette 49, Side A, 000-149, 181-END;
Cassette 48, Side B, ALL)
Mar 25: p. 1-7   (Also on Cassette 69, Side A & B, ALL;
Cassette 70, Side A & B, ALL;
Cassette 71, Side A, 000-061)

Exhibit file contains:

1. EXH A of 3/06: Proposed amendments submitted by
    OEA. 4 pages.

2. EXH A of 3/25: Proposed amendments submitted by
    Jerry Brown, Workers' Compensation Department.
    7 pages.

3. EXH B of 3/25: Testimony by Jim Edmunson. 2 pages.

4. EXH C of 3/25: Supreme Court decision, Dethlefs v
    Hyster submitted by Edmunson. 7 pages.

5. EXH D of 3/25: Supreme Court decision, Castro v
    Saif. 10 pages.

6. EXH E of 3/25: WC Board Hearings Division, Opinion
    and Order submitted by Evelyn Ferris. 11 pages.

7. EXH F of 3/25: Testimony by Steve Socotch, Oregon
    AFL-CIO. 9 pages.

SENATE LABOR COMMITTEE MINUTES:

Apr 23: p. 1-7   (Also on Cassette 120, Sides A & B, ALL;
Cassette 121, Sides A & B, ALL;
Cassette 122, Side A, 000-253)
Apr 30: p. 7-9   (Also on Cassette 132, Side B, 073-END;
Cassette 133, Side A, 000-417)
May 26, p. 13&14 (Also on Cassette 170, Side A, 010-042)
Jun 8: p. 1&2   (Also on Cassette 201, Side A, 034-412)
June 9: p. 1-4   (Also on Cassette 202, Side A, ALL;
(3:00pm)   Cassette 203. Side A, ALL;
Cassette 202, Side B, 000-ca200)

Exhibit file contains:

1. EXH B of 4/23: Testimony with proposed amendments
    by Dennis Olson,the Chamber of Meford/Jackson
    County. 12 pages.

2. EXH C of 4/23: Testimony by Joe Gilliam,
    Contractors for Reform. 1 page.

3. EXH D of 4/23: Testimony by Steve Sacotch, Oregon
    AFL-CIO. 9 pages.

4. EXH E of 4/23: Dr. Frank Colistro and others
    letters. 6 pages.

5. EXH H of 4/30: Testimony by Colleen Hoss, League of
    Oregon Cities. 2 pg

6. EXH I of 4/30: Proposed amendments submitted by
    Diana Godwin, OPA, etc. 2 pages.

7. EXH J of 4/30: Proposed amendments submitted by
    Diana Godwin. 1 page.

8. EXH A of 6/08: Hand engrossed version submitted by
    staff. 6 pages.

9. EXH A of 6/09: Hand engrossed version submitted by
    staff. 6 pages.

10. EXH B of 6/09: Memo from Roger A. Luedtke, submitted by
    staff. 5 pages.

Compiled by: M. McQuade, Reference Archivist
15 December 1987

The ORS is available back to 1953 through the Oregon State Library at http://library.state.or.us/repository/2014/201402281543535/.

Chapter 6

Administrative Law

I. Administrative Law and Governmental Agencies

Administrative law encompasses the rules and decisions of governmental agencies. Agencies include boards, commissions, and departments that are part of the executive branch of government.[1] Chapter 182 of *Oregon Revised Statutes* (ORS) lists the agencies found in Oregon. Examples include the Department of Transportation, the Public Utility Commission, and the Board of Nursing.[2] Table 6-1 shows the laws that give agencies their power and the functions that agencies perform.

Although agencies are administered by the executive branch, they are generally established by the legislature through *enabling statutes*. In Oregon, some agencies are created by the state constitution; for example, the State Lottery Commission was created through the initiative process that amended the Oregon Constitution.[3] The statutory or constitutional provisions that create agencies establish the powers and duties of the agencies. Each agency must work within the limits set by its enabling statute or constitutional provision.

Administrative law is primary authority like statutes and cases. It is unique because agencies perform functions of all three branches of government. Agen-

---

1. An agency is "any state board, commission, department, or division thereof, or officer authorized by law to make rules or to issue orders, except those in the legislative and judicial branches." ORS 183.310(1).

2. The *Oregon Blue Book* lists state agencies and provides a short description for each. The online *Blue Book* is available at www.bluebook.state.or.us; click on "State agencies A-Z."

3. *See* Or Const, Art XV, § 4. Following passage of that amendment, the legislature enacted chapter 461 of ORS to implement it. Remember to research statutes even if an agency was created by constitutional amendment.

Table 6-1. Agency Power and Functions

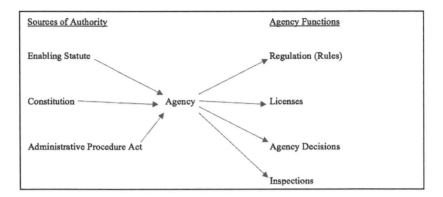

cies write *rules* (also called *regulations*) that interpret and apply statutes in the agencies' jurisdictions; these rules are similar in form and in authority to statutes enacted by the legislature. In Oregon, these rules are published by the Secretary of State in the *Oregon Administrative Rules Compilation*. As part of the executive branch, agencies issue licenses (such as those permitting citizens to drive) and conduct investigations to see whether laws are being followed (e.g., inspecting environmental sites). Agencies also hold quasi-judicial hearings, deciding cases that involve the agency's rules or its mission (e.g., to suspend a dental license or award unemployment benefits). These hearings are similar to court proceedings, but less formal.

In general, agencies function within the bounds of an Administrative Procedures Act (APA), such as Oregon's APA, found at chapter 183 of ORS.[4] The APA requires that the public be involved in developing agency policy and drafting rules. Agencies are encouraged "to seek public input to the maximum extent possible before giving notice of intent to adopt a rule."[5] To meet this goal, agencies schedule public hearings where interested entities or individuals may make suggestions or express concerns before a rule is finally adopted or changed. The APA also sets requirements for administrative hearings to ensure they are conducted fairly.[6]

Each of the three branches of government has some oversight of agency functions. The legislative branch generally grants agencies the power to perform

---

4. Some agencies are exempt from portions of the Oregon APA. ORS 183.315.

5. ORS 183.333(1).

6. *See* ORS 183.413 *et seq.*

Table 6-2. Example of Relationship between Statutes and Rules

---

An Oregon statute provides that an individual is disqualified from receiving unemployment compensation benefits if the individual left work voluntarily "without good cause."

An Oregon rule issued by the Employment Department enumerates the following examples of leaving work "without good cause":

(A) Leaving suitable work to seek other work;

(B) Leaving work rather than paying union membership dues;

(C) Refusing to join a bona fide labor organization when membership therein was a condition of employment; [and]

(D) Leaving to attend school, unless required by law.

Sources: *Oregon Revised Statutes* 657.176(2)(c); *Oregon Administrative Rules* 471-030-0038(5)(b) (excerpt).

their duties and provides funding for the agencies to operate. The courts may determine in contested cases whether agencies' rules are valid. The Governor is the supervisor of all state agencies, and the executive branch exercises control over some agencies by appointing their highest officials.

II. Administrative Rules

Administrative agencies promulgate rules, similar to the legislature enacting statutes. Administrative rules are written in an outline-numbering format similar to that of statutes. Rules are defined by Oregon statute to include "any agency directive, standard, regulation or statement of general applicability that implements, interprets or prescribes law or policy, or describes the procedure or practice requirements of any agency."[7] Many rules supply details that the legislative branch is not able to include in statutes. Since agencies are the experts in particular legal areas, they are well suited for supplying specific details to general statutes. See Table 6-2 for an example of the relationship between a statute and a rule. Rules also may provide guidance based on an agency's understanding of a relevant statute or determine procedural deadlines and format for agency filings.

Although rules and statutes are both primary authority, rules are subordinate to statutes. In any inconsistency between a rule and a statute, the

---

7. ORS 183.310(9).

Table 6-3. Example of Oregon Administrative Rule Numbering

The rules of the Board of Massage Therapists are contained in chapter 334 of *Oregon Administrative Rules Compilation*. Rules are separated into five divisions:

Division 1: Procedural Rules

Division 10: Massage Licensing

Division 20: Sanitation, Facility and Building Requirements

Division 30: Ethical Standards

Division 40: Complaints and Discipline

Within division 10, OAR 334-010-0005 contains rules for applying to take the exam to be licensed as a massage therapist; it requires certain forms to be submitted with the required fee, a copy of photo identification, class transcripts, etc. A later rule in that division, OAR 334-010-0012, sets out the appeal procedures for an applicant who fails the examination.

statute wins. Moreover, a rule cannot "cure" a statute that a court has held to be unconstitutional.

Administrative rules in Oregon are designated by a ten-digit number in the form 000-000-0000. The first three digits are the agency chapter number. The next three digits are a division number, which groups related rules together. The last four digits are the number assigned to a particular rule. See Table 6-3. In Oregon, the abbreviation "OAR" is used before regulations.[8] Note that the agency chapter number is not related to the chapter of ORS that created the agency or the chapter of the enabling statute in *Oregon Laws*.

---

8. The *ALWD Guide* and the *Bluebook* require the abbreviation "Or. Admin. R."

III. Researching Oregon Administrative Law

Oregon administrative law research has five essential steps:

A. Research the enabling act — find the statutory or constitutional provision granting the agency power to act

B. Find the rule — find the text of the rule in the *Oregon Administrative Rules Compilation* (OAR) for the year at issue

C. Update the rule to find proposed changes

D. Find agency and judicial decisions applying the rule

E. Consult agency websites and other resources

These steps are explained in detail below.

A. Researching the Enabling Act

Analytically, the initial question with any agency action is whether the agency acted within its power. If that is in doubt, the first step in administrative law research is to find the statute or constitutional provision that gives the agency power and to find cases interpreting that provision. Chapters 3 and 4 explain the process of researching constitutional provisions and statutes, respectively. Chapter 7 explains how to find cases in addition to those listed in annotated codes. If the agency's power is clear, skip this inquiry and move directly to finding relevant rules, as explained next.

B. Finding the Relevant Rule

Oregon's permanent rules are published annually by the Oregon Secretary of State in *Oregon Administrative Rules Compilation* (known as OAR, not OARC).[9] It includes the full text of rules as of November 15 of the previous

---

9. As stated in the text, the Oregon Secretary of State's office publishes both print and online versions of Oregon rules. Note, however, that the official copies of those rules are contained in administrative orders filed at the Secretary of State's Archives Division. Any discrepancy between those orders and the published versions are satisfied in favor of the orders. Copies of these orders are available for a fee.

year. Volume 1 contains an alphabetical list of agencies and a numerical index of chapters. OAR does not, however, contain an index for locating rules on a particular topic. When using only print sources, skim the list of agencies and determine which would be likely to make rules relevant to your client's situation. Turn to that agency's rules in OAR and skim them to see which ones apply.

A better approach for researching OAR is to use the Oregon Secretary of State's website at sos.oregon.gov. On that site, as of November, 2017, you can access rules through the Oregon Administrative Rules Database (OARD), a dynamic database that is updated as rules are received and approved. You can browse by chapter number or chapter name (based on the name of the agency), or search by rule number. On the home page of the Secretary of State website, a search box allows you to enter terms to search the text of Oregon's rules.

The OARD also provides access to the Annual Compilation. The online Compilation is published on the Oregon Secretary of State website on January 1 and contains the rules effective as of January 1. For example, the 2018 Compilation contains all rules effective as of January 1, 2018.

Oregon administrative rules are available on both Lexis and Westlaw.[10] Both services allow searching the full text of the rules as well as browsing the OAR table of contents. On Lexis, go to "Browse Sources" and type *Oregon administrative rules* into the search bar. Alternatively, enter terms into the universal search bar, limit the search to "Administrative Codes and Regulations," and select "Oregon" as the jurisdiction. The Lexis material is updated monthly. On Westlaw, type *Oregon regulations* into the universal search bar to locate relevant databases. To browse through sources, you could begin with "Content types," then "Regulations" and "Oregon"; you will end up in the same place if you begin with "State Materials," selecting "Oregon" and then "Oregon Regulations." To determine the scope of regulations, you can select the information icon that appears at the top of the page under the "Oregon Regulations" heading. In the Oregon Regulations Scope Information, expanding the "Contents" subheading displays information on the current coverage date.[11] To ensure currency on Westlaw, use the KeyCite function, which generally includes the most recent changes to Oregon rules.

---

10. Note that some university and county law libraries provide administrative material to researchers for free through commercial databases such as Westlaw.

11. For example, in February of 2018, the regulations were current through December 1, 2017.

Table 6-4. Example of an Oregon Rule

845-025-5500. Marijuana Worker Permit and Retailer Requirements

(1) A marijuana worker permit is required for any individual who performs work for or on behalf of a marijuana retailer, producer, processor or wholesaler if the individual participates in:

(a) The possession, securing or selling of marijuana items at the premises for which the license has been issued;

(b) The recording of the possession, securing or selling of marijuana items at the premises for which the license has been issued;

(c) The verification of any document described in ORS 475B.170; or

(d) The direct supervision of a person described in subsections (a) to (c) of this section.

(2) An individual who is required by section (1) of this rule to hold a marijuana worker permit must carry that permit on his or her person at all times when performing work on behalf of a marijuana retailer.

(3) A person who holds a marijuana worker permit must notify the Commission in writing within 10 days of any conviction for a misdemeanor or felony.

(4) A marijuana retailer, producer, processor or wholesaler must verify that an individual has a valid marijuana worker permit issued in accordance with OAR 845-025-5500 to 845-025-5590 before allowing the individual to perform work at the licensed premises.

Source: Oregon Administrative Rules, at arcweb.sos.state.or.us.

For previous versions of OAR, Lexis provides archival material dating from 2000, while Westlaw's coverage dates back to 2002, and the state website goes back to just 2010. Note that, on Westlaw, the prior OAR compilations are grouped together under "Oregon Historical Regulations."

After finding relevant rules, read the text of each rule carefully. Many techniques used for reading statutes apply equally well to reading administrative rules.[12] In particular, always look for a separate rule that provides definitions, be aware of cross references, read the text several times, and outline any complicated provisions. Table 6-4 provides an example of an Oregon rule.

Following the text of each rule is the history of that rule. This history can be important in determining when a rule was promulgated, amended, or

---

12. These techniques are explained in Chapter 4, Section I.A.1.b.

renumbered. Since a legal issue will be controlled by the rules in effect when the issue arose, you need to read the history note to learn of any changes to the rule since that time. The history begins with the statutory or constitutional authority for the rule, as well as statutes implemented by the rule. Then the rule's history lists in chronological order any changes to the rule. An explanation of the abbreviations used in the history note is included in the introduction to each print volume of OAR and on the state's website under "Understanding the History of an Administrative Rule," which is linked under "About the OARs."

C. Updating the Rule

Updating rules is accomplished by using the *Oregon Bulletin*, or by using a citator in Westlaw or Lexis that will reflect recent action in the *Bulletin*. This section first provides foundational information about the *Oregon Bulletin*, and then an overview of the methods used to update rules.

1. *Oregon Bulletin*

The *Oregon Bulletin* is a monthly online publication providing the text of new rules, notice of proposed action on rules by various agencies, and other helpful material. On the Oregon Secretary of State website, the *Bulletins* published prior to November 2017 appear as PDF documents with a table of contents and an OAR Revision Cumulative Index. Beginning in November of 2017, the *Bulletin* interface links through the OARD and displays the actual rule filings, which you can browse by chapter number or agency. The monthly issue contains filings from the previous month. For example, filings from February 1 through 28 appear in the March 1 *Bulletin*.

The *Bulletin* is available on Lexis in the "Oregon Bulletin" database within one week of publication. On Westlaw, the database "Oregon Proposed and Adopted Regulations" contains the text of the state's proposed and recently adopted administrative rules.[13]

The text of a new or modified rule will be published in the *Bulletin*. In addition, the *Bulletin* gives notice of proposed action on rules by various agencies. Agencies must announce when they intend to introduce new rules or modify

---

13. Although Westlaw does not contain the *Bulletin* itself, updates are incorporated into Westlaw's KeyCite citator each month, typically within three business days of the *Bulletin*'s publication.

existing rules. The *Bulletin* lists "Notices of Proposed Rulemaking Hearings/ Notices," which allow for public comment. The *Bulletin* contains other notices as well. For instance, the Department of Environmental Quality may publish notices of its proposed action on various cleanup sites around the state.

Executive orders also are included in the *Bulletin*. As one example, when the Governor declares a state of emergency due to flooding in an area of the state, the executive order is printed in the *Bulletin*.

The *Bulletin* occasionally provides synopses of Attorney General opinions, although these opinions are not published as part of OAR. Part IV of this chapter explains these opinions and where to find them.

2. Methods of Updating an Oregon Rule

Beginning in November of 2017, the online OAR on the state's website is updated continuously as rules are filed and approved.

Lexis and Westlaw are both updated regularly, although you should use each service's citator to ensure that you know about recent action published in the *Bulletin*.

The print OAR is current only through November 15 of the prior year, meaning that you must update it with the *Bulletin*. Use the link to the most recent issue of the *Bulletin*, then search by chapter number or agency and look for the link to the PDF for the first three digits of the rule you wish to update (e.g., 100s, 200s).

D. Finding Agency and Judicial Decisions

In addition to their rulemaking function, agencies also act in a quasi-judicial role, adjudicating cases pertaining to agency rules or actions. There may be several levels of agency review, depending on the agency. Check with a particular agency to learn the procedure it follows. The first level may involve a reviewer or adjudicator considering the claimant's file and making a recommendation or determination. Subsequently, a hearing may be held before an Administrative Law Judge (ALJ);[14] these proceedings may resemble short, in-

---

14. Most Oregon agencies are required to use Administrative Law Judges (ALJs) from the Office of Administrative Hearings (OAH). For more information, see *Oregon Administrative Law* (OSB Legal Pubs. 2010) (Hans Linde et al. eds.) and the OAH website at www.oregon.gov/oah. Note that ALJs are not required to be attorneys, although most are.

formal trials. At the conclusion of the hearing, the ALJ may issue a final order or a proposed order. A proposed order may be reviewed by the agency, which will issue a final order.

Some agency orders are widely available in print and online, while others are more difficult to locate.

Print Reporters

Print reporters containing agency decisions are not widely available. Only a few agencies publish decisions in print reporters. Where print reporters are available, they may not be updated. For example, the Land Use Board of Appeals (LUBA) and the Workers' Compensation Board each have their own print reporters.

Westlaw and Lexis

Westlaw and Lexis provide access to agency decisions and guidance for certain agencies such as Oregon Bureau of Labor & Industries, Oregon Environmental Quality Commission, Oregon Land Use Board of Appeals, and the Oregon Public Utility Commission, among others.

Agency Websites

Orders of some agencies may be available on the deciding agency's website, while still others may be available only from the agency itself. For example, the Oregon Land Use Board of Appeals website provides access to final opinions and published orders for certain years.

Judicial Review of Administrative Orders

Administrative orders may be appealed to the Oregon Court of Appeals for review.[15] Oregon courts have jurisdiction to review both the validity of agency rules and final orders.[16] Conducting case research may reveal cases that address the agency rules and orders relevant to your research. Case research is covered in Chapter 7, Part V.

The interplay between agency rulemaking and judicial interpretation is beyond the scope of this book, but note that the *PGE* framework (modified by

---

15. Some orders are appealable to circuit court, the Tax Court, or an appeals board of the agency. The final order should contain information about appeals.
16. ORS 183.400, 183.480.

Gaines) that was explained in Chapter 4, Part II, applies to interpretation of administrative rules as well as statutes. The seminal case on agency rulemaking is *Springfield Education Association v. Springfield School District*, 290 Or 217 (1980). For guidance on an agency's rulemaking authority and the court's role in judicial review, see Chapter 14, Judicial Review of Administrative Decisions, by James E. Mountain, Jr. and Sivhwa (Hwa) Gho, in *Oregon Administrative Law* (OSB Legal Pubs. 2010) (Hans Linde et al. eds.).

E. Consulting Agency Websites and Other Resources

The most valuable resource in administrative law research is often the agency itself. While statutes and rules are relatively easy to find, be aware that additional policies, guidelines, and decisions exist that may be difficult to access. A large part of your research should be reviewing the agency's website; all Oregon agencies are linked from the state's website at www.oregon.gov. Also consider talking to the agency's representatives to find out what material is available. For example, a handbook provided by the agency may outline the steps in filing a claim. The Secretary of State's website has a page called "State Agency Rules Coordinator Contact List" that provides the name and phone number for a contact person in each agency.

A useful tool for general administrative law practice in Oregon is the Oregon Attorney General's *Administrative Law Manual and Uniform and Model Rules of Procedure Under the Administrative Procedures Act*. It is updated every two years and published by the Oregon Department of Justice. Another helpful handbook in this area is *Oregon Administrative Law* (OSB Legal Pubs. 2010). The editors of this edition are Hans Linde, Steven R. Schell, and Alison G. Webster. For insights on questions that are not addressed specifically by Oregon law, consider Richard J. Pierce, Jr., *Administrative Law Treatise* (5th ed 2010), which has often been referred to by Oregon courts.

The Secretary of State's website contains more than the OAR and *Bulletin*. Agency forms, checklists, contact information, and other useful material are also available. In addition, the Oregon State Bar's website at www.osbar.org provides information and links to relevant sites. Click on "Member Groups" and "Sections," and then go to the Administrative Law Section's page.

Table 6-5. Sources of Formal and Informal Attorney General Opinions

1. Oregon Department of Justice Website
2. Westlaw — Oregon Administrative Decisions and Guidance
3. Lexis — All Oregon Administrative Materials
4. Opinions of the Attorney General of the State of Oregon (print)

IV. Attorney General Opinions

The Attorney General is the state's lawyer. In that role, the Attorney General provides formal and informal opinions to the state that are similar to the advice of an attorney to a client.[17]

A formal opinion responds to a specific question posed by the Governor, an agency official, or a legislator. As examples, an agency director may ask whether the federal constitution preempts the state constitution in a particular matter, or a senator may ask about the impact of a statute if enacted. The Attorney General's responses to these inquiries are available from the Department of Justice's website at www.doj.state.or.us; under the link for "Legal Resources," click on "Attorney General Opinions" in the bar on the right side of the screen.[18] These opinions are also available on Lexis and Westlaw. Table 6-5 summarizes the resources for locating Attorney General Opinions in Oregon.

Formal opinions are currently designated by a four-digit number. For example, No. 8287 was issued in 2008 in response to a question about the statu-

---

17. For more information on Attorney General opinions, see *Oregon Administrative Law, supra* note 14 (Chapter 9 by David K. Gerstenfeld addresses "Attorney General Opinions and Rules").

18. Some of the Attorney General's formal opinions are published in *Opinions of the Attorney General of the State of Oregon* and cited by volume and page number of the bound volumes. The print version of these opinions is official, available from the Department of Justice for a fee. Volumes of formal opinions are not kept current; formal opinions are currently being sent to libraries in PDF format for the library to print and place in a binder. Indexing is not current.

tory qualifications to be a county sheriff in Oregon. The question was raised by the Department of Public Safety Standards and Training.

While formal opinions address issues of general concern, informal opinions are likely to affect only the party requesting the opinion. Informal opinions are signed not by the Attorney General but by the Chief Counsel of the Department of Justice's General Counsel Division. Some letter opinions are available on the web with formal opinions.[19] Informal opinions are designated by year plus an identifying number (e.g., 2007-1).

V. Practice Example

Your client is interested in working in a recreational marijuana dispensary and needs to know the documentation, licensing, training, or permit she needs in order to do that kind of work.

A. Finding the Enabling Statute

Using the Oregon Legislature website, go to the "Bills and Laws" tab and click on the most recent edition of Oregon Revised Statutes (ORS). Browsing the table of contents, you see Volume 12 "Drugs and Alcohol, Fire Protection, Natural Resources (Chapters 471-535)." Expanding the view of that volume by clicking on the plus sign, you see that Chapter 475B is entitled "Cannabis Regulation." Under Chapter 475B, Recreational Use of Cannabis is covered by sections 475B.050 through 475B.395. Scanning the table of contents alerts you to Powers and Duties of Oregon Liquor Control Commission, 475B.025, which you will want to consult. Scanning further, you see sections on "Employees and Other Workers," with sections 475B.261 covering the "permit required to perform work for or on behalf of marijuana retailer." After reading OSB 475B.025, you know that the Oregon Liquor Control Commission (OLCC) has the power and authority to regulate the recreational use of cannabis, so you will want to look for rules issued by the OLCC.

---

19. Some of these informal opinions are compiled as *Letters of Advice* and are available in libraries in bound volumes or in loose-leaf binders. The same caveats about currency and indexing referenced in footnote 18 for formal opinions also apply to informal opinions.

B. Finding the Relevant Rule(s)

Go to the Oregon Secretary of State website, sos.oregon.gov, to find relevant rules regarding the work permit. On the opening page, select Oregon Administrative Rules (OARs). You can use the search box by typing in terms such as *marijuana work permit*, or you can select "Public Access" and search for rules by browsing the chapter name, *Oregon Liquor Control Commission*. If you search using terms, you will get a result of 845-025-5500, Marijuana Worker Permit and Retailer Requirements. After reading the regulation, look at surrounding sections to see if there are any other relevant regulations. For example, subsequent sections cover marijuana worker applications, worker permit denial criteria, examination requirements, renewal requirements, and suspension or revocation.

C. Updating the Rule(s)

You can stay on the Oregon Secretary of State website to update the rules using the *Bulletin*. To search for updates in February 2018, for example, you would first scroll to the end of the text of 845-025-5500 and see that an amendment was filed on December 22, 2017, effective December 28, 2017. You would want to look at the February *Bulletin* to find any proposed rules from January of 2018.

D. Finding Agency and Judicial Decisions, and

E. Consulting the Agency Website and Other Resources

Checking Westlaw and Lexis, you see that those services do not cover agency decisions and guidance for the OLCC, specifically. If you conduct a terms and connectors search on Westlaw, for example, you can find some results related to administrative decisions and guidance for recreational marijuana. The OLCC website, oregon.gov/olcc, is a good place to check for decisions and guidance. On the left-hand side of the OLCC home page, there is a link for recreational marijuana. From there, you can access recreational marijuana program bulletins, forms and publications, recreational marijuana laws and rules (including audio recordings of Marijuana Rules Advisory Committee meetings and Rule Hearings agendas and materials). While the website does not contain a collection of commission decisions, the bulletins as well as Rule Hearings agendas and materials provide guidance from the OLCC. To find judicial decisions, if any, follow the processes explained in Chapter 7, Part V.

F. Finding Attorney General Opinions

On Westlaw or Lexis, or on the Oregon Department of Justice website, you can use terms to search for opinions by the Attorney General regarding recreational marijuana work permits. Keep in mind that you might need to try various combinations of search terms to find relevant results.

Chapter 7

Oregon Courts, Judicial Opinions, and Case Research

A judicial opinion, also called a case, is written by a court to explain its decision in a particular dispute. Cases are available online on court websites, free sources like Google Scholar, and commercial sites including Lexis and Westlaw. In print, cases are published in rough chronological order in books called *reporters*. Even researchers working primarily with online resources must be familiar with reporters because case citation formats and pagination are still based on print reporters. This chapter begins with an overview of the Oregon court system. Then it explains reporters and online sources used to locate Oregon cases when you have a citation. Next, this chapter explains how to read and analyze cases. The last part describes how to research cases using full-text searches, topic searching, and digests.

I. Courts in Oregon

The basic court structure includes a trial court, an intermediate court of appeals, and an ultimate appellate court, often called the "supreme" court. These courts exist at both the state and federal levels.[1] The Oregon state court system is explained below;[2] federal courts are discussed in Appendix A.

---

1. Most states have the three-tier court system of Oregon and the federal judiciary. A few do not have an intermediate appellate court, just as Oregon did not until 1969.

2. Also located in Oregon are local courts and tribal courts. Local courts include county courts, municipal courts, and justice of the peace courts. These are not part of the state court system, but basic information about their jurisdiction is available in the *Oregon Blue Book* at www.bluebook.state.or.us; click on "State," then "Judicial branch." Similar information is posted on the Oregon Judicial Department's website; click on "Find a Court" under the "How Do I" tab and scroll down to "Other Courts." Information on tribal courts is available on the state's *Blue Book* website; click on "National," then "Indian Tribes."

In the Oregon state system, the trial courts are called *circuit courts*. These courts exist in each of Oregon's thirty-six counties; some counties are combined to result in twenty-seven judicial districts. In addition to the circuit courts, the Oregon Tax Court serves as the trial court for all state cases in which Oregon tax law is at issue.[3]

Oregon's intermediate court is called the Court of Appeals. Located in Salem, the Court of Appeals is composed of thirteen elected judges.[4] Cases decided by this intermediate court of appeals are heard by three judges sitting as a *panel* of the full court; the chief judge acts as a substitute when needed.

The Supreme Court of Oregon is the court of last resort.[5] It also sits primarily in Salem and has seven elected justices.[6] The seven justices sit *en banc* to hear all cases, unless a justice is recused.

The website for the Oregon Judicial Department contains useful information:
- An explanation of the jurisdiction of state courts
- A map of Oregon's circuit courts
- Links to state courts' websites
- Lists of court personnel
- Recent opinions of the appellate courts.

II. Sources for Oregon Cases

Oregon cases are available in print and online. Even when working online, you will most often find cases by references to the volume and page number where those cases appear in print reporters. This part of the chapter introduces official reporters, commercially produced regional reporters, and online sources for Oregon cases.

---

3. The Tax Court has existed since 1961. Appeals from decisions of this court go to the Oregon Supreme Court, not the Court of Appeals.

4. Frequently, a judge will retire in the middle of a term, allowing the governor to appoint a judge to complete that term. The new judge would then run in the next election.

5. Note that in some court systems the "supreme" court is not the highest court. In New York, the trial courts are called supreme courts, and the highest court is the Court of Appeals. Two other states, Massachusetts and Maine, call their highest court the Supreme Judicial Court.

6. A jurist on the highest court is called a "justice," while on lower courts the term "judge" is used.

A. Official Reporters for Oregon Cases

Oregon Reports and *Oregon Reports, Court of Appeals* are the official reporters for Oregon appellate cases. All cases decided by the Oregon Supreme Court are published in *Oregon Reports*. The abbreviation for this reporter is "Or." The case *Stranahan v. Fred Meyer, Inc.* can be found in volume 331 of the series *Oregon Reports*, starting on page 38. The case was decided in 2000.

Oregon's intermediate appellate court opinions are published in a separate reporter called *Oregon Reports, Court of Appeals*. "Or App" is the abbreviation for this reporter. The case *State v. Hart* was published in volume 222 of the reporter series *Oregon Reports, Court of Appeals*, beginning on page 285. It was decided in 2008. Almost all opinions of the Court of Appeals are published.[7] The first page of this case is shown in Figure 7-1. The case as it appears on Lexis appears in Appendix 7-A of this chapter; the Westlaw version is in Appendix 7-B.

> EXAMPLES: *Stranahan v. Fred Meyer, Inc.*, 331 Or 38 (2000).[8]
> *State v. Hart*, 222 Or App 285 (2008).

Cases from state trial courts in Oregon are not published but may be obtained directly from the court that decided the case, or sometimes online. As noted earlier, Oregon has a separate court that addresses matters of taxation. The decisions of the Oregon Tax Court are reported in *Oregon Tax Reports*, abbreviated "OTR."[9]

B. Regional Reporters and Oregon Cases

Cases from Oregon's appellate courts are also reported in a commercially produced regional reporter called *West's Pacific Reporter*. While the text of the court's opinion is the same in the official and unofficial reporters, the appearance, pagination, and editorial research aids may be different. Because Oregon's

---

7. Sometimes the Court of Appeals affirms a case without writing an opinion; these cases are "affirmed without opinion" and are referred to as "AWOPs." They are listed in a table in *Oregon Reports, Court of Appeals* and on the court's website, but they should not be cited.

8. Under Oregon courts' rules for citation, no periods are used in reporter abbreviations. This rule differs from other states' citation rules and from the national citation systems, as explained in Appendix B of this book. Outside of Oregon, the citation for the *Stranahan* case would be 331 Or. 38 (2000).

9. Oregon lawyers abbreviate this reporter as "OTR," but the national citation abbreviation is "Or. Tax."

Figure 7-1. Case Excerpt in Official Reporter

Dates ⟶ Submitted October 31, 2007, affirmed September 10, 2008

Parties and procedural
designations ⟶

STATE OF OREGON,
Plaintiff-Respondent,

v.

PAMELA ANN HART,
Defendant-Appellant.

Washington County Circuit Court

Docket numbers ⟶ D055175M; A130811

Parallel cite ⟶ 193 P3d 42

Background ⟶ **Background:** Defendant was convicted in the Circuit Court, Washington County, Donald R. Letourneau, J., of fourth-degree assault. Defendant appealed.

Holding: The Court of Appeals, Rosenblum, J. held that evidence was sufficient to support conviction.

Affirmed.

1. Criminal Law — Review — Scope of Review in General — Nature of Decision Appealed from as Affecting Scope of Review — In General — Criminal Law — Review — Presumptions — Facts or Proceedings Not Shown by Record — Sufficiency of Evidence — Inferences or Deductions from Evidence.

Court of Appeals reviews the denial of a motion for judgment of acquittal to determine whether the record contains evidence from which a rational trier of fact, drawing all reasonable inferences in the light most favorable to the state, could find all elements of the charged crime beyond a reasonable doubt.

2. Assault and Battery — Criminal Responsibility — Prosecution — Weight and Sufficiency of Evidence — Assault Causing, or Intended to Cause, Great Bodily Harm.

Headnotes ⟶ Assuming that rational factfinder could have determined that assault victim suffered substantial pain, as element of charged offense, such determination could not serve as basis for appellate affirmance of defendant's conviction, where factfinder clearly found that there was no evidence that victim suffered substantial pain. ORS 161.015(7).

3. Assault and Battery — Criminal Responsibility — Prosecution — Weight and Sufficiency of Evidence — Assault Causing, or Intended to Cause, Great Bodily Harm.

Evidence that victim sustained half-inch cut to the back of his head, which was still bleeding when police arrived, and was advised by medical personnel to go to the hospital, was sufficient to support finding that victim suffered "impairment of physical condition," as element of fourth-degree assault, as injury interfered with body's ability to function in normal manner by protecting inner body from infection. ORS 161.015(7).

Trial judge ⟶ Donald R. Letourneau, Judge.

Attorneys ⟶ Peter Ozanne, Executive Director, Peter Gartlan, Chief Defender, Legal Services Division, and Kristin Carveth,

Source: *Oregon Reports, Court of Appeals.*

courts cite to the official reporters, lawyers submitting briefs to those courts often cite the official reporters, too, but lawyers in other states are most likely to cite Oregon cases to the regional reporter.

West's Pacific Reporter publishes appellate cases from the courts of fifteen states. It is one of seven regional reporters that publish state appellate cases.[10] West decided which states' cases to publish together in its regional reporters, so these groupings have no legal impact.[11] Moreover, the coverage of each regional reporter is not the same as the composition of the federal circuits. The Ninth Circuit includes Alaska, Arizona, California, Hawaii, Idaho, Montana, Nevada, Oregon, and Washington, as well as Guam and the Northern Mariana Islands. It does not include Colorado, Kansas, New Mexico, Oklahoma, Utah, or Wyoming, yet those states' cases are reported in *Pacific Reporter*.

Sometimes when a reporter reaches a certain volume number, the publisher begins another series. In 1931, after publishing volume 300 of *Pacific Reporter*, West began again with volume one of *Pacific Reporter, Second Series*. In 2000, following publication of volume 999 in the second series, West started a third series, *Pacific Reporter, Third Series*. To find a case in a reporter with multiple series—whether searching print reporters or online—you must know which series the case was reported in. To indicate which state's courts decided the cases, a case citation includes an abbreviation at the beginning of the date par-

---

10. These reporters are part of West's vast National Reporter System, which reports and indexes most of the published cases of American courts.
   - *Atlantic Reporter* (A., A.2d, A.3d): Connecticut, Delaware, District of Columbia, Maine, Maryland, New Hampshire, New Jersey, Pennsylvania, Rhode Island, Vermont;
   - *North Eastern Reporter* (N.E., N.E.2d, N.E.3d): Illinois, Indiana, Massachusetts, New York, Ohio;
   - *North Western Reporter* (N.W., N.W.2d): Iowa, Michigan, Minnesota, Nebraska, North Dakota, South Dakota, Wisconsin
   - *Pacific Reporter* (P., P.2d, P.3d): Alaska, Arizona, California, Colorado, Hawaii, Idaho, Kansas, Montana, Nevada, New Mexico, Oklahoma, Oregon, Utah, Washington, Wyoming
   - *Southern Reporter* (So., So. 2d, So. 3d): Alabama, Florida, Louisiana, and Mississippi
   - *South Eastern Reporter* (S.E., S.E.2d): Georgia, North Carolina, South Carolina, Virginia, West Virginia
   - *South Western Reporter* (S.W., S.W.2d, S.W.3d): Arkansas, Kentucky, Missouri, Tennessee, Texas

11. In fact, because West grouped states into reporters during the 1800s, some placements now seem nonsensical, for example, placing Kansas cases in the *Pacific Reporter* and Kentucky cases in the *South Western Reporter*.

enthetical. (Note that the following examples follow the national citation format of using periods in reporter abbreviations.)

> EXAMPLES: *Stranahan v. Fred Meyer, Inc.*, 11 P.3d 228 (Or. 2000).
> *State v. Hart*, 193 P.3d 42 (Or. App. 2008).

If you are not sure which reporter a reader may prefer, you may want to include citations to both reporters. Two citations that refer to the same case in different reporters are called *parallel citations.*

> EXAMPLES: *Stranahan v. Fred Meyer, Inc.*, 11 P.3d 228, 331 Or. 38 (2000).
> *State v. Hart*, 193 P.3d 42, 222 Or. App. 285 (2008).

C. Online Sources for Oregon Cases

The full text of Oregon cases is also available for free from the Oregon Courts' website,[12] on Google Scholar, and (for members of the Oregon Bar) from Fastcase. Online services like VersusLaw require paid subscriptions, but they are less expensive than Lexis or Westlaw. Bloomberg BNA is a relatively new provider of legal documents, including Oregon cases.[13] Appendices to this chapter show the first screen of the *Hart* case on Lexis and Westlaw.

When working with cases from any online provider, be aware of pagination markers because information must be cited to a specific page in the print reporter. To show where a page change occurs, online services use *star paging.* Whenever text in the print reporter runs to the next page, that page number will be embedded in the text of the online version and preceded by an asterisk or "star." To give star pagination for multiple reporters, an online provider may assign a different number of asterisks to each reporter. Whenever a certain reporter changes pages, the new page number will follow the related number of stars. Text following that marker appears on the next page in the reporter. Figure 7-2 shows a Westlaw case with star paging. The text at the bottom of the screen supports the first headnote West has assigned to the case, as shown

---

12. A *slip opinion* is the actual document produced by the court, with no editorial enhancements. Oregon's appellate courts make opinions available on the Oregon Judicial Department's website. The state website is updated weekly.

13. Additionally, Willamette University College of Law provides an online service called Willamette Law Online at www.willamette.edu/law/resources/journals/wlo. This service provides summaries of cases from the Oregon Supreme Court, the Oregon Court of Appeals, the Oregon Land Use Board of Appeals, the United States Supreme Court, and the Ninth Circuit Court of Appeals, as well as leading intellectual property cases.

Figure 7-2. Star Paging

State v. Hart
Court of Appeals of Oregon. | September 10, 2008 | 222 Or.App. 285   193 P.3d 42   *(Approx. 6 pages)*

| ent | Filings (3) | Negative Treatment (3) | History (0) | Citing References (120) ▾ | Table of Authorities | Powered by KeyCite |

Go to ▾

***287** Defendant appeals a judgment of conviction for one count of fourth-degree assault. ORS 163.160(1)(a). She argues that the trial court erred in denying her motion for judgment of acquittal on the ground that there is insufficient evidence in the record that the victim sustained any physical injury. Specifically, she contends that the state failed to adduce any evidence that the victim suffered substantial pain or an impairment of his physical condition. We conclude that there is sufficient evidence of impairment of physical condition and therefore affirm.

The facts are undisputed. The victim is defendant's husband. During an argument, defendant pushed the victim, who was intoxicated, in the chest, causing him to fall over backward in the chair in which he was sitting. He hit his head on a windowsill and sustained a cut on the back of his head. Defendant's son called the police. Deputy Humphrey responded to the call. He testified that, when he arrived, the victim was bleeding and was holding a tissue to the wound. He described the wound as "about a half an inch gash" above the hairline. Humphrey called for medical personnel to examine the victim. They advised the victim to go to the hospital, which he declined to do.

Defendant was charged with fourth-degree assault and two counts of harassment, ORS 166.065, [1] and tried in a bench trial. The state's evidence consisted entirely of Humphrey's testimony. After the state rested, defendant moved for judgment of acquittal, arguing that the state had adduced no evidence that the victim suffered substantial pain or an impairment of physical condition and, thus, had not proved any physical injury, as required by ORS 163.160(1)(a). The trial court agreed that there was no evidence of substantial pain, but it concluded that the evidence of the cut on the victim's head constituted evidence of physical impairment, so it denied the motion. After the defense rested, the court convicted defendant.

***288** On appeal, defendant renews her challenge to the sufficiency of the evidence. The state responds that there is sufficient evidence ****44** in the record of both substantial pain and impairment of physical condition, arguing that we can affirm on either of those alternative bases.

[1]   We review the denial of a motion for judgment of acquittal to determine whether the record contains evidence from which a rational trier of fact, drawing all reasonable inferences in the light most favorable to the state, could find all elements of the charged crime beyond a reasonable doubt. *State v. Simons,* 214 Or.App. 675, 677, 167 P.3d 476 (2007), *rev. den.,* 344 Or. 43, 178 P.3d 247 (2008). ORS 163.160(1)(a) provides that a person commits fourth-degree assault if the person intentionally, knowingly, or recklessly causes physical injury to another. ORS 161.015(7), in turn, defines "physical injury" as "impairment of physical condition or substantial pain."

Source: Westlaw. Reprinted with permission of Thomson Reuters.

by the number "1." That text appears on page 288 of *Oregon Reports, Court of Appeals* and on page 44 of *Pacific Reporter, Third Series.*

Note that some of the more advanced online services allow you to select which reporter's pagination you want to have indicated, and then show only those pages. On Lexis, the page numbers for the selected reporter are presented in brackets, without asterisks.

III. The Anatomy of a Reported Case

Each reported case contains the exact language of the court's opinion, but the publisher also provides supplemental information intended to aid researchers in learning about the case, locating the relevant parts of the case, and finding similar cases. Some of these research aids are gleaned from the court record of the case, while others are written by the publisher's editorial staff.

The following discussion explains the information and enhancements for cases published with an Oregon Court of Appeals case, *State v. Hart.* To best understand the discussion, refer to Figure 7-1 or to the appendices at the end of this chapter, which include the first screen of this case on Lexis and Westlaw. Most online resources and print reporters will include most of this information and similar enhancements, although perhaps in a different order.

Dates. Reporters typically provide the date the case was argued and submitted to the court, and the date of the court's decision. In *State v. Hart,* the case was submitted on October 31, 2007, and the court issued its decision on September 10, 2008. For most citation purposes, only the year a published case was decided is important.

Parties and procedural designations. All of the parties are listed with their procedural designations. In general, if a losing party has a right to appeal, she will be called the *appellant* and the opposing party will be called the *respondent.*[14] If the losing party must ask the court to review the case, he is the *petitioner* and the opposing party will be the *respondent.* The *State v. Hart* case shows that the State of Oregon was the plaintiff but is now the respondent. Pamela Ann Hart was the defendant and is now the appellant.

Docket numbers. The tracking number assigned to the case by a court is called a docket number. Each court assigns a different docket number to the case, just as colleges and universities assign each student a different student identification number. In Oregon, the circuit court docket numbers begin with CC; Court of Appeals docket numbers begin with CA; and Supreme Court docket numbers begin with SC.

Docket numbers are helpful in locating the parties' briefs, a court's orders, or other documents related to that case. Because some of these documents are not published, they can be obtained only from the court that decided the case. To request these documents, you must have the appropriate docket number or, in some instances, the parties' names.

Parallel citations. Cases are often published in multiple reporters or online databases. The citations to these various sources for the same case are *parallel*

---

14. In other jurisdictions, the term *appellee* is used for respondent in this situation.

citations. The parallel citations for the *State v. Hart* decision from the Oregon Court of Appeals are 222 Or App 285 and 193 P3d 42.

Synopsis. One of the most helpful research aids included by a publisher's editorial staff is a very brief summary of the case; it may be called a synopsis, background, syllabus, or overview. Westlaw's version is called a *synopsis,* and Lexis's version is called an *overview.* It quickly summarizes the key facts, procedural posture, legal points, and disposition of the case. Reading a synopsis can quickly show whether a case is on point for your research issue. You cannot rely exclusively on a synopsis and must never cite the synopsis, even when it gives an excellent summary of the case.

Headnotes. A headnote is a sentence or short paragraph that sets out a single point of law in a case. Most cases will have several headnotes because most cases discuss several points of law. The number of headnotes varies by publisher, meaning the number of headnotes for a case on Westlaw will likely be different from the number of headnotes for the same case on Lexis.[15]

The text of each headnote often comes directly from the text of the opinion. But because only the opinion itself is authoritative, do not rely on headnotes in doing research and do not cite them in legal documents.

At the beginning of each headnote is a number identifying it in sequence with other headnotes. Within the text of the opinion, the same sequence number will appear in bold font or be enclosed in brackets print at the point in the text supporting the headnote. Online, the sequence number may link directly from the headnote to the relevant portion of the text. Read and cite that text, not the headnote.

Just after the sequence number, each headnote begins with a word or phrase in bold print. These are used in subject indexes to locate other cases that discuss similar points of law. For example, the image for *State v. Hart* in Figure 7-1 shows the first headnote is about Criminal Law. In the Westlaw image in Appendix 7-B, the phrases to the right of the key icon provide two specific criminal law topics that the headnote addresses. Clicking on Criminal Law or on one of the subtopics would take you to a database where Westlaw has compiled other headnotes on the same topics.

You can use headnotes as research tools in the following ways:

---

15. In Oregon, the headnotes of the official reporters and the headnotes of *West's Pacific Reporter* are essentially the same. Moreover, the headnotes in *West's Pacific Reporter* will be the same as those on Westlaw.

- Use the headnote reference as a searchable term.
- Click on a relevant headnote in a case you have already found.
- Look in a database containing headnotes (sometimes called a digest).

Library references. Some reporters give cross references to the relevant sections of a legal encyclopedia like *Corpus Juris Secundum* (CJS). A summary of the law in a legal encyclopedia could provide valuable background information and refer to additional cases or statutes that are on point.

Procedural information. Reporters contain a variety of procedural information on each case, including the court from which the case was appealed, the name of the trial court judge, the appellate judges who heard the case, and the judge who wrote the appellate decision. Note that following a judge's name may be "C.J." for the chief judge, "P.J." for the presiding judge in the Court of Appeals, or "J." for another judge.

When a case is decided *per curiam,* no judge is given credit as author of the court's opinion. If a case includes concurring or dissenting opinions, they will be noted in the procedural listings. Also in this section will be the attorneys who argued for each party.

Disposition. The disposition of the case is the court's decision to affirm, reverse, remand, or vacate the decision below. If the appellate court agrees with only part of the lower court's decision, the appellate court may affirm in part and reverse in part.

Opinion. The actual opinion of the court begins with the name of the judge who wrote the opinion, given in bold. If the appellate judges who heard the case do not agree on the outcome or the reasons for the outcome, they may write separate opinions. An appellate case may have one opinion or several:

- The opinion supported by a majority of the judges is called the *majority opinion.*
- An opinion written to agree with the outcome but not the reasoning of the majority is called a *concurring opinion.*
- Opinions written by judges who disagree with the outcome supported by the majority of the judges are *dissenting opinions.* While only the majority opinion is binding precedent, the other opinions provide valuable insights and may be cited as persuasive authority.
- If there is no majority on both the outcome and the reasoning, the case will be decided by whichever opinion garners the most support and is called a *plurality decision.*

IV. Reading and Analyzing Cases

After locating a case, you must read it, understand it, and analyze its potential relevance to the problem you are researching. This is an intense process. It is not unusual for a lawyer to spend hours reading and re-reading a complex case. For a novice, this reading is frequently interrupted by referring to a law dictionary to look up unfamiliar terms.

To aid your early efforts to understand cases, the following sections explain basic concepts of civil procedure and case analysis. This part ends with strategies for reading cases effectively.

A. A Thimbleful of Civil Procedure

The person who believes he was harmed begins civil litigation by filing a *complaint* in the court he selects. The *plaintiff* is the person who files the complaint; the person against whom the complaint is filed is the *defendant*. The complaint names the parties, states the facts, notes the relevant laws, and asks for relief. Courts vary considerably in how much information is required at this stage of the litigation, but the complaint must be specific enough to put the defendant on notice of the legal concerns at issue and to allow her to prepare a defense. In Oregon, more specific pleading is required.

The defendant has a limited amount of time in which to file a response to this complaint. (If the defendant does nothing within the prescribed time, the plaintiff can ask the court for a *default judgment*, which would grant the plaintiff the relief sought in the complaint.) One form of response to the complaint is an *answer*. In the answer, the defendant admits to the parts of the complaint that she knows are true, denies those things that she disputes, and asserts no knowledge of other allegations. The defendant may also raise affirmative defenses.

Throughout the litigation, parties submit a variety of papers to the court for its consideration. Some require no action or response from the court (e.g., the filing of the complaint). In other instances, a party asks the court to make a decision or take action. An example is a motion for summary judgment, where a party asks the court to decide the case in that party's favor without holding a trial.

When the trial judge grants a motion that ends a case, the losing party can appeal.[16] The appealing party is called the *appellant*; the other party is the *respondent*.[17] In deciding an appeal from an order granting a motion, the appellate court is deciding whether the trial judge was correct in issuing the order at that stage of the litigation. If the appellate court agrees with the decision of the trial judge, it will *affirm*. If not, the court will *reverse* the order granting the motion and, in some instances, *remand* the case back to the trial court.

Even during trial, the parties can make motions and appeal the judge's ruling. For example, at trial, the plaintiff presents his evidence first. After all of the plaintiff's witnesses have testified, the defendant may move for a *judgment as a matter of law*, arguing that the plaintiff cannot win based on the evidence presented and asking the judge for an immediate decision. The judge's order granting that motion would end the case, and the plaintiff could appeal. (If the judge denied the motion, the trial would continue.)

Most reported cases are appeals of orders granting motions. These cases apply different standards of review, depending on the motion that is the object of the appeal. While standards of review are beyond the scope of this book, understanding the procedural posture of the case is crucial to understanding the court's holding. The relevant rules of civil procedure will guide your analysis. Texts listed in Appendix C of this book contain helpful explanations as well.

B. Analyzing the Substance of Cases

Determining whether a case is relevant to your research problem can be difficult. If the case concerns the same legally significant facts as your client's

---

16. It is also possible that the parties will be inclined to settle following a court's order deciding a motion. For instance, a plaintiff who survives summary judgment will likely be offered a settlement to dispose of the case faster. In addition to saving money and time, defendants may also offer to settle to preserve favorable appellate law that could be reversed in an appeal. For example, in a case brought under Oregon's statute on uninsured drivers, ORS 742.504(4)(b), insurance companies may want to preserve the interpretation currently applied by the Oregon Supreme Court, which is more favorable to insurance providers. For this reason, insurance companies have an incentive to settle prior to an appellate decision overturning the current law.

17. In most jurisdictions, the terms appellant-appellee are used when a party has a right to appeal, while the terms petitioner-respondent apply to parties when the court has discretion to hear the appeal. Oregon uses the term respondent for the non-moving party in both instances.

situation and the court applies law on point for your problem, then the case is relevant. "Legally significant facts" are those that affect the court's decision. Some attorneys call these "outcome-determinative facts" or "key facts." Which facts are legally significant depends on the case. The height of the defendant in a contract dispute is unlikely to be legally significant, but that fact may be critical in a criminal case where the only eyewitness testified that the thief was about five feet tall.

Rarely will research reveal a case with facts that are exactly the same as your client's situation. Rather, several cases may involve facts that are similar to your client's situation but not exactly the same. Your job is to determine whether the facts are similar enough for a court to apply the law in the same way and reach the same outcome. If the court reached a decision favorable to your client, you will highlight the similarities. If, on the other hand, the court reached an unfavorable decision from your client's perspective, you may argue that the case is distinguishable from yours based on its facts or that its reasoning is faulty. You have an ethical duty to ensure that the court knows about a case directly on point, even if the outcome of that case is adverse to your client.

It is also unlikely that one case will fully address all aspects of your client's situation. Most legal claims have several elements or factors. *Elements* are required subparts of a claim (e.g., the statutory requirements for burglary), while *factors* are important considerations that are not all required (e.g., components in determining which custody arrangement is in the best interests of a child). If a court decides that one element is not met, it may not discuss others. In a different case, the court may decide that two factors are so overwhelming that others have no impact on the outcome. In these circumstances, you would have to find additional cases that analyze the other elements or factors.

Once you determine that a case is relevant to some portion of your analysis, you must decide how heavily it will weigh in your analysis. Two important points need to be considered here. One is the concept of *stare decisis;* the other is the difference between the holding of the case and dicta within that case.

Stare decisis means "to stand by things decided."[18] This means that courts must follow prior opinions, ensuring consistency in the application of the law. This requirement, however, is limited to the courts within one jurisdiction. The Oregon Court of Appeals must follow the decisions of the Oregon Supreme Court, but not those of the courts of any other state. The concept of *stare*

---

18. *Black's Law Dictionary* 1626 (10th ed 2014).

decisis also refers to a court with respect to its own opinions. Thus, the Court of Appeals should follow its own earlier cases in deciding new matters. A court may decide not to continue following its earlier cases because of changes in society that have outdated that law, or because a new statute has been enacted that changes the legal landscape.

Under *stare decisis*, courts are required to follow the holding of prior cases. The *holding* is the court's ultimate decision on the matter of law at issue in the case. Other statements or observations included in the opinion are not binding; they are referred to as *dicta*. For example, a court in a property dispute may hold that the land belongs to Martinez. In reaching that decision, the court may note that had the facts been slightly different it would have decided the land belonged to Seifer. That observation is not binding on future courts, though it may be cited as persuasive authority.

After finding a number of cases that have similar facts, that discuss the same legal issue, and that are binding on your client, the next step is to synthesize the cases to state and explain the legal rule. Sometimes a court states the rule clearly and completely; if not, you will need to piece together the information from the relevant cases to state the rule concisely. Then use the analysis and facts of various cases to explain the law. Decide how the rule applies to the client's facts and determine your conclusion. Note that this method of synthesis is much more than merely summarizing all of the various cases. Legal analysis texts in Appendix C of this book explain synthesis in detail.

C. Strategies for Reading Cases

As you begin reading cases, the following strategies may help you understand them more quickly and more thoroughly.

- Quickly determine whether the case seems to be on point, either by reading the synopsis or by reading the portion of the case that contains your research terms. Online services will highlight search terms both in headnotes and the text of the opinion.
- If the case seems to be on point, skim the entire case for an overview of what happened and why, focusing on the most relevant portion of the case. This portion might be identified by an online service because it contains your search terms, or it might be identified by a relevant headnote. Remember that one case may discuss several issues of law, only one or two of which may interest you.
- Read the case slowly and carefully. Skip the parts that are obviously not pertinent to your problem. For example, when researching a property

question, there is no need to scrutinize the tort issue that is not pertinent to your property question.

- At the end of each paragraph, page, or screen, consider what you have read. If you cannot summarize it, try reading the text again.
- The next time you read the case, make notes. The notes may be in the form of a formal "case brief" or they may be scribbles that only you can understand. Regardless of the form, the process of taking notes will help you parse through, identify, and comprehend the essential concepts of the case. In law school, the notes will record your understanding of the case both for class discussion and for the end of the semester when you begin to review for exams. When preparing to write a legal document, the notes will assist you in organizing your analysis into an outline.
- Deep concentration is required to achieve thorough comprehension of judicial opinions. Some researchers prefer to print key cases, as reading them in hard copy enhances understanding. Other researchers read cases online; if you do so, note that closing other windows helps to avoid interruptions and distractions. When reading cases online, using a larger screen helps you see more context and understand the text better. Using an online service's features that allow you to highlight and annotate text can also ensure that you are reading actively.

Reading cases and understanding the law will be easier with an organized approach, so begin by sorting cases according to jurisdiction and then by decision date. If the law at issue has several elements or factors, you might also organize the cases according to the elements or factors they discuss. Then, begin with the most recent case to find the current rule of law and read the rest in reverse chronological order. As an alternative, some researchers read cases chronologically to learn how the law developed over time. The key is to define your goal and organize the order in which you read the cases accordingly.

Pay attention to how the cases fit together. Has the law remained unchanged or have new elements been introduced? Has the meaning of an important term been redefined? Have certain facts virtually guaranteed success for one party while other facts have tended to cause difficulties? Does one case summarize the current rule or do you have to synthesize a rule from several cases that each address part of the rule? Look for trends in the law and in the facts of the cases. Then carefully consider how the synthesized cases affect your research project.

V. Researching Judicial Opinions

Lawyers typically find references to relevant cases throughout the research process: Many secondary sources provide links to relevant cases, and some secondary sources analyze cases in depth. Annotated statutes are valuable in large part because they contain "Notes of Decisions"—short summaries of and links to cases that interpret or apply statutes. Cases cite precedent, so reading one case might reveal several others that are also relevant. Citators like Shepard's and KeyCite provide lists of subsequent cases that cite one particular case. These approaches to researching cases are covered in other chapters.[19]

This part of the chapter explains three additional ways to research case law to be sure that your research is thorough: (1) full-text searching for cases using either terms and connectors searching or natural language searching, both of which were introduced in Chapter 1; (2) topical searching for cases online, also introduced briefly in Chapter 1; and (3) searching an index of cases, which is sometimes called a *digest*. Digests organize the headnotes from cases on similar subjects to create the index. Digests exist both online and in print. The West digest system is the most widely recognized, so it receives the most attention here.

Each of these approaches will produce a list of potentially relevant cases. In deciding which cases in the results list to read, consider the following guidelines:

- Read first those cases that are binding authority in your jurisdiction.
- Within that subset, read the more recent cases because they reflect the current state of the law.
- Consider the facts of the cases, as you should include in your analysis any cases with facts similar to your client's facts. You can identify factually similar cases either by skimming their headnotes or by narrowing the results by entering terms in a search box.

Never disregard a binding or factually similar case simply because that case reaches a result that would be bad for your client. You must either find a way to distinguish that case or find an alternative legal basis for your claim.

---

19. If the area of law you are researching is not covered by a statute, you will not find statutory annotations, and if you are researching a new area of law, you might find few secondary sources on point and few references in citators.

A. Full-Text Searching for Cases

Regardless of the service you are using for full-text searching, creating effective searches can yield the most useful cases. If you are unsure what you are looking for, start with broad terms, perhaps in a natural language search. Sometimes, entering a few words in the search bar can get you started. To be thorough, though, create a list of potential searches using different search terms and connectors. In creating these searches, anticipate the types of documents that might be relevant to your issues and where key terms might appear in those documents. Be specific enough to avoid getting results that will not be helpful. Having a list of effective searches for your issue early in the research process makes it easier for you to plug that search into multiple different databases or relevant jurisdictions.

1. Searching Westlaw

Westlaw has several databases containing Oregon cases. One large database contains cases from Oregon's state and federal courts. A narrower database contains just Oregon state cases. In addition, separate state databases exist for cases from the Oregon Supreme Court, the Oregon Court of Appeals, and the Oregon Tax Court. Other databases contain cases of federal courts located in Oregon (e.g., the federal district court, the federal bankruptcy court).

You can find these databases in several ways. First, in the universal search bar, begin typing *Oregon cases* (or a more specific search for a particular court) and you will see a list of relevant databases. Click on the title of the database you wish to search. Second, on the Westlaw home page, click on the link "State Materials" and then "Oregon," and review the databases listed under "Cases." Alternatively, from "Content types," click on "Cases," and then "Oregon." Whichever approach you take, always click the small "i" icon to learn the exact coverage of each database.

Once you have selected a database, it will be noted in a tab to the left of the universal search bar. In Figure 7-3, the database "Oregon State and Federal Cases" has been selected. When you then enter a search in the universal search bar, the results will be drawn only from the selected database, not from other materials in Westlaw's vast collection of documents.

Another approach is to type a search query into the universal search bar and select "Oregon" as the jurisdiction, using the drop-down menu to the right of the search bar. The results would be drawn from across the content areas in Westlaw. To search specifically for cases, click on "Cases" under "View" in the left margin. Scroll down farther in the left margin to find filters for narrowing the search by jurisdiction and court, to limit the date range, to search for specific terms, etc.

Figure 7-3. Selecting Oregon Case Databases on Westlaw

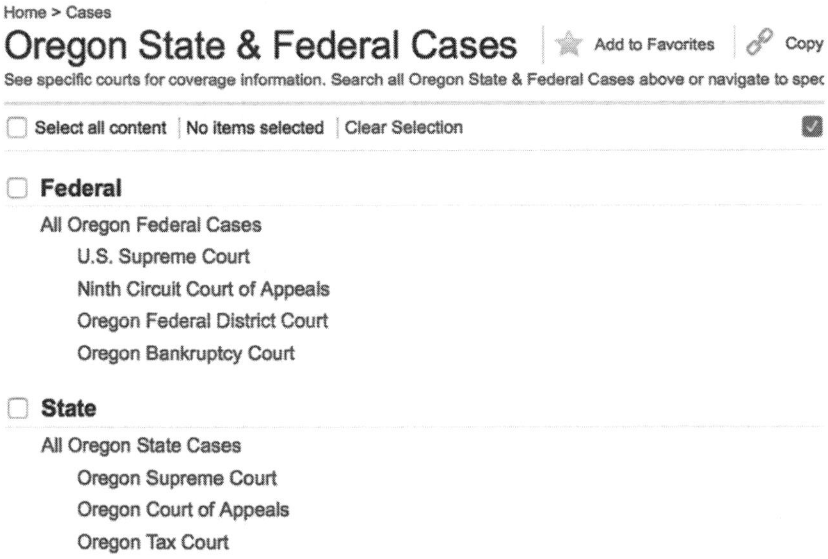

Home > Cases

Oregon State & Federal Cases   ☆ Add to Favorites   🔗 Copy

See specific courts for coverage information. Search all Oregon State & Federal Cases above or navigate to spec

☐ Select all content │ No items selected │ Clear Selection   ☑

☐ **Federal**

    All Oregon Federal Cases

        U.S. Supreme Court

        Ninth Circuit Court of Appeals

        Oregon Federal District Court

        Oregon Bankruptcy Court

☐ **State**

    All Oregon State Cases

        Oregon Supreme Court

        Oregon Court of Appeals

        Oregon Tax Court

Source: Westlaw. Reprinted with permission of Thomson Reuters.

2. Searching Lexis Sources

Lexis allows you to restrict a search to Oregon cases in two primary ways: (1) using limitations on the main research screen and (2) adding a source to your search.

First, from the "Explore Content" tab under the universal search bar or the "Search" box to the right of the search bar, you can limit by content type or category (select "Cases") and jurisdiction (select "Oregon"). Additionally, you can select from a list of forty practice areas and topics (e.g., "Real Property"). Figure 7-4 shows these pre-search filters selected from the "Search" box. Then type your search into the universal search bar, using either a terms and connectors query or a natural language query. The results will be limited to Oregon cases, as well as any topic restriction you included.

You can further narrow results by court, by date (e.g., 1980 forward) and by term (e.g., exclusive possession), using filters in the left margin. Results for a search of *title by adverse possession* using these filters are shown in Figure 7-4. The initial limitations appear just under the universal search bar; the date and search term filters for the search results appear under "More."

You can sort the list of search results by relevance, document title, jurisdiction, court, and date. The "Sort by" menu is at the right of the screen, just

Figure 7-4. Lexis Searching for Oregon Cases

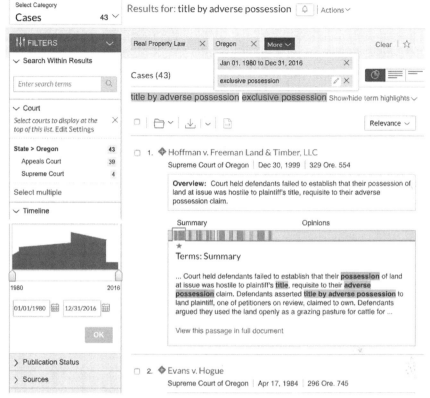

above the search results. You can also control the information displayed in the results: just an overview, an overview showing your search terms, or an overview with a portion of the case containing the most search terms. These options are linked from a drop-down menu on the right side of Figure 7-4.

A second option is to include a source in your search. From the top of the main research page, open the link to "Browse." Enter a search for sources related to Oregon cases in the search box in the left frame. After you click the search icon, you will have the option of adding the source as a restriction to the search, meaning that only documents in that source will be in your search results. (Figure 4-12 in Chapter 4 illustrates the drop-down menu in "Browse Sources," in the context of statutory research.)

Again, Lexis allows you to run full-text searches without any restrictions. The results will be drawn from all Lexis sources within your subscription. You can then open the tab for "Cases" and further restrict by jurisdiction and other filters. (Figure 9-2 near the end of this book demonstrates this type of unrestricted search.)

B. Online Topic Searching for Cases

1. Topical Searching on Westlaw

Westlaw provides topic searching primarily through two tools: a "Practice areas" link on the main page and the "Key Numbers" link under "Content areas."

a. Practice Areas Tab

The Westlaw home page provides "Practice areas" that link to over thirty topics, including Bankruptcy, Criminal Law, Family Law, Intellectual Property, Securities Enforcement and Litigation, and Tax. To find cases within one of the broad subjects listed, click on its name, and then click on the link for "Cases," as shown in Figure 7-5. Recognize that the various practice areas have different interfaces, and not all will look like Figure 7-5.

Figure 7-5. Searching Real Property Topic on Westlaw

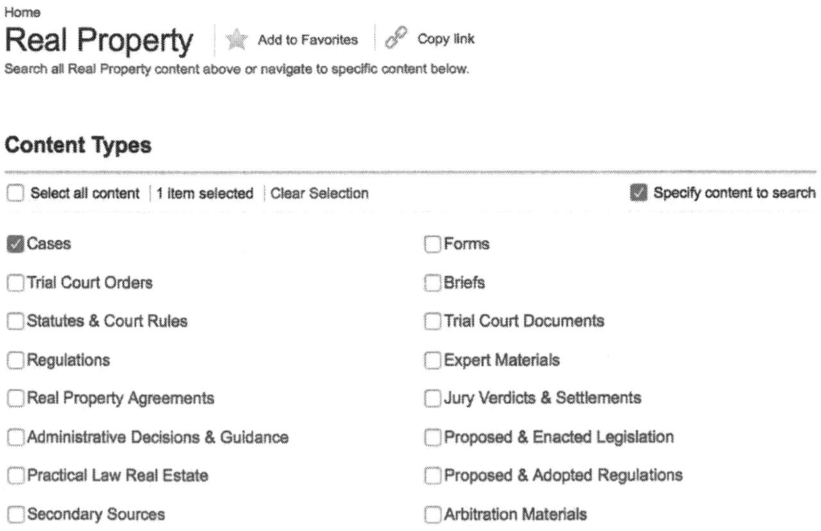

Home

Real Property   ⭐ Add to Favorites   🔗 Copy link

Search all Real Property content above or navigate to specific content below.

Content Types

☐ Select all content	1 item selected	Clear Selection	☑ Specify content to search

☑ Cases	☐ Forms
☐ Trial Court Orders	☐ Briefs
☐ Statutes & Court Rules	☐ Trial Court Documents
☐ Regulations	☐ Expert Materials
☐ Real Property Agreements	☐ Jury Verdicts & Settlements
☐ Administrative Decisions & Guidance	☐ Proposed & Enacted Legislation
☐ Practical Law Real Estate	☐ Proposed & Adopted Regulations
☐ Secondary Sources	☐ Arbitration Materials

Source: Westlaw. Reprinted with permission of Thomson Reuters.

The next screen shows a list of the ten most recent cases on that topic, from any jurisdiction.[20] You may browse these documents, but in most instances you will want to use the search bar to conduct a search of all cases grouped under that topic. Before doing so, click on the small "i" icon at the top of the screen for information about the date and source of documents the search engine is considering.

The search bar at the top of the screen should show a tab with the topic you selected. Figure 7-5 shows the area "Real Property," and the box next to "Cases" has been checked. To search for cases on a specific real property claim within a particular jurisdiction, enter terms in the search bar and select the jurisdiction from the drop-down menu to the right of the search bar.

For example, one claim for gaining legal title to real property is adverse possession, and one element of that claim is exclusive possession. Entering the term *exclusive possession* in the search box and selecting "Oregon" as the jurisdiction results in almost 200 documents—all of which are real property cases. You can sort the cases by relevance, by date, by how often they have been cited, or by how often they have been used by West's customers (note that "use" of a document includes downloading, emailing, etc.). In the left margin, you can narrow the results by the Oregon court that decided each case, as well as by date, judge, attorney, etc.

b. West Key Number System

One of the most effective ways to search Westlaw is with Key Numbers, available under "Content types" on the home page of Westlaw. This digest indexes cases from all American jurisdictions according to more than 400 "Topics."[21] Each Topic is an area of law, and Topics range from "Abandoned and Lost Property" to "Zoning and Planning."[22]

---

20. In some practice areas, you can avoid the screen with the most recent cases. In Figure 7-5, for example, after clicking on the topic "Real Property," check the box for "Cases." To ensure that your search results include only cases, be sure that other boxes are unchecked (e.g., "Statutes and Court Rules," "Regulations," "Secondary Sources," "Forms," "Jury Verdicts," "Arbitration Agreements").

21. In this book, the term "Topics" is capitalized when it refers specifically to these components of West's digest. The term is not capitalized when it refers to topics in a general sense.

22. These Topics are much narrower than the categories listed under the "Practice Areas" link on Westlaw. As a comparison, the "Practice Areas" link contained the broad legal area "Real Property." You might go through that broad category to search more narrowly for cases on adverse possession, boundaries, common lands, public lands, and quieting title. In the Key Number System, each of those is a distinct Topic.

West assigns a number to each of its 400+ Topics, placing them in alphabetical order. Adverse Possession, for example, has been assigned number 20. Within each Topic, the area of law is broken down into discrete subtopics. These subtopics are called "Key Numbers" and each begins with the letter "k." Key Numbers can be represented by descriptive words (e.g., Exclusion of Others, Necessity) or the number assigned by West (e.g., 36, 58).[23] An example of a Topic and Key Number for Adverse Possession cases dealing with exclusion of others from the property is 20k36. Figure 7-6 shows some of the broad categories of Key Numbers under the Topic "Adverse Possession," each of which can be searched or expanded. Often there are additional, even more discrete outline numbers in the Topics and Key Numbers on Westlaw. For example, the Topic and Key Number for Adverse Possession 16, "Acts of Ownership in General," has three subheadings: (1) In general; (2) Marking boundaries and entry to make survey; and (3) Wild lands.

West indexes each headnote of each case reported in West's vast National Reporter System according to these Topics and Key Numbers. The headnotes that appear in the Key Number digest are the same headnotes that appear at the beginning of West cases. As a demonstration, compare the two headnotes for *Schoeller* in the digest excerpt in Figure 7-7 with headnotes 9 and 10 in the excerpt from that case shown in Figure 7-8.

1. Searching the Key Number System

You can begin searching the Key Number System (1) using the "Key Numbers" link, (2) using a relevant headnote from a case you know is on point, and (3) using Topics and Key Numbers as terms in a search query.

First, you can simply go to the "Key Numbers" link under "Content types" and open a directory of all 400+ Topics. Browse the directory, and select those Topics that seem most relevant to your work. Then you have several choices:

- *Open Topics and Key Numbers.* Open a Topic by clicking on it. Within the Topic, click on the relevant Key Number (or the range of Key Numbers). As an example, to find cases about the necessity of proving hostile possession in an adverse possession claim, and what that element requires, go to West's list of Topics and select "Adverse Possession." Then click on the portion of the outline labeled "Hostile Character of Possession" (it appears in Part I, Section F). Clicking on "58 Necessity" will lead you to a list of the headnotes of all cases that West has indexed

---

23. Figure 7-9, a bit later in this chapter, shows two headnotes with both the descriptive words and the assigned numbers.

Figure 7-6. Westlaw Key Numbers for "Adverse Possession"

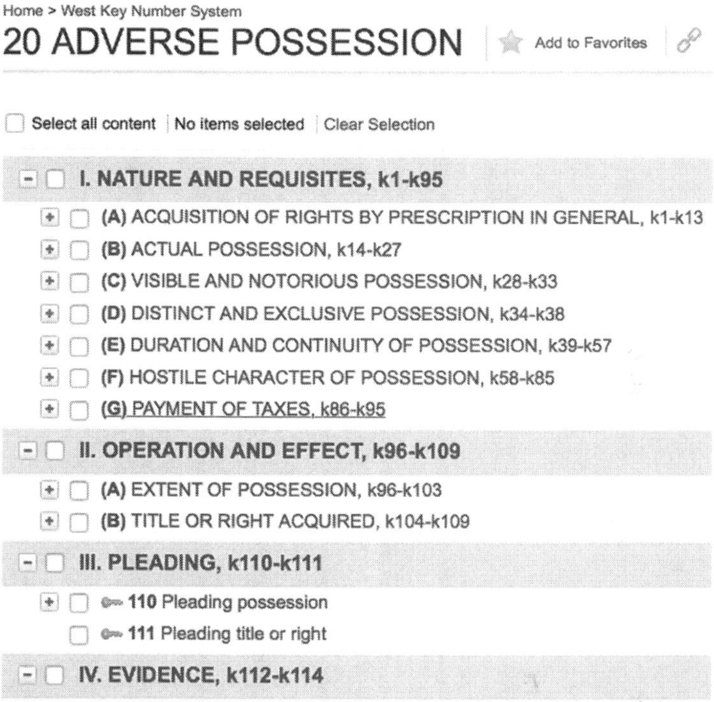

Home > West Key Number System

20 ADVERSE POSSESSION   ☆ Add to Favorites   ⚲

☐ Select all content │ No items selected │ Clear Selection

▣ ☐ **I. NATURE AND REQUISITES, k1-k95**
  ⊞ ☐ **(A)** ACQUISITION OF RIGHTS BY PRESCRIPTION IN GENERAL, k1-k13
  ⊞ ☐ **(B)** ACTUAL POSSESSION, k14-k27
  ⊞ ☐ **(C)** VISIBLE AND NOTORIOUS POSSESSION, k28-k33
  ⊞ ☐ **(D)** DISTINCT AND EXCLUSIVE POSSESSION, k34-k38
  ⊞ ☐ **(E)** DURATION AND CONTINUITY OF POSSESSION, k39-k57
  ⊞ ☐ **(F)** HOSTILE CHARACTER OF POSSESSION, k58-k85
  ⊞ ☐ **(G)** PAYMENT OF TAXES, k86-k95

▣ ☐ **II. OPERATION AND EFFECT, k96-k109**
  ⊞ ☐ **(A)** EXTENT OF POSSESSION, k96-k103
  ⊞ ☐ **(B)** TITLE OR RIGHT ACQUIRED, k104-k109

▣ ☐ **III. PLEADING, k110-k111**
  ⊞ ☐ ⚷ **110** Pleading possession
  ☐ ⚷ **111** Pleading title or right

▣ ☐ **IV. EVIDENCE, k112-k114**

Source: Westlaw. Reprinted with permission of Thomson Reuters.

under that one particular Topic and Key Number. Scrolling through the results will lead to the headnotes shown in Figure 7-7. Note that a case will be listed in the digest for each of its headnotes that is indexed under that Topic and Key Number; thus, a case may appear more than once.

- *Conduct a "Title Search" of the Topics or of specific Key Numbers within a Topic.* After opening the list of Topics from the "Tools" link, you can search the titles by using a box on the right side of the screen. Note that this search does not review the text of the headnotes listed under each Topic and Key Number; instead, it looks only at the words in the Topics and Key Numbers themselves.

2. Starting with a Known Case

Another approach to using the Key Number System is to start with a Topic and Key Number from a relevant case. Once you have a case that is relevant

Figure 7-7. West Digest Headnotes on Westlaw

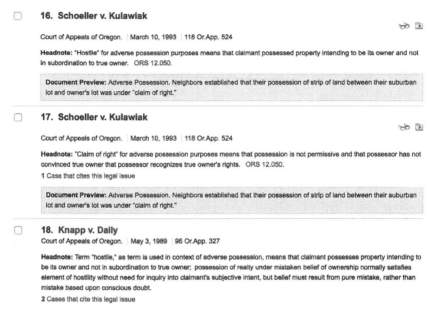

Source: Westlaw. Reprinted with permission of Thomson Reuters.

Figure 7-8. Linking to Key Number System from a Known Case

Source: *Schoeller v. Kulawiak*, 118 Or. App. 524 (1993), on Westlaw. Reprinted with permission of Thomson Reuters.

to your work, review its headnotes. When you find a headnote that is on point, clicking on the Topic or on one level of the Key Numbers will lead to the list of cases indexed by the Key Number System under the related Topic and Key Number. In Figure 7-8, clicking on 20k58 next to the word "Necessity" in headnote 9 or 10 will lead to the list of headnotes excerpted in Figure 7-7. Similarly, clicking the Topic "Adverse Possession" will lead to the Topic outline in Figure 7-6. Finding a useful headnote from a case can also help with subsequent research projects, so you should be sure to keep track of Topics and Key Numbers that lead you to relevant authority.

3. Using the Topics and Key Numbers as Search Terms

A third way to use the Topics and Key Numbers from West's Key Number System is to conduct a search with a relevant Topic and Key Number as the search term. For best results, use this option only as an advanced search, either entering "adv:" before the Topics and Key Numbers or clicking on "advanced" to the right of the search bar. For example, the search *adv: 20k58* produces a highly relevant, small set of cases about hostile possession in an adverse possession claim. In order to use this method effectively, you should keep a running list of relevant Topics and Key Numbers. This allows you to utilize Topics and Key Numbers throughout the research process and can be useful for future research projects if you have a repeat issue.

4. Uniformity of West's Key Numbers Across Jurisdictions

Regardless of how you access and use the Key Number System, remember that the Topics and Key Numbers are the same in all American jurisdictions. If you needed to find California cases on adverse possession, simply follow the steps outlined above, but change the jurisdiction to California. The resulting Topics and Key Numbers will be the same, but the cases indexed will be from California.

2. Topical Searching on Lexis

Lexis provides several tools for searching for cases by topic. You can "Browse" or use headnotes from a known case. Additionally, Lexis allows you to limit searches by topic using tabs under the universal search bar.

a. Browsing Topics

To begin, click the "Browse" link at the top of the main page, and then "Topics." You can either scroll through the list of over forty topics or enter terms into the "Find a topic" box. Using the adverse possession example, you might

Figure 7-9. Searching within a Topic on Lexis

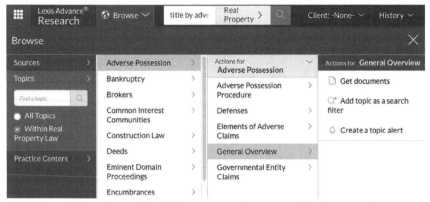

scroll through the list of topics and recognize that "Real Property Law" is most likely to index relevant cases. Alternatively, you could enter the term *adverse possession* into the search box and scroll through a shorter list of potentially relevant topics.

With either approach, you can open subtopics (as long as an arrow appears) until you reach the end of the outline. Clicking on a topic or subtopic will open a drop-down menu with three "actions," which are shown in Figure 7-9.

Clicking on "Get documents" from the drop-down menu will produce search results for all documents that Lexis has indexed under that topic. You can restrict the results to just cases by clicking the "Cases" tab. You can also restrict by search term, court, date, and other filters, listed in the left margin. Figure 7-10 shows the results of a topic search for "Adverse Possession, General Overview." The initial search produced over 20,000 cases. The results shown have been narrowed to cases in Oregon since 1994, indicated by the filters in the left frame. The number of results—fifty with these filters applied—is reasonable, and the results are on point.

The second option in the drop-down menu displayed in Figure 7-9 is to add the topic to your search. The topic displays next to the universal search bar. You then enter search terms in the universal search bar and continue with a more narrowed search. Of course, the results will include documents from throughout the Lexis databases, but as shown above, you can filter them to locate just cases, from a certain jurisdiction, during a defined period, etc.

Figure 7-10. Results of Lexis Topic Search

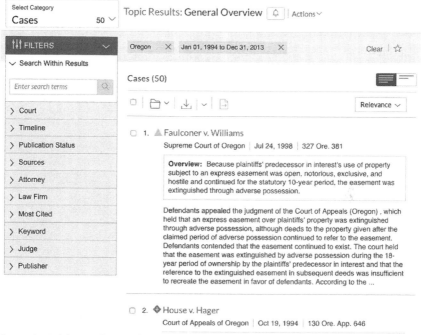

The third option shown in Figure 7-9, creating an alert, asks the service to contact you with new material in this topic. You can limit the alert to only cases, excluding statutes, administrative material, secondary sources, and other documents.

b. Starting with a Known Case

Once you have a relevant case, you can use its headnotes to guide you to other relevant cases. As shown in Figure 7-11, you can either Shepardize by the headnote (explained in Chapter 8) or click on the topics following the headnote. Clicking on the topic will produce three options: "Get documents," "Create an alert," or "View in topic index."

c. Restricting from the Main Search Bar

This chapter's discussion of Lexis began with pre-search limitations, shown in Figure 7-4. One of the pre-search limitations is "Practice Areas and Topics," which allows you to choose from a list of forty practice areas and topics to re-

Figure 7-11. Using Lexis Headnotes from a Known Case

Evidence > Inferences & Presumptions ▾ > General Overview ▾
Real Property Law > Adverse Possession ▾ > General Overview ▾

HN3 Evidence, Inferences & Presumpt[☐ Get documents]
For purposes of establishing title by adverse [⬚ Create an alert]nts must show
that their possession of the property is the ki[⚏ View in topic index]characterize an owner's use.
⚲ More like this Headnote

Shepardize - Narrow by this Headnote (1)

Real Property Law > Adverse Possession ▾ > General Overview ▾

HN4 Real Property Law, Adverse Possession
In Oregon the statutory period for adverse possession is 10 years. Or. Rev. Stat. § 12.050. ⚲ More like this Headnote

Shepardize - Narrow by this Headnote (0)

Real Property Law > Adverse Possession ▾ > Elements of Adverse Claims ▾
View more legal topics

HN5 Adverse Possession, Elements of Adverse Claims
For purposes of establishing title by adverse possession, whether use has been continuous depends on the kind of land involved.The fact that an adverse possessor only cultivates and harvests agricultural land in season does not interrupt the required continuity. ⚲ More like this Headnote

Shepardize - Narrow by this Headnote (1)   ◈ 1

Source: *Schoeller v. Kulawiak,* 118 Or App 524 (1993), on Lexis Advance. Reprinted with permission of LexisNexis. All rights reserved.

strict the search results. For example, select "Real Property Law" along with "Cases" under "Category" and "Oregon" as the "Jurisdiction." After running the search, you can further narrow results by date (e.g., 1980 forward) and by term (e.g., exclusive possession). Results for this search are shown in Figure 7-4, earlier in this chapter. The initial restrictions appear under the universal search bar; additional filters are available in the left margin.

You can sort the list of search results by relevance, document title, jurisdiction, court, and date. The "Sort by" link is at the right of the screen, just above the search results, and in Figure 7-4 is set to "Relevance." You can also control the information displayed in the results: graphic view, full view or title view. These options are shown on the right side of Figure 7-4.

C. West Digests in Print

Although most researchers prefer the ease of searching this digest system on Westlaw, this portion of the chapter briefly introduces print digests. *Oregon Digest 2d* includes headnotes of cases from state and federal courts in Oregon; headnotes from Ninth Circuit and U.S. Supreme Court cases that originated in Oregon; and references to Oregon Tax Court cases, opinions of the Oregon Attorney General, and articles published by Oregon law reviews.[24] *Oregon Digest 2d* is cumulative from 1843 to the present.

Like all other West digests, *Oregon Digest 2d* indexes cases according to the West system of Topics and Key Numbers, as explained earlier in Part V.B.1.b of this chapter. Entries in the digest are the actual headnotes found in cases, indexed according to the Topic and Key Number assigned by West to each headnote.[25]

There are several approaches for using print digests to conduct research.

• Beginning with the Descriptive-Word Index

When beginning research with only a fact pattern and a legal issue, start with the Descriptive-Word Index. Search that index for your research terms and record the Topics and Key Numbers provided. As with all print research, check the back of each volume for pocket parts. Find the volume that contains one of your Topics, and quickly review its list of "Subjects Included," as well as "Subjects Excluded and Covered by Other Topics." After these lists is the Key Number outline of the topic, under the heading "Analysis," which you should skim to ensure that you found in the Descriptive-Word Index all the relevant Key Numbers within that Topic. Then turn to each of the relevant Key Numbers, review the case headnotes, and record citations for any relevant cases. Check each volume's pocket parts and look for any soft-cover booklets of updated material for the volume or the digest series.

---

24. Some digests index cases from a number of different jurisdictions. For instance, *Pacific Digest* contains headnotes of cases that are reported in *Pacific Reporter*, which were decided by many different state courts. Other digests are limited by topic, such as *Bankruptcy Digest* and *Military Justice Digest*.

25. Although cases published in *Oregon Tax Reports* do not receive Topics and Key Numbers, some are included in *Oregon Digest 2d* as "Library References" under Topics and Key Numbers that are relevant to the subject matter of the case.

• Beginning with a Relevant Case

When reading a case in a West reporter or on Westlaw, identify the headnotes that are relevant to your issue. Note the Topics and Key Numbers given for the relevant headnotes. Then select a digest volume containing one of the Topics. Within that Topic, find the Key Number given in the related headnote and review the cases indexed there.

• Using the Words and Phrases Volumes

To learn whether a court has defined a term, refer to the Words and Phrases volumes. While a legal dictionary like *Black's Law Dictionary* will provide a general definition of a term, Words and Phrases will lead to cases that define the term for a particular jurisdiction. Judicial definitions are especially helpful when an important term in a statute is vague. At the end of each entry in the Words and Phrases volumes, West lists the Topics and Key Numbers used for that case's headnotes (e.g., "Parent & Child 2(1)" and "Domicile 5").

• Using the Table of Cases

The Table of Cases lists all the cases indexed in a particular digest series by both the primary plaintiff's name and the primary defendant's name. This table is helpful when you know the name of one of the parties but not its citation.

Appendix 7-A. Case Excerpt from Lexis

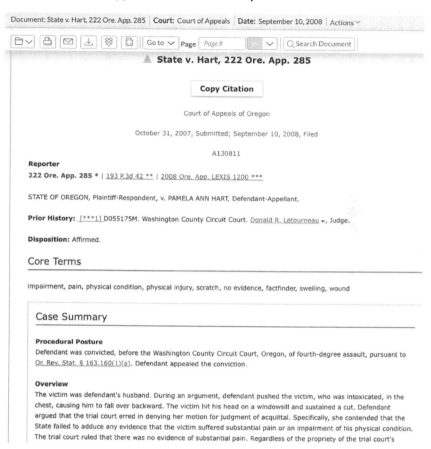

Source: Lexis Advance. Reprinted with the permission of LexisNexis. All rights reserved.

Appendix 7-B. Case Excerpt from Westlaw

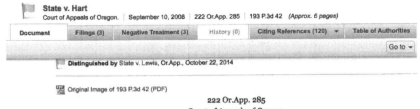

State v. Hart
Court of Appeals of Oregon. | September 10, 2008 | 222 Or.App. 285 | 193 P.3d 42   *(Approx. 6 pages)*

| Document | Filings (3) | Negative Treatment (3) | History (0) | Citing References (120) ▾ | Table of Authorities |

Go to ▾

Distinguished by State v. Lewis, Or.App., October 22, 2014

Original Image of 193 P.3d 42 (PDF)

222 Or.App. 285
Court of Appeals of Oregon.

STATE of Oregon, Plaintiff–Respondent,

v.

Pamela Ann HART, Defendant–Appellant.

D055175M; A130811.
Submitted on Oct. 31, 2007.
Decided Sept. 10, 2008.

Synopsis
Background: Defendant was convicted in the Circuit Court, Washington County, Donald R. Letourneau, J., of fourth-degree assault. Defendant appealed.

Holding: The Court of Appeals, Rosenblum, J. held that evidence was sufficient to support conviction.

Affirmed.

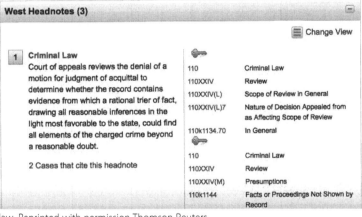

West Headnotes (3)

▤ Change View

1 **Criminal Law**
Court of appeals reviews the denial of a motion for judgment of acquittal to determine whether the record contains evidence from which a rational trier of fact, drawing all reasonable inferences in the light most favorable to the state, could find all elements of the charged crime beyond a reasonable doubt.

2 Cases that cite this headnote

⚷		
110	Criminal Law	
110XXIV	Review	
110XXIV(L)	Scope of Review in General	
110XXIV(L)7	Nature of Decision Appealed from as Affecting Scope of Review	
110k1134.70	In General	

⚷		
110	Criminal Law	
110XXIV	Review	
110XXIV(M)	Presumptions	
110k1144	Facts or Proceedings Not Shown by Record	

Chapter 8

Updating with Citators

Before relying on any legal authority, a researcher must know how that authority has subsequently been treated by courts, legislatures, or agencies. A case may have been reversed on appeal; a statute may have been amended by a later legislature or declared unconstitutional by a court. To be sure that cases, statutes, and other authorities represent the current law requires "updating." The tools used for updating are called "citators." Citators list all of the documents that have subsequently cited the authority being updated. The more sophisticated citators also indicate the possible impact of those documents on the authority.[1]

"Shepard's" is the citator available on Lexis; Westlaw's citator is called "KeyCite." These are the premier online citators and the focus of this chapter, but others are available. For example, Bloomberg provides "BCite," Fastcase uses "Authority Check," and Google Scholar has "How cited." Using any of these services to retrieve a list of citations is quite easy, often simply requiring you to click on a link, select a tab, or type in a citation. Analyzing the citator results and reading the authorities listed is the challenging—and the rewarding—part of updating. Even sophisticated citators like Shepard's and KeyCite are just tools to aid you in determining whether an authority is still respected as "good law."

This chapter uses a case to illustrate updating, but many types of state and federal authorities can be updated using the same process. Statutes, constitutions, regulations, administrative decisions, patents, and secondary sources are among the many authorities included in KeyCite and Shepard's.[2]

---

1. Print citators called *Shepard's Citations* are still available in some libraries. You should seek the assistance of a law reference librarian if you need to update an authority using these books.

2. While updating process is the same, the citators use different symbols for some authorities. See, for example, Figure 8-7 later in this chapter, which shows that an exclamation point indicates negative treatment for a statute.

Courts expect lawyers to update authorities to ensure that the lawyers' arguments are well supported and present the current state of the law.[3] Beyond meeting this ethical obligation, you should use citators to expand your research; reading additional authorities identified by citators can lead to additional support for your argument and might open new lines of analysis.

I. Four Times to Update

Although updating is included in Chapter 1 as the fifth step of the research process, it is important at four different points. First, always glance at a citator's overall assessment of a case as you begin to read it. If the case has received negative treatment, explore that treatment before spending much time reading the case.

Second, after reading a case thoroughly and deciding that it is important for your analysis, update it carefully to be sure that it is still good law. Read any sources that criticize, explain, or distinguish it, as those arguments might be raised against your client as well.

Then, use each relevant case to expand your research. A list of authorities that cite a case you know is relevant to your analysis might include additional resources that you have not uncovered through other steps in your research. Carefully review the list of citing sources to find other cases and secondary sources that discuss the same points of law as the first case. Reading these citing sources could lead to cases with clearer reasoning or with facts more similar to your client's situation.

Finally, update your key cases, statutes, and other important authorities just before you submit your final document or present your argument orally. KeyCite and Shepard's are continually publishing new information, and your leading case could have been overruled yesterday.

II. Updating Outline

Updating an authority requires you to first retrieve a list of documents that cite that authority (sometimes called "citing sources," "citing references" or "citing authorities"). Then you must analyze the symbols provided by the citator, limit the results on the citator list (if necessary), and read the citing

---

3. The Oregon Court of Appeals has noted that failing to update is "not excusable." *See McCarthy v. Oregon Freeze Dry, Inc.*, 158 Or App 654, 656 (1999).

Table 8-1. Outline for Updating Online

A. Access the citator list containing the information you need.

B. Analyze the symbols provided by the citator for each source.

C. Consider limiting the list of citing sources by jurisdiction, date, or other function.

D. Prioritize and read the citing sources. Analyze the impact, if any, these sources have on the authority you are updating.

sources to determine their impact on your authority. This process is outlined in Table 8-1. While the outline is generic, this chapter uses an Oregon case as the authority being updated.

The more sophisticated citators provide several lists of citing references. Some lists give only negative treatment, while others include only cases or only secondary sources. A list commonly included is a "Table of Authorities," which lists the authorities your case cited. While other citator lists look forward from the case you are updating to show all subsequent action, the Table of Authorities looks backward by listing authorities that your case cited. The list can be helpful as you decide which of the older, perhaps foundational, authorities you need to read. The Table of Authorities can also alert you to hidden weaknesses in a case. Even if your case has not been overruled, if the cases it cited as authoritative have been called into question (e.g., reversed, overruled, distinguished), your case may no longer be valid.

The most important aspect of updating is the final step: reading the citing sources. A citator is an invaluable tool for determining which sources might deserve your attention. But then you must read the relevant citing authorities to determine the impact of each on your analysis. Clicking on an authority's reference in a citator list will typically take you to the point in the corresponding document where your case is cited. Quickly skim that portion of the document to determine its relevance to your research. If a source is on point, carefully analyze its impact on your case. The new source might change the legal rule in your case, either explicitly by reversing it or overruling it or implicitly by distinguishing it or explaining it in a new way. In contrast, the new source might follow the legal rule in your case but apply it to a new set of facts; if those facts are closer to your client's situation, the case can be very helpful to your argument. As a third example, the new source might distinguish or criticize your case. If the criticism is relevant to your argument, you will need to be able to explain why the criticism is not harmful to your client's claim.

Figure 8-1. KeyCite on Westlaw

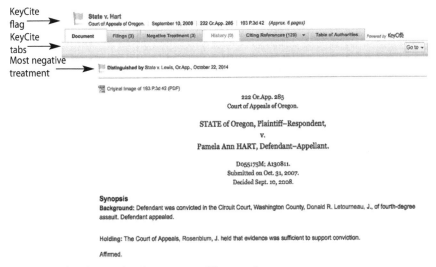

KeyCite flag →

KeyCite tabs →

Most negative treatment →

Source: Westlaw. Reprinted with permission of Thomson Reuters.

III. Updating with KeyCite on Westlaw

The following discussion uses *State v. Hart*, 222 Or App 285 (2008), as an example of updating a case.

A. Access the Citator Lists

You can access KeyCite on Westlaw in three ways:

- Retrieve the document and click on one of the KeyCite tabs at the top of the Westlaw screen, just above the document's heading. See Figure 8-1. Each case has several tabs: Filings, Negative Treatment, History, Citing References, and Table of Authorities. To the right of the tabs is the icon "Powered by KeyCite"; clicking on that icon gives helpful information about the KeyCite system.
- Click on a KeyCite status flag, such as the yellow flag at the top left of the screen shown in Figure 8-1.
- Type *kc* or *keycite* followed by the case citation in Westlaw's universal search box.

Westlaw provides five different tabs for retrieving citator information through KeyCite. "Filings" includes links to briefs and motions filed in the litigation of

Figure 8-2. KeyCite Negative Treatment on Westlaw

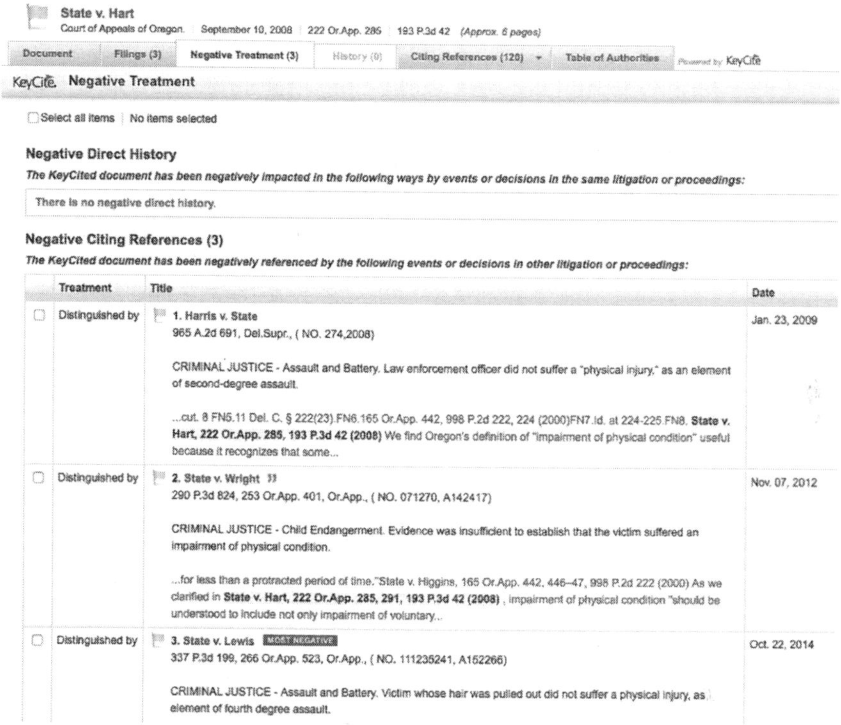

Source: Westlaw. Reprinted with permission of Thomson Reuters.

the case. You might read these briefs to see which additional arguments were made and which authorities support them.

The two tabs that are most helpful in determining whether your case is still good law are "History" and "Negative Treatment." The History tab includes opinions in the same litigation as your case (if any exist). This tab will lead, for example, to the opinion on a different motion earlier in the litigation as well as a subsequent appellate decision. Some of those cases might have a negative impact (e.g., an early motion to dismiss was denied) while others might have a positive impact (e.g., the appellate court affirmed summary judgment). The History cases are available in both list and graphic format. You can restrict the History list even further from the drop-down menu next to "View," by selecting from Principal History, Previous History, Subsequent History, or Negative Direct History. The Negative Treatment tab lists cases with negative impact on your case, whether in the same litigation or in dif-

Figure 8-3. Citing References on Westlaw

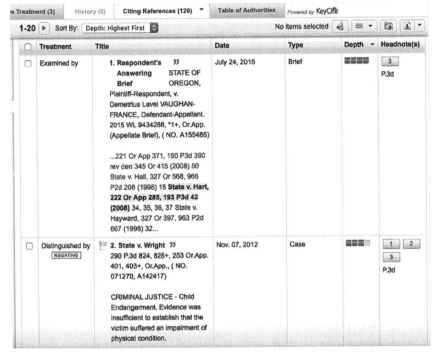

Source: Westlaw. Reprinted with permission of Thomson Reuters.

ferent litigation (i.e., between other parties). See Figure 8-2 for the negative treatment of the *Hart* case.

The KeyCite tab that is most useful in expanding your research is "Citing References." It includes all cases, administrative decisions, secondary sources, court filings from other litigation, and other documents that have cited the case you are updating. Figure 8-3 illustrates the citing references for the *Hart* case. A drop-down menu shows the number of documents in each category (e.g., cases, secondary sources).

The final tab is the "Table of Authorities," explained earlier.

B. Analyze the Citator Symbols

Westlaw uses a variety of symbols to help you (a) analyze the validity of the case you are updating and (b) determine which authorities you need to read. Flags show negative treatment or indicate a case has been appealed.

- A red flag means that West has determined the case is no longer good law for at least one legal point, perhaps because it was overruled or reversed. The case might still be binding authority for other points, so you must read and analyze each citing source yourself.
- A yellow flag means that West has found some negative authority for the case, but it has not been overruled or reversed. See Figures 8-1 and 8-2 for screenshots illustrating the yellow flag for the *Hart* case.
- A blue and white striped flag shows a case is on appeal to a federal circuit court or to the U.S. Supreme Court.
- An orange exclamation point warns that a case relies on an authority that has been overruled or is invalid, undermining the case.

A case that West has assigned a red or yellow flag will have the most harmful negative treatment noted at the top when you open the case. The negative treatment could be that the case has subsequently been overruled, reversed, or distinguished. As shown in Figure 8-1, West suggests that *Hart* was distinguished by a 2012 case, its most negative treatment.

You can sort the documents in a list of citing references by date or by depth of treatment, using the drop-down menu under "Sort By." The list of citing references gives treatment, title, date, type of document, depth of treatment, and headnote sections for each citing source, as seen in the bar near the top of Figure 8-3. Some of those headings deserve explanation. "Treatment" states how the citing source treated your case (e.g., reversed, distinguished, discussed, cited). "Title" gives the name of the document that cites your case. Underneath the title is a citation to that document and, if you choose "More detail" or "Most detail" from a drop-down menu, a brief excerpt where the document cited your case. (This icon is between the bell and the folder; when you select "Most detail," the icon will show three horizontal lines.) "Depth" indicates how much each citing reference discusses your case:

4 bars = more than one page
3 bars = more than one paragraph
2 bars = less than one paragraph
1 bar = a brief mention (typically in a string citation)

Assuming that the longer discussion contains the more thorough analysis, a case with four bars will be more helpful to your research than a case with one bar. "Headnote" lists each of the headnote topics covered by a citing source. As you point to each headnote number, the headnote text appears, making it easy to determine whether that point of law is relevant to your research.

Finally, quotation marks included in a KeyCite list show that the source quoted your case. In Figure 8-3, the first two citing sources quote *Hart*.

C. Limit the Citator Results

You can view a subset of the documents in the KeyCite list by using filters in the left frame. Initially, you can narrow the list by a document type, such as cases, secondary sources, or court documents. Once you have chosen a document type, you can narrow the list by specific terms (in the "Search within results" box) and by filters specific to that document type. Filters for cases include jurisdiction, date, depth of treatment, headnote topic, treatment status, and whether the citing reference is a reported or an unreported case. A "+" symbol in front of a filter provides more possibilities. Opening the filter for jurisdiction, for example, allows restricting by the federal or state jurisdictions in which courts have cited your case. Figure 8-4 shows the options for limiting results under the "Citing References" tab for the *Hart* case, with the state jurisdiction option opened. Section V.C. of this chapter explains how to prioritize the citator results that you read, which is closely related to limiting your citator results.

Figure 8-4. Limiting KeyCite Results on Westlaw

Source: Westlaw. Reprinted with permission of Thomson Reuters.

Figure 8-5. Shepard's on Lexis Advance

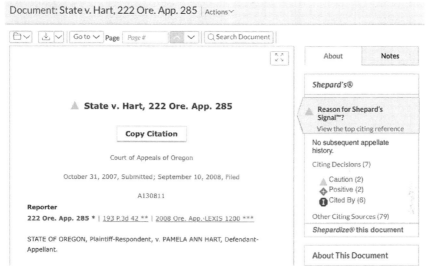

IV. Updating with Shepard's on Lexis

The following explanation uses *State v. Hart*, 222 Or App 285 (2008), to demonstrate updating with Shepard's on Lexis.

A. Access the Citator Lists

Shepard's is available in three ways.

- When viewing the document, click on the "Shepardize this document" link that appears near the top right of the screen. You could also go directly to a specific Shepard's list (e.g., "Citing Decisions").
- Click the Shepard's symbol that appears near the title of a document. In Figure 8-5, clicking the yellow triangle will open the Shepard's report for "Citing Decisions" for the *Hart* case.
- Type into the universal search bar *shep:* followed by the citation (e.g., *shep: 222 Or App 285*).[4]

---

4. If Lexis does not recognize the abbreviation "Or App," add an "e" and use "Ore App."

Figure 8-6. Shepard's Citing Decisions

Lexis provides four Shepard's links for a case: (1) Appellate History; (2) Citing Decisions; (3) Other Citing Sources; and (4) Table of Authorities. See the top left of Figure 8-6. You can view Appellate History—the full story of this case's litigation—either as a list or as a map, which can be especially helpful for complex litigation with many motions and appeals. The Citing Decisions link lists all of the cases that have cited the case you are updating. This list will be most helpful in expanding your research. A separate link, shown as "Other Citing Sources," has secondary sources and annotated statutes that have cited your case. The final link is Table of Authorities, which lists the cases cited by your case.

Figure 8-7. Shepard's Legend

Legend			✕

Shepard's Signal™ indicator

● **Warning: Negative treatment is indicated.**

The red *Shepard's* SignalTM indicator indicates that citing references in the *Shepard's®* Citations Service contain strong negative history or treatment of your case (for example, overruled by or reversed).

ⓘ **Warning**

The red *Shepard's* Signal™ indicator indicates that citing references in the *Shepard's®* Citations Service contain strong negative treatment of the section (for example, the section may have been found to be unconstitutional or void).

▣ **Questioned: Validity questioned by citing reference.**

The orange *Shepard's* SignalTM indicator indicates that the citing references in the *Shepard's®* Citations Service contain treatment

Analysis

■ Red	Warning
■ Orange	Questioned
■ Yellow	Caution
■ Green	Positive
■ Blue	Neutral
■ Light Blue	No phrase exists

Depth of Discussion

■■■■■■ Analysed

■■■■■ Discussed

■■■ Mentioned

You can sort the display of documents in the list of Citing Decisions using a menu to the right of the screen. The choices are level of court, date, type of analysis, and length of discussion.

You can control the amount of information displayed in a list of Citing Decisions, as well as the presentation of that information, by selecting icons on the top right of the screen. To view a list of citing decisions, along with their citations and brief excerpts, select "Full View." To see just the titles and citations of the Citing Decisions, click "Title View." You can choose "Grid View" for an alternate format.

B. Analyze the Citator Symbols

Shepard's uses symbols to help you interpret the validity of the case you are updating and determine whether additional authorities are important for your research. The "Legend" link at the bottom right of every Shepard's screen explains each symbol. An excerpt from that link is copied in Figure 8-7.

C. Limit the Citator Results

Shepard's provides filters in the left frame for limiting the number of documents you review. For Citing Decisions, these filters include the type of analysis given by the citing case, the citing court's jurisdiction, the length of discussion, and the headnotes involved. You can also narrow the list by specific terms and within a certain timeframe. The arrow to the left of the filter allows you to expand or collapse each one. See Figure 8-6 earlier in this chapter.

V. Updating Details

A. Citator Symbols — Significance and Location

The colored symbols provided by both KeyCite and Shepard's carry more weight with some researchers than perhaps is warranted. A red symbol could mean that a case has been reversed (meaning you should not rely on it), but that symbol could also mean that a court in another state disagreed with the analysis of the case you are updating (which would have no impact on the validity of your case). Similarly, the absence of a red or yellow symbol may provide more comfort than is warranted. Be sure to read the citing references and decide for yourself whether your case is still good law.

The location of symbols on the citator screen is important. A symbol next to a citing source (before the source on KeyCite and after the source on Shepard's), refers to that citing source, not to the case you are updating. As an example, look at the *State v. Hendricks* case in Figure 8-6. The words below *Hendricks* show it cites and follows *Hart*. The green diamond with a plus appearing to the right of *Hendricks* shows that it has received positive treatment. However, the yellow triangle at the top of the page and in the left margin shows the overall assessment of *Hart*—researchers should be cautious because the case has received some negative treatment (specifically from *Wright*).

B. Headnote References

When you are updating a case, both KeyCite and Shepard's allow you to filter your citator results by headnote. If only two of fourteen headnotes in the case that you are updating are on point, this filter can be quite valuable. Assume, for example, that your most important case delves into an unrelated issue of civil procedure before addressing the merits of a tort claim. If you are interested only in the tort claim, you can limit your citator results to just cases that discuss the point of law in the two relevant headnotes in your case.

Remember that you must stay within one service publisher to use the headnote references effectively. The headnotes in Westlaw are different from the headnotes in Lexis. Realize, too, that headnote numbers differ among cases; in other words, the point of law in the third headnote of your case might be covered by headnote five in another case and by headnote two in yet another case. It helps to recall that you know only the headnotes of the case that you have read, i.e., the case that you are updating—you do not know the headnotes of the citing sources.

C. Prioritizing Cases

If time allows, consider reading every citing source (1) to determine its impact on the case you are updating, (2) to see whether it assists in your analysis, and (3) to expand your research universe. With limited time, prioritize the citing sources according to the following criteria (assuming you are researching an Oregon state issue):

- *Jurisdiction:* Cases from Oregon will almost always be more important than cases decided elsewhere, which are just persuasive authority.
- *Treatment:* Look for negative treatment, indicating that a later case has reversed, overruled, criticized, or distinguished your case.
- *Court:* Begin reading cases from the Oregon Supreme Court, then the Oregon Court of Appeals. (When working on a federal issue or in a state that publishes its trial court decisions, read those trial court decisions last.)
- *Date:* Start with more recent cases rather than older cases.
- *Headnotes:* Select cases that were cited for the headnotes that are most relevant to your project.
- *Keywords:* Use keywords to narrow the citator results to those that contain an important fact or legal term.
- *Depth of Treatment:* Cases that devote more space to your case (shown by depth of treatment indicators) are likely to be more helpful than others that merely cite your case.

In reading the citing sources, look for trends in how often each case is cited and what treatment it receives. You should generally base your analysis on cases that have been cited and followed frequently.

D. Setting Alerts

The "alert" function in a citator notifies researchers of later action on authorities of interest. For instance, if you will be working for several weeks on an argument that hinges on a particular case, you might set an alert to tell you of any new action that affects the case. On KeyCite and Shepard's, setting an alert is as easy as clicking on the bell icon and choosing the information you want to receive, for example only negative action on the point of law in a particular headnote or only cases from your jurisdiction. You can also set how frequently you want to receive notices (e.g., daily, weekly) and set the beginning and end dates for the alert.

Chapter 9

Research Process Examples

Chapter 1 introduced a process of legal research, and subsequent chapters have explained details of how to search for particular documents (e.g., secondary sources, statutes, cases) using a variety of resources and search techniques. This chapter pulls all of that information together to illustrate how to research an issue of Oregon state law in a legal area you have not researched previously. The illustrations here are generic so that they can be easily transferred to different projects.

The rest of the chapter outlines three possible approaches. The first uses Westlaw to conduct Boolean searches in selected databases. The second uses Lexis to run guided word searches (sometimes called "open water searching"). The third uses a range of free online sources. Each of these three examples uses one service or type of sources — Westlaw, Lexis, and free sources — to illustrate its use at each step of the research process. In practice, you are more likely to use a variety of sources in researching a single project, moving from Oregon BarBooks, to Westlaw's Key Number System, to Shepard's on Lexis.

The following approaches are intended to be illustrative, not limiting. Thus, an approach described for one source is probably available for others. For example, the approach described below for Westlaw — using Boolean searches in selected databases — will also work on Lexis. Moreover, each of the three approaches shows just one of many possible routes a good researcher might follow in each service or type of source.

I. Boolean Searching of Selected Databases (Westlaw)

In this approach, you will primarily use Boolean searches that you run in selected databases on Westlaw. You will thus exercise a great deal of control over the searches that the computer runs, with the goal of producing comprehensive but very focused results.

A. Conducting Pre-Research Tasks

Before opening Westlaw, complete four pre-research tasks. First, you are researching Oregon law. From the facts and research questions, develop a list of search terms, as explained in Chapter 1. Next, using those terms, create Boolean searches by deciding which proximity connectors will be most useful. Will these terms likely appear within the same sentence or the same paragraph?

Third, decide which databases are likely to contain your target documents. In researching an Oregon state law issue, review the sources under the tab "State Materials" and "Oregon," some of which are shown in Figure 9-1, and select appropriate databases for each step of the research process. Think critically about whether to use a general or specific database. You might decide to begin searching general secondary sources, as there are few specifically on Oregon law. Then you might decide to search only Oregon Supreme Court and Court of Appeals cases, excluding cases from federal courts or the Oregon Tax Court.

Finally, create a folder in Westlaw where you will keep documents related to this research project. Either now, or as the need arises during your research, create subfolders. The subfolders could be based on different issues (e.g., if you have two tort claims and a related contracts claim), on the components of a single claim (e.g., the elements of negligence), or on general divisions that make sense to you (e.g., primary authority, secondary authority, unhelpful resources).

B. Researching Secondary Sources

From "Content types," select "Secondary Sources." Because you are researching in an area of law that is new to you, consider beginning with a treatise or an encyclopedia by selecting "Texts and Treatises" or "Jurisprudence and Encyclopedias" in the left margin. You can search across all publications within those categories, or you can narrow to a single publication (e.g., *American Jurisprudence 2d*). When you select a category or a specific publication, its name will appear to the left of the universal search bar.

Enter your Boolean search query in the universal search bar. If you receive a large number of results, use the tools in the left margin to narrow your search results. Skim each document in the narrowed results list, reading the title and then the excerpt provided to determine whether it seems relevant. Look carefully at footnotes, where you are most likely to find references to cases. If a source

Figure 9-1. Oregon State Sources on Westlaw

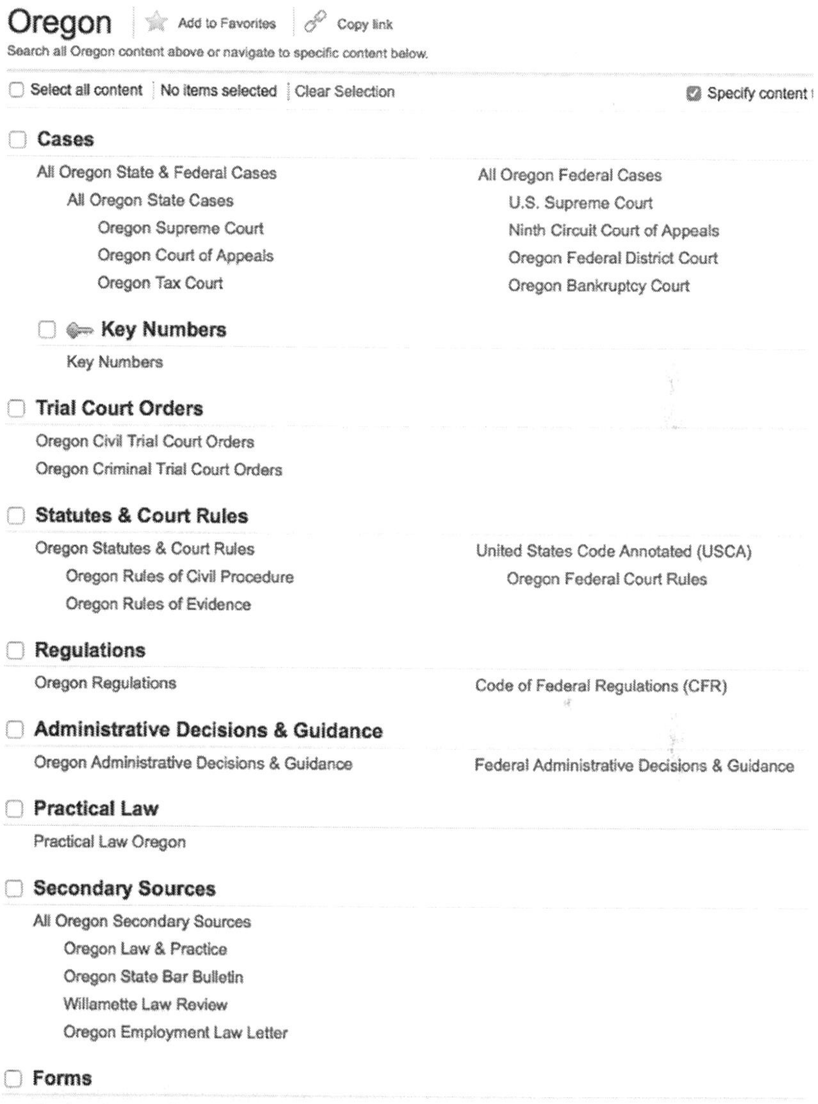

Oregon   ☆ Add to Favorites   🔗 Copy link

Search all Oregon content above or navigate to specific content below.

☐ Select all content │ No items selected │ Clear Selection   ☑ Specify content

☐ **Cases**

All Oregon State & Federal Cases	All Oregon Federal Cases
All Oregon State Cases	U.S. Supreme Court
Oregon Supreme Court	Ninth Circuit Court of Appeals
Oregon Court of Appeals	Oregon Federal District Court
Oregon Tax Court	Oregon Bankruptcy Court

☐ 🔑 **Key Numbers**

Key Numbers

☐ **Trial Court Orders**

Oregon Civil Trial Court Orders
Oregon Criminal Trial Court Orders

☐ **Statutes & Court Rules**

Oregon Statutes & Court Rules	United States Code Annotated (USCA)
Oregon Rules of Civil Procedure	Oregon Federal Court Rules
Oregon Rules of Evidence	

☐ **Regulations**

Oregon Regulations	Code of Federal Regulations (CFR)

☐ **Administrative Decisions & Guidance**

Oregon Administrative Decisions & Guidance	Federal Administrative Decisions & Guidance

☐ **Practical Law**

Practical Law Oregon

☐ **Secondary Sources**

All Oregon Secondary Sources
Oregon Law & Practice
Oregon State Bar Bulletin
Willamette Law Review
Oregon Employment Law Letter

☐ **Forms**

Source: Westlaw. Reprinted with permission of Thomson Reuters.

seems relevant, annotate it briefly to state how it applies and save it to your folder.

If you are finding nothing relevant, revise your search query or look in a different source. As examples, you might move from an encyclopedia to a treatise, or if you started in an Oregon-specific treatise, you might move to a general treatise. After spending twenty or thirty minutes skimming (depending on the complexity of the project, this time will vary), stop to read in depth the most relevant secondary sources. Make note of any cross references to primary authorities that you should read. Continue working with secondary sources until you have a good understanding of the area of law and perhaps have citations to a few relevant cases or statutes.

C. Researching Enacted Law and Related Cases

If the secondary source referred to a relevant constitutional provision or statute, read it immediately. But also conduct independent research to ensure that you have not overlooked another relevant provision or statute.

Open an Oregon statutes database; remember that you can access it in several ways: by typing *Oregon statutes* into the universal search bar; by browsing under "Content types" for "Statutes & Court Rules" then "Oregon"; or by browsing under "State Materials" and "Oregon." Enter your Boolean search query in the universal search bar, realizing that you might be able to refine it after your work in secondary sources. Skim the research results. Most likely, they will not contain relevant constitutional provisions. They will likely include both statutes and notes of decisions, but focus first on those that refer to statutes. Once you have identified a relevant statute, read it carefully at least twice. Outline it if it is long or complex. Read any statutes that it cross references. Click on "Table of Contents" to see whether other nearby statutes are also relevant. Check any KeyCite indicator to ensure that the statute is current and has no negative treatment by cases in your jurisdiction.

Open the "Notes of Decisions" from the link at the top of the screen or the box under the statutory text. If there are many cases indexed with this statute, you might be able to narrow your search using a list of subheadings. Skim the notes for relevant cases. Even if all of the cases in "Notes of Decisions" seem dated, you can use them as a springboard to other research by using their Topics and Key Numbers in the West digest or by using KeyCite. Save the statute(s) and relevant cases to your folder.

At this point, consider researching administrative law. Relevant regulations might have been mentioned already in a secondary source, annotations to a statute, or a related case. To conduct a fresh search, type *Oregon regulations* in the universal search bar or browse below the search bar for databases with Oregon state regulations. Continue with the detailed instructions provided in Chapter 6, Section V.

If you don't find any relevant statutes, modify your search query. If you still don't find anything, consider the possibility that the area is controlled by common law.

D. Finding Cases with Topic and Key Number Digests

Although you might have already found a number of cases from secondary sources and annotated statutes, you should still check a digest for additional cases. Note that if your research issue is controlled by common law, you will not find a statute or related annotations, and using the digest will be even more important.

Using "Content types," click on "Key Numbers." Either search for your terms using the box at the top of the page, or skim the list of Topics and expand relevant headings. The results of your search will be a list of headnotes from cases that West has indexed under a particular Topic and Key Number. Skim the headnotes and determine which cases are relevant. Annotate those and save them to your folder. Remember that an eyeglasses icon means that you have already viewed a document. If you begin to see the same relevant cases repeatedly, you should feel good about the effectiveness of your research.

E. Reading Cases

By this point, your folder should have a number of cases that you have determined are relevant. Take time now to read each one carefully, using the techniques explained in Chapter 7, Section IV.C. If you determine a case is not relevant, add an annotation to the first page of the case briefly stating why and move it to another folder. Keeping a folder of discarded cases can help you avoid rereading cases later that you have already determined are not useful.

As you determine the most relevant cases, consider printing them. You might find that reading in print helps you concentrate on the text, or that you are able to annotate printouts with arrows and other symbols that are not available in Westlaw's annotation system.

F. Updating with KeyCite

As you encountered each statute or case that you thought was relevant, you should have quickly checked to see whether it had a red or yellow symbol indicating negative treatment that could affect that authority's impact on your analysis. Now, for each case that you have decided to rely on, use KeyCite to ensure that the case is still good law. Check the history and negative treatment as well as the table of authorities (if other authorities that this case relied on are no longer valid, this case might not be either). Then expand your research by clicking on "Citing References." You might find additional cases that are more recent, that have clearer analyses, or that have facts closer to your issue.

G. Ending Research

When you have completed each step of the process and you have begun to see the same relevant sources appear in various steps, you might be nearing the end of your research. Sketch an outline of the elements or key arguments, and see whether you have sufficient statutory, administrative, or case law to support each. If not, continue research, trying new sources and new search terms. If so, move into organizing your analysis for either a final document or an oral presentation.

II. Guided Word Searching (Lexis)

Guided word searching takes advantage of the powerful search engines provided by Lexis and other premier services. Each search is likely to produce a large number of results in a variety of sources, but at each step the researcher "guides" the process by making choices about which sources and which documents to review. This is very different from a haphazard word search, which can be very time consuming and produce unreliable results.

A. Conducting Pre-Research Tasks and Running the First Search

Clarify your issue and generate search terms based on the facts and the research question. Consider carefully the terms likely to appear in relevant documents. If proximity of terms is important, create a search query with Boolean connectors to control the results; review search tips to ensure that you are using the correct connectors for this service.

Enter your search query in the universal search bar. Because this is your first search and Oregon is a small jurisdiction, do not limit your search by ju-

Figure 9-2. Categories on Lexis Advance

Select Category		Results for: b₁
Cases	3,430 ∨	⌂ ‖ Actions∨
Cases		**3,430**
Statutes and Legislation		1,158
Secondary Materials		622
Administrative Materials		47
Briefs, Pleadings and Motions		526
Administrative Codes and Regulations		399
Forms		1
News		Get
Legal News		461
Dockets		Get
Jury Verdicts and Settlements		4
Jury Instructions		13
Expert Witness Materials		13
Company and Financial		Get
Directories		86

risdiction (because non-jurisdictional material can provide good background, especially in secondary sources); do not limit by category of document (e.g., cases, statutes), or by practice area or topic.

Your search results will be divided by category of documents (e.g., Secondary Materials, Statutes and Legislation, Cases), as shown in Figure 9-2.

B. Researching Secondary Sources

Review secondary materials (you might need to open a drop-down menu to select this category). Consider narrowing by jurisdiction, depending on the number of results returned. Decide which type of secondary source is most likely to be helpful for your project. If you need an authoritative overview, for example, begin with a treatise. Alternatively, a database containing *American Jurisprudence* or *American Law Reports* could provide a less detailed explanation of the law, but more references to primary authorities in a number of jurisdictions. Because you are just beginning to research and this is a new area of law, do not start by looking at law review articles as they tend to be too specific. You might come back to these later, for example, if you need analysis of how different jurisdictions interpret a certain law.

Work methodically through each treatise or other secondary source that seems relevant. Skim the headings, and then read the text for those results that seem on point. Note potentially relevant statutes and cases referenced in the text or in footnotes.

Decide which documents to open or save to a folder. Some researchers like to simply open tabs for all possibly relevant statutes or cases until they have finished reading the treatise, and then read the authorities all together and save the relevant ones to a folder. Other researchers prefer to quickly skim each statute or case as they encounter it, saving relevant ones to a folder. Briefly annotate or highlight each document so that when you return to it later you will remember why it seemed relevant.

C. Researching Enacted Law and Related Cases

Select the category "Statutes and Legislation."[1] Narrow the results to contain only statutes from Oregon (you might need to click "More" to see this option). If there are still too many for you to review, filter by keyword. You might first skim a few statutes in the results to determine which keywords will filter the results list most effectively. For each entry in your filtered results list, read the title and the blurb carefully. Determine whether the entry is a statute or an annotation to a case discussing a statute; focus first on statutes.

When you find a relevant statute, read it carefully. Then read it again. Consider outlining it, unless it is very short and simple. Read statutes before and after each relevant statute, browsing with the "Previous" and "Next" arrows or using the "Table of Contents" tab. Also read any statutes cross-referenced in a relevant statute.

To see how courts have interpreted and applied the statute, study the annotations. Use the "Go to" link to drop down to the annotations from the screen containing the statutory text. Realize that annotations might be numbered, or there might be an index of annotations, grouping them under related categories. These numbers and categories are not part of the statutory code, but aids to research that can help you identify the most useful annotations for your project.

---

1. To find any relevant constitutional provisions, you may need to use "Browse" and "Sources." Under "Oregon" and "Statutes and Legislation" is a table of contents for the Oregon Constitution.

You might also Shepardize the statute at this point, both to ensure that it is still current and to find more cases that have applied it. You should expect overlap between cases you find in the case notes for the statute and in Shepard's. This overlap should make you feel confident in your research, but look carefully for cases included in one source but not the other.

Next, return to your initial search and select the category "Administrative Codes and Regulations." Review the results for the text of relevant regulations or agency action included in the *Oregon Bulletin*. Then select the category "Administrative Materials" for related agency decisions.

D. Finding Additional Cases

Return to your initial search (either using the "History" link or clicking back) and open the "Cases" category. Again, narrow the results by using the filters in the left margin; with the research you have done so far, you should be able to narrow effectively by court, search terms, date, etc. Your goal is to have a results list with a manageable number of cases that appear to be relevant.

Two alternative approaches might also be effective in locating additional cases. First, using the cases that you have determined are relevant, link from important headnotes into the Lexis index by using "More like this Headnote." Second, highlight relevant text of a key case and use the drop-down option to "Add to search"; this approach will locate additional cases that Lexis identifies as related to or similar to the text you selected.

E. Reading Cases

This step — reading cases — is different from the quick skimming of cases you have done in the earlier steps of the research process. Now, you must read each case very closely, understand how it affects your client's issue, and decide whether it should be part of your analysis. Begin by skimming the synopsis of each case to get an overview. Read the headnotes to determine all of the significant portions of the case (because if one portion does not contain your search terms, it will not have been highlighted from the word search but might still be significant). Jump from possibly relevant headnotes to the linked portion of the case, reading that portion carefully to determine its impact on your project. Additionally, a colored bar code will identify those parts of the case that contain more of your search terms, which may be good places to begin.

Read each relevant case in full at least once. After deciding that a few paragraphs or a few pages of a case discuss an unimportant procedural issue or another cause of action, you can avoid those pages in future readings. Consider crossing them out on printed pages or annotating them online.

When you decide a case is relevant, quickly check its Shepard's status to ensure that the portion you plan to rely on is still good law.

F. Updating with Shepard's

As noted above, you should have been glancing at the Shepard's symbols on statutes and cases to determine whether they have negative or pending treatment. Now you have three more tasks to complete for each case you intend to rely on. First, ensure that your case is still good law by using the tab for "Appellate History." Remember that you can Shepardize using headnotes so that you validate only the portion of the case that is relevant to your work, saving you time.

Next, check the "Table of Authorities" for hidden weaknesses. If the key cases that your case relied on have a long line of negative treatment, your case may no longer be based on good law. Moreover, because the Table of Authorities lists each case cited by the case you are Shepardizing, you might skim it for additional cases to read.

Third, expand your research with the tab for "Citing Decisions." If there are many citing decisions, use the filters to restrict to a reasonable number of recent cases from your jurisdiction that discuss similar facts. Your goal here is to find additional cases that might be even more important than those you found earlier in the process. Be sure not to disregard a case with negative facts or negative analysis for the outcome your client desires; you will have to address those weaknesses.

G. Ending Research

You can be confident in your research when you begin to see the same relevant sources come up repeatedly and when you can complete your analysis with the authorities you have found.

Figure 9-3. Oregon BarBooks Titles

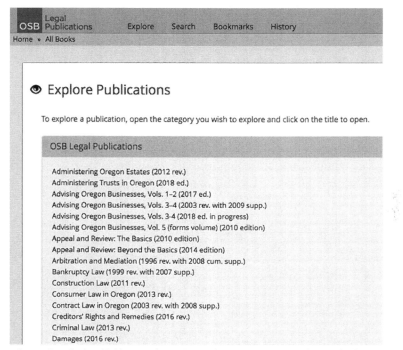

Source: Oregon State Bar Legal Publications, https://www.osbar.org/secured/barbooksapp/#/books.

III. Free Searching with Oregon-Specific Materials

A. Conducting Pre-Research Tasks

Many of the sources you will search in this third approach are restricted to Oregon. Consult with a law reference librarian to ensure that you know which Oregon resources are available and how to use them. Try to write your issue in one short, clear sentence.

B. Researching Secondary Sources

Begin with a Google search, using your issue statement as the search query. Skim the first twenty results quickly to see whether any seem helpful and reliable. If so, read them and record any references to primary sources (which you will need to confirm later as both accurate and current). Create a Word document with a list of helpful Google results, including each source's URL and a short note about why it is helpful. Your goal at this point is simply to get oriented.

Go to the Oregon BarBooks website. Click on "Explore Books" and review the list of titles for a few that seem to cover your issue. See Figure 9-3 for a partial list of titles. Open the link for each of those books, read the short description of its coverage, and skim the table of contents. Once you find a relevant book (or two), either download it and review its table of contents or index for relevant portions, or go to "Search Books." With the latter option, you can run searches in a particular book (or several) to locate specific sections that seem helpful. Early on in your research, you should read the first chapter of a relevant BarBook to get a clear overview of this area of law.

If this area is covered by an Oregon-specific treatise, spend some time researching the treatise relevant to your issue. For example, no research on an Oregon evidentiary issue should begin without a review of Laird Kirkpatrick's treatise.[2] If you have not found anything helpful in the BarBooks or an Oregon treatise, turn to a general secondary source. Print versions of Am Jur, CJS, ALR, etc. are available in some law school and county law libraries.

C. Researching Oregon's Constitution, Statutes, and Regulations

If a constitutional provision is on point, you should have encountered it in researching secondary sources. Use the Oregon State Legislature's website to review the text of that provision and to find annotations to cases that discuss it. To be thorough, check the ORS index, which could include references to additional provisions of the constitution.

You might have encountered an Oregon statute while researching secondary sources. If so, begin your statutory research by finding the statute. Be sure to read the current statute if you are giving advice prospectively, or to read the version of the statute in force when a past situation arose. Using the Oregon State Legislature's website, enter the statute's citation in the appropriate box and read the statute's language carefully. Then read any cross-referenced statutes, as well as statutes appearing just before or after the statute. Find the table of contents for this portion of ORS and skim it, both to get an overview of the area of law and to see whether other statutes are on point.

---

2. Laird C. Kirkpatrick, *Oregon Evidence* (2013).

Even if you started this step with a citation to a particular statute, spend a few minutes with the ORS index to ensure that you haven't missed another statute that is also relevant.

To find cases related to the statutes that apply to your issue, click on "Annotations" (currently, this appears in the left margin). While the ORS Annotations are not comprehensive, you might find a few cases that are on point or that will lead to other, relevant cases.

To determine if any regulations are on point, use the Oregon Secretary of State' website. You can search for keywords in the OARs, or you can browse by chapter name if you know the name of the relevant administrative agency. Update administrative rules by using the link to the *Oregon Bulletin* on the Secretary of State's website. Administrative agency decisions may be available on individual agency websites.

D. Finding Cases

Google Scholar can be an effective tool for locating cases. From the home page, click on "Cases," and then select Oregon cases. Enter your issue statement in the search box, refining it based on what you have learned so far in your research. Using links in the left margin, limit the results by date, and sort results by relevance or date. Read the cases that seem relevant, noting that they may have star paging available only for *Pacific Reporter*, not an official Oregon reporter. Although Google Scholar does not have headnotes for expanding your research, each case will have hyperlinks to other cases. You can expand your research using the "How cited" link that appears at the top left when you are viewing a case.

In addition to conducting new research, you can try typing into the search bar the citation to cases you found in earlier steps; realize that sometimes Google Scholar does not return the case you intended.

E. Reading Cases

You can read cases in Google Scholar, or (for some physical activity) go to the library and pull volumes from the shelves. For older reporter volumes that are not on the shelves, ask at the circulation desk if the volumes are easy to retrieve from storage. Print or photocopy cases that seem especially important.

F. Updating Cases

Google Scholar provides a citator called "How cited," mentioned above for expanding your research. You could use it to begin the process of ensuring your case is still good law. However, to ensure the validity of cases and to check the validity of statutes, you should use KeyCite or Shepard's.

Another possibility is to use Fastcase, which is free to members of the Oregon State Bar. It offers a citator called "Authority Check," but it is not nearly as comprehensive as the citators provided by Lexis and Westlaw.

G. Ending Research

You can feel confident that your research is nearing an end when you begin to see the same sources cited repeatedly. That is, if the secondary sources all refer to the same key authorities, and your most important cases all cite the same statutes and each other, and all of the cases and statutes are good law, you have likely been thorough. Outline your analysis; if any holes remain — meaning that you are missing an analytical link or that you do not have support for a particular element or factor — return to the research process.

IV. Conclusion

Like most skills, legal research improves with practice. Try to view each frustrating experience with a search engine or resource as an opportunity to learn more about the research process. Most of all, remember that professional reference librarians are available to assist you, whether you are a novice or an experienced researcher.

Appendix A

Federal Research

The legal research process and the techniques discussed throughout this book are effective in researching federal law as well as Oregon law. This appendix introduces the fundamental sources of federal law:

- the U.S. Constitution
- federal statutes and legislative history
- court rules for federal courts
- federal administrative regulations and agency decisions
- cases from federal courts

I. United States Constitution

The federal constitution is widely available online and in print; each publication offers something unique. For example, the United States Senate's website at www.senate.gov (click on "Reference" then "The Constitution") includes two annotated versions, one of which provides a brief introduction and an explanation of each article and amendment to the constitution.[1] Lexis and Westlaw provide the federal constitution and make it easy to search for related cases, treatises, and other sources that interpret and explain particular provisions. In print, the federal constitution is published along with the Oregon Constitution in *Oregon Revised Statutes* and in *West's Oregon Revised Statutes Annotated*. There is an index immediately following the federal constitution, and annotations are provided just as they are for statutes. The federal constitution is also available in print in the first few volumes of two commercial publications of federal statutes, *United States Code Annotated* and *United States*

---

1. Currently, the link is under the "Annotated Constitutions" section of that web page, entitled "The Constitution of the United States of America, S. Pub. 103–21 (1994)."

Code Service, as a convenience for readers. These series are explained in the next part of this appendix.

Many books, law review articles, and judicial opinions have been devoted to interpretation of the federal constitution. Refer to discussions in other chapters of this book for instruction on searching these resources.[2]

II. Federal Statutes

The *United States Code* (USC) codifies federal statutes under fifty-four titles. Within each title, individual statutes are assigned section numbers. To cite a federal statute, include both the title and the section number, and insert periods in the code abbreviation. The federal statute granting appellate jurisdiction to federal appellate courts is 28 U.S.C. § 1291 (2012); title 28 is devoted to courts and judicial matters, and 1291 is the section number assigned to this statute.[3] The year 2012 denotes the edition of the code, which contains laws passed through that year, though publication actually occurred in 2013 or later.[4]

The USC is the official codified version of the federal code and is issued in print every six years. Cumulative annual supplements provide laws passed between the six-year editions. An authenticated version is available online from the Government Publishing Office (GPO) at www.govinfo.gov. That material is currently available on govinfo, a GPO website.

The more commonly used sources for researching federal statutes are commercially produced and extensively annotated: *United States Code Annotated* (USCA) and *United States Code Service* (USCS). Both are available online as well as in print. USCA is on Westlaw, and USCS is on Lexis. Even if you use a commercial source to research a federal statute, try to confirm the text in the official USC (in print or on GPO's website) and cite it.

Both USCA and USCS contain the text of federal statutes, federal court rules, and the U.S. Constitution. They also provide references to related research sources:

---

2. For a more extensive discussion, see Mary Garvey Algero et al., *Federal Legal Research* (2d ed. 2015). Chapter 4, Constitutional Law Research, was written by Sarah E. Ricks.

3. Remember that Oregon citation does not use periods in abbreviations, so the citation would be 28 USC § 1291 (2012).

4. The *United States Code* will be updated in 2018. The 2018 edition will be published in 2019.

- cases interpreting or applying each federal statute, rule, or the Constitution;
- secondary sources on related topics;
- federal regulations and executive orders;
- tables listing statutes by popular names.

Some researchers feel that USCA provides more case annotations than USCS, while USCS provides better information on court rules and administrative regulations. Often the two are of equal value, so use whichever one is available.

When working online, check the date through which the statute is current; often this information is given at the top of the screen. In print, USCA and USCS are updated through pocket parts and paperback supplements. When only portions of a statute have changed, the pocket part may refer to the unchanged language in the hardbound volume. Other pocket parts are cumulative, so a modified statute will be reprinted in full.

III. Federal Legislative Research

The legislative process in Congress is similar to that described in Table 5-1 for enacting Oregon statutes. The Library of Congress website at Congress.gov includes a section on "The Legislative Process," with links to detailed videos (and transcripts) explaining each step of the process.

Each Congress meets for two years, in two year-long sessions that match the calendar year. For example, the 115th Congress held its first session in 2017 and its second session in 2018.[5] Federal bills are numbered sequentially in each chamber of Congress. Generally, Senate bill numbers are preceded by an "S." and House of Representatives bill numbers are preceded by "H.R." A bill that is not enacted in a particular two-year cycle dies and must be reintroduced in the following Congress.

A. Federal Bill Tracking

Much Congressional material is available from government websites. The Library of Congress site at Congress.gov provides bill summaries and status, committee reports, and the *Congressional Record* (which records debate in the House and Senate). The website is free and updated daily. It contains material back to 1995.

---

5. As a quick reference and mnemonic device, the 113th Congress convened in 2013.

Lexis and Westlaw provide federal bill tracking through databases named "Bill Tracking Report—Current Congress" and "Federal Bill Tracking," respectively. Each has historical bill tracking material available, with varying dates of coverage.

B. Federal Legislative History

Researching federal legislative history involves roughly the same steps as researching Oregon's laws, although some of the terminology is different. When a federal statute is enacted, it is assigned a *public law number*. This number is in the form Pub. L. No. 101-336, where the numerals before the hyphen are the number of the Congress in which the law was enacted and the numerals after the hyphen are assigned chronologically as bills are enacted. The public law number given above is for the *Americans with Disabilities Act* (ADA), which was passed in 1990 during the 101st Congress.

The new statute is later published as a *session law* in *United States Statutes at Large*, which is the federal counterpart of *Oregon Laws*. Session laws are designated by volume and page in *Statutes at Large*, e.g., 104 Stat. 328. Finally, the new statute is assigned a *section number* when it is codified with statutes on similar topics in the *United States Code*. The citation for the first section of the ADA is 42 U.S.C. § 12101.

To summarize with a more recent example, the *Patient Protection and Affordable Care Act* (known as "Obamacare") was enacted in 2010. The bill was H.R. 3590. The public law number is Pub. L. No. 111-148, showing it was the 148th statute enacted in the 111th Congress. Its session law citation is 124 Stat. 119. It is codified at 42 U.S.C. 18001 *et seq.*

As with Oregon legislative history, federal legislative history research typically begins with a statute number. If you do not know the statute number, use an annotated code or online service to find it (as described in Chapter 4). With a statute number, you can find the session law citation and public law number, which will lead to the legislative history of the bill as it worked its way through Congress. Table A-1 compares sources for Oregon and federal legislative history.

1. Sources of Federal Legislative History

The goal of federal legislative history research is to find committee reports, materials from committee hearings, and transcripts of floor debates. *Committee reports* are considered the most persuasive authority. Unlike Oregon's committee reports, which are short forms, Congressional committee reports are often lengthy documents. These reports contain the committee's analysis of the bill,

**Table A-1. Comparison of Sources for Oregon and
Federal Legislative History**

Action	Oregon Sources	Federal Sources
Committee work	Minutes and audio logs; audio recordings; exhibits of hearings	Committee reports; transcripts, video, or live streams of hearings; committee prints
Floor debate and votes	*Journal of the Senate* *Journal of the House*	*Congressional Record*
Session law	*Oregon Laws*	*Statutes at Large*
Codified version	*Oregon Revised Statutes* (official in print and unofficial online) *West's Oregon Revised Statutes Annotated* (unofficial in print and online through Westlaw products) Lexis (online only)	*United States Code* (official) *United States Code Annotated* (West in print and online) *United States Code Service* (LexisNexis in print and on-line)

the reasons for enacting it, and the views of any committee members who dis-agree with those reasons. Congressional hearing materials include transcripts from the proceedings and documents such as prepared testimony and exhibits. A *committee print* may publish the staff's research and supporting documents.

Floor debates are published in the *Congressional Record*. Be wary in relying on these statements as they may not have actually been delivered in the House or Senate; members of Congress can amend their remarks and even submit written statements that are published in transcript form as if they were spoken.

2. Compiled Legislative History

Similar to the Oregon archivist staff compiling tracings of certain Oregon statutes, some researchers have compiled legislative history for certain federal statutes. A widely known reference book that compiles legislative histories of major federal statutes is *Sources of Compiled Legislative Histories*.[6] It is worth-

---

6. Nancy P. Johnson, *Sources of Compiled Legislative Histories: A Bibliography of Government Documents, Periodical Articles, and Books* (AALL 1979–present) (also available at www.heinonline.org).

while to see whether a compiled legislative history exists before identifying all of the documents yourself.

3. Resources for Federal Legislative History

The sites noted earlier in this appendix for tracking federal legislation also provide useful information for legislative history research. The Library of Congress site at Congress.gov provides bill summaries, text, amendments, and status; cosponsors and related bills; committee reports; and the *Congressional Record*. Much federal legislative history is available on Lexis and Westlaw, both in general databases devoted to legislation and in topical databases. In addition, ProQuest Congressional and ProQuest Legislative Insight are two of the most comprehensive sites, with the latter focusing on activity that led to enacted law.[7]

IV. Federal Court Rules

Federal courts have court rules, similar to the rules for Oregon courts. Many rules that apply to federal courts in Oregon (and to all federal courts) will be found in USC, USCA, and USCS. To locate the rules for individual federal courts in Oregon, you may need to consult either comprehensive databases, such as Lexis or Westlaw, or the jurisdiction-specific deskbook *Oregon Rules of Court: Federal*. Additionally, courts frequently post their rules on their websites. For example, rules for the United States District Court for the District of Oregon are on its website at http://www.ord.uscourts.gov/.

A well known treatise on federal rules, *Federal Practice and Procedure*, is introduced in Chapter 2 of this book.

V. Federal Administrative Law

The federal government's agencies function much like Oregon's. Agencies such as the Civil Rights Division of the Department of Justice, the Internal Revenue Service, and the U.S. Fish and Wildlife Service are invaluable parts of the executive branch.

The federal Administrative Procedure Act (APA) is codified at 5 U.S.C. § 551 *et seq*. Like Oregon's APA, its goals are to promote uniformity, public partic-

---

7. Most of the sources covered in this chapter exist in print. To conduct federal legislative history research in print, consult a reference librarian or one of the texts noted in Appendix B of this book.

ipation, and public confidence in the fairness of the procedures used by agencies of the federal government.

A. *Code of Federal Regulations*

Federal administrative rules are called *regulations*. Federal regulations are published by the Government Publishing Office (GPO) in the *Code of Federal Regulations* (CFR). They are also available online on the govinfo site and, through 2018, the Federal Digital System (FDsys). Additionally, you can access the CFR at www.ecfr.gov, an unofficial compilation of federal regulations that is kept current daily. The CFR is also available on Lexis and Westlaw, which keep their databases fairly current.

Similar to rules in OAR in Oregon, regulations in CFR are organized by agency and subject. The titles of CFR do not necessarily correspond to the titles of the *United States Code* (USC), although some subjects do fall under the same title number. For instance, title 7 in both CFR and USC pertain to agriculture, but title 11 of USC addresses bankruptcy, while the same title in CFR deals with federal elections. See Table A-2 for an example of a federal regulation, with its citation in national format.

B. *Federal Register*

New regulations and proposed changes to existing regulations are published in the *Federal Register*, the federal equivalent of the *Oregon Bulletin*. The *Federal Register* is the first print source to publish regulations in their final form when they are adopted (i.e., before they are codified in CFR). In addition to providing the text of regulations, the *Federal Register* contains notices of hearings, responses to public comments on proposed regulations, executive orders, and helpful tables and indexes. It is published almost every weekday, with continuous pagination throughout the year. This means that citation to page numbers in the thousands is common. The *Federal Register* is available online through the government sites and on Lexis and Westlaw.

C. Decisions of Federal Agencies

Like Oregon agencies, federal agencies hold quasi-judicial hearings to decide cases that arise under the agencies' regulations. Some of these decisions are published in reporters specific to each agency, for example, *Decisions and Orders of the National Labor Relations Board* (NLRB). Increasingly, agency decisions are available on agency websites and from Lexis and Westlaw.

Table A-2. Example of a Federal Regulation

---

29 C.F.R. § 825.104

Title 29: Labor

PART 825 — THE FAMILY AND MEDICAL LEAVE ACT OF 1993

Subpart A — Coverage Under the Family and Medical Leave Act

§ 825.104 Covered employer.

(a) An employer covered by FMLA is any person engaged in commerce or in any industry or activity affecting commerce, who employs 50 or more employees for each working day during each of 20 or more calendar workweeks in the current or preceding calendar year. Employers covered by FMLA also include any person acting, directly or indirectly, in the interest of a covered employer to any of the employees of the employer, any successor in interest of a covered employer, and any public agency. Public agencies are covered employers without regard to the number of employees employed. Public as well as private elementary and secondary schools are also covered employers without regard to the number of employees employed.

See § 825.600.

Source: Electronic Code of Federal Regulations, www.ecfr.gov.

VI. Federal Courts and Cases

A. Federal Trial Courts

The trial courts in the federal system are called United States District Courts. There are ninety-four district courts in the federal system, with each district drawn from a particular state. A state with a relatively small population might not be subdivided into smaller geographic regions. The entire state of Oregon, for example, makes up the federal District of Oregon. Even so, district courts are located in three cities: Portland, Eugene, and Medford. States with larger populations and higher caseloads are subdivided into more districts. For example, California has four federal districts: northern, central, southern, and eastern. Washington has two federal districts: eastern and western.

Selected cases from the United States District Courts, the federal trial courts, are reported in *Federal Supplement, Federal Supplement, Second Series,* and *Federal Supplement, Third Series,* published by West. Some opinions from the *Federal Supplement* series are available on the U.S. Courts website, as well as Google Scholar and other online providers. Lexis and Westlaw tend to make available more U.S. District Court cases, but these "unpublished" decisions carry less authoritative weight than those published in *Federal Supplement*.

B. Federal Circuit Courts of Appeals

Intermediate appellate courts in the federal system are called United States Courts of Appeals. There are courts of appeals for each of the thirteen federal circuits. Twelve of these circuits are based on geographic jurisdiction. Eleven numbered circuits cover groups of states; the twelfth is the District of Columbia Circuit. The thirteenth federal circuit, called the Federal Circuit, hears appeals from district courts in all other circuits on issues related to patent law and from certain specialized courts and agencies.

Oregon is in the Ninth Circuit, so cases from the United States District Court for the District of Oregon are appealed to the United States Court of Appeals for the Ninth Circuit. This circuit encompasses Alaska, Arizona, California, Hawaii, Idaho, Montana, Nevada, Oregon, and Washington, as well as Guam and the Northern Mariana Islands.

Cases decided by the intermediate appellate courts in the federal system are published in West's *Federal Reporter*, now in its third series. Federal appeals courts maintain their own websites that provide access to recent cases for free. A gateway to each court is available at www.uscourts.gov. Both Lexis and Westlaw include cases from federal courts of appeals in several databases. Other online providers typically provide access to federal appellate cases, too. Some appellate cases that were not selected for publication in *Federal Reporter* may be published by West in *Federal Appendix*. Additional cases may be available on Lexis and Westlaw. Be careful, however. If a case does not have a citation to *Federal Reporter*, the case may be of limited authority in some jurisdictions.[8]

---

8. Opinions published in *Federal Appendix* and other cases available only online may be considered "unpublished" and of limited precedential value. Check the rules of the relevant court as there is no national consistency. *See, e.g.*, Fed R App P 32.1 (authorizing litigants in the federal Courts of Appeals to cite unpublished opinions of those courts beginning in 2007, but allowing courts to determine the weight of unpublished opinions); David R. Cleveland, *Local Rules in the Wake of Federal Rule of Appellate Procedure 32.1*, 11 J App Prac & Process 19 (Spring 2010) (examining local rules regarding precedential value of unpublished opinions and finding lack of uniformity).

C. Supreme Court of the United States

The highest court in the federal system is the United States Supreme Court. It decides cases concerning the United States Constitution and federal statutes. This court does not have the final say on matters of purely state law; that authority rests with the highest court of each state. Parties who wish to have the U.S. Supreme Court hear their cases must file a petition for *certiorari*, as the court has discretion over which cases it hears.

Decisions of the United States Supreme Court are reported in *United States Reports*, the official reporter; *Supreme Court Reporter*, a West publication; and *United States Supreme Court Reports, Lawyers' Edition*, published by LexisNexis and in its second series. Although *United States Reports* is the official reporter, meaning that you should cite it if possible, that series frequently publishes cases several years after they are decided. Thus, for recent cases, lawyers often cite the *Supreme Court Reporter*. You can access a PDF version of *United States Reports* for many cases on HeinOnline. Another source for recent cases from the Supreme Court is *United States Law Week*. This service publishes the full text of cases from the Supreme Court and provides summaries of important decisions of state and federal courts.

There are a number of free online sources for Supreme Court opinions, including the Court's website, the Cornell Law School's Legal Information Institute, and Google Scholar. Both Lexis and Westlaw provide quick access to Supreme Court opinions, as well as to briefs filed by the parties.

The United States Courts' website contains a map showing the federal circuits and districts, court addresses (with maps), explanations of jurisdiction, and other helpful information. The address is www.uscourts.gov. Reporters for cases decided by federal courts are listed in Table A-3, along with their national citation abbreviations. Citation to these cases is introduced in Appendix B of this book.

D. Topical Reporters

Some reporters publish cases on a particular topic, rather than cases from a specific court or region. For example, *Federal Rules Decisions* includes federal trial court cases that analyze federal rules of civil and criminal procedure that do not appear in *Federal Supplement*. Similarly, *West's Bankruptcy Reporter* includes cases from United States Bankruptcy Courts, including those in Oregon. West publishes both of these reporters, so they contain West's editorial enhancements. Other publishers also provide reporters in topical areas. An example is Bloomberg BNA's *Media Law Reporter*, which publishes all relevant

Table A-3. Reporters for Federal Court Cases

Court	Reporter Name	Abbreviation
U.S. Supreme Court	*United States Reports* (official)	U.S.
	Supreme Court Reporter	S. Ct.
	United States Supreme Court Reports, Lawyers' Edition	L. Ed. or L. Ed. 2d
U.S. Courts of Appeals	*Federal Reporter*	F. or F.2d or F.3d
U.S. District Courts	*Federal Supplement*	F. Supp. or F. Supp. 2d or F. Supp. 3d

opinions of the United States Supreme Court as well as significant opinions of federal and state courts on the topic of media law.

Appendix B

Legal Citation

When writing about legal research and analysis, lawyers use *legal citations* to refer to the authorities used to develop that analysis and reach the conclusion. Legal citations tell readers where to find the authorities relied on and indicate the level of analytical support the authorities provide. Citations allow legal writers to give credit for every idea borrowed from a case, statute, or other source.[1] In a legal document, every legal rule and every explanation of the law must be cited.

Legal citations are included in the text of legal documents rather than being saved for a bibliography. To minimize the space devoted to citations, lawyers use abbreviations and formatting conventions that are generally well known. Consistent citation format within a document makes reading and understanding citations easy. While many different citation systems exist, they tend to follow well established formats and conventions.

This chapter addresses Oregon state citation rules as well as the two national citation manuals, the *ALWD Guide to Legal Citation*[2] and *The Bluebook: A Uniform System of Citation*.[3] In law practice, you may encounter state statutes, court rules, and style manuals that dictate the form of citation used before the courts of different states.[4] You may find that each firm or agency that you

---

1. ALWD & Coleen M. Barger, *ALWD Guide to Legal Citation* 2 (6th ed 2017) ("*ALWD Guide*").

2. The first four editions were written by Darby Dickerson and published as the *ALWD Citation Manual: A Professional System of Citation*. The fifth edition was renamed *ALWD Guide to Legal Citation*.

3. *The Bluebook: A Uniform System of Citation* (The Columbia Law Review et al. eds., 20th ed 2015) ("*Bluebook*").

4. In the state of Washington, for example, the Office of Reporter of Decisions publishes a "style sheet" that determines citations to be used in documents submitted to Washington courts. The abbreviations required by that style sheet are familiar to lawyers practicing in Washington, but lawyers elsewhere may be unaccustomed to them.

Table B-1. Example Citations Under Oregon Local Rules

Statutes	ORS 164.225.
Cases	*Hoffman v. Freeman Land and Timber, LLC.,* 329 Or 554 (1999).
	State v. Reid, 36 Or App 417 (1978).
	Linder v. Dept. of Rev., 18 OTR 11 (2004).
	Brown v. Bd. of Educ., 349 US 294 (1955).
State Rules	OAR 808-003-0010. [Oregon Administrative Rules]
	ORCP 71 B(1)(b). [Oregon Rules of Civil Procedure]
Federal Rules	FRE 802. [Federal Rules of Evidence]

work for has its own preference for citation or makes minor variations to generally accepted format. Some law offices have their own style manuals, drawn from state rules and national manuals. Once you are aware of the basic function and format of citation, adapting to a slightly different set of rules is not difficult.

I. Oregon Citation Rules

In Oregon, two sources of citation rules are the *Uniform Trial Court Rules* (UTCR) and the *Oregon Appellate Courts Style Manual* (OSM).[5] Lawyers practicing in Oregon generally follow these rules, even when they are not submitting documents to Oregon courts. Examples are given in Table B-1.

Under these rules, no periods are used in reporter abbreviations. Thus, *Oregon Reports* and *Oregon Reports, Court of Appeals* are abbreviated "Or" and "Or App" without punctuation. When citing *Oregon Revised Statutes* while working in Oregon, use the abbreviation "ORS." Do not include the date when referring to the current code. After using an online service or *West's Oregon*

---

5. The *Oregon Appellate Courts Style Manual* guides the state's appellate courts in writing decisions. Oregon Rule of Appellate Procedure 5.20(4) refers to the manual, but both the rule and the manual itself make clear that its style is not mandatory for counsel. For additional Oregon citation rules, see Uniform Trial Court Rule 1.070 and Oregon Tax Court Rule 61. Note, too, that some sources determine how they are to be cited. The preface to *Oregon Revised Statutes* requires that they be cited, for example, as ORS 758.505. Oregon Rule of Civil Procedure 1G states that those rules may be cited according to the following example: ORCP 7 D(3)(a)(iv)(A).

Revised Statutes Annotated (WORSA) to conduct your research, confirm the statutory language in ORS and cite to that official source.

The OSM includes examples of citations for constitutions, legislative material, rules of civil procedure and evidence, administrative rules, and much more. It also contains a writing style guide that addresses such things as capitalization, punctuation, word usage, and parallel construction. The OSM is available online from the Oregon Judicial Department links.

II. The National Citation Manuals

While state citation rules often provide only rules and examples, national citation manuals also attempt to explain in some detail the components of citations. The two national citation manuals that are currently popular are the *ALWD Guide* and the *Bluebook*. The content and format of citations produced by the two manuals is almost always identical; note in Table B-2, however, that different typeface is required for citations in practice documents and for footnotes in law review articles. The biggest difference for the student is that the *ALWD Guide* focuses its examples and explanations on the style of citation used in legal memoranda and briefs, while the *Bluebook*'s focus is on citation format used in law review articles and other academic publications.

Table B-2. Comparison of Citation Formats

Oregon Style Manual	ORS 164.225.
ALWD and *Bluebook* Practice Documents	Or. Rev. Stat. § 164.225 (2017).
ALWD and *Bluebook* Law Review Articles	Or. Rev. Stat. § 164.225 (2017).

A. *ALWD Guide*

The Association of Legal Writing Directors (ALWD) publishes a citation manual that is intended to make citation instruction straightforward. Both the instructions and the examples focus on the citations used in legal practice; an alternate format for academic citations is designated "Academic Formatting." The sixth edition was published in 2017 under the name *ALWD Guide to Legal Citation*.

Three finding tools lead to relevant rules in the *ALWD Guide*:

- the table of contents, laying out the organization of the rules in the guide
- the index at the back of the guide
- a table of "Fast Formats," inside the front cover, which refers to example citations.

In the guide's index, most references are to rules or to specific sidebars, charts, appendices, or other features. References to a page are preceded by "p."

Appendix 1 at the back of the guide lists abbreviations for primary sources of law for each state, presented alphabetically, along with resources for federal, Native American, and territorial law. For Oregon, this appendix includes abbreviations for state and regional reporters, state statutes and regulations, the state constitution, etc. Appendix 3E gives abbreviations to use for case names in citations, Appendix 4 provides abbreviations for courts, and Appendix 5 includes abbreviations for law journals.

B. *Bluebook*

Student editors of four Ivy League law reviews have developed citation rules that are published as *The Bluebook: A Uniform System of Citation*. The *Oregon Appellate Courts Style Manual* defers to the *Bluebook* for rules not covered in the state manual.[6] Many law firms, agencies, and organizations consider *Bluebook* citations the norm; it is the oldest citation manual still in general use. Although the rules change with each new edition, most attorneys assume that the *Bluebook* has not changed since they were in law school.

For practicing attorneys, the primary difficulty with the *Bluebook* is that its focus is on the citation style used in law review articles, not the format used for legal memoranda and court documents. Because almost all of the *Bluebook* examples are in law review format, a student or lawyer using the *Bluebook* has to translate each example into the format used in legal practice documents.

Perhaps the most helpful information in the *Bluebook* is the reference guide on the inside back cover of the book, which gives examples of citations used

---

6. When writing to Oregon courts, be sure to resolve any inconsistencies between the two manuals in favor of the *Oregon Style Manual*. For example, Oregon style abbreviates the word "Department" in case names as "Dept." with a period, while the *Bluebook* uses "Dep't" with an apostrophe.

in court documents and legal memoranda.[7] Another helpful section of the *Bluebook* appears on pages 3 through 56; these are the "Bluepages." This section provides information for and additional examples of citations used in documents other than law review articles.

The index at the back of the *Bluebook* is quite extensive, and in most instances is more helpful than the table of contents. Most often, you should begin working with the *Bluebook* by referring to the index. Entries given in black type refer to citation instructions, while entries in blue refer to examples. Note that the references in the index are to page numbers, not rule numbers.

Blue-bordered pages at the back of the *Bluebook* contain tables with jurisdictional material (federal and states), and abbreviations for case names, courts, and law journals.

C. Citation Essentials

1. Citing Oregon Materials with National Citation Formats

Because the *ALWD Guide* and the *Bluebook* are designed for national use, they use different abbreviations for some Oregon materials. The most obvious difference is that *Oregon Revised Statutes* is abbreviated "Or. Rev. Stat." instead of "ORS." Since an attorney working outside of Oregon would not be expected to know whether ORS referred to the statutes of Ohio, Oklahoma, or Oregon, the clarity of the longer abbreviation is necessary.

Another small difference is that in the national manuals all reporter abbreviations include periods. Thus, the Oregon reporters are abbreviated "Or." for *Oregon Reports* and "Or. App." for *Oregon Reports, Court of Appeals*. Similarly, *Pacific Reporter, Third Series* would be abbreviated "P.3d" rather than "P3d" (as under Oregon rules).

2. Incorporating Citations into a Document

A legal document must provide a citation for each idea that comes from a case, statute, article, or other source. Thus, paragraphs that state legal rules and explain the law should contain many citations.

A citation may offer support for an entire sentence or for an idea expressed in part of a sentence. If the citation supports the entire sentence, it is placed

---

7. Examples of law review citations are found on the inside front cover.

Table B-3. Examples of Citation Sentences and Citation Clauses

---

Citation Sentences: First-degree burglary involves a building that is a dwelling. Or. Rev. Stat. § 164.225 (2017). The term dwelling is defined as "a building which regularly or intermittently is occupied by a person lodging therein at night, whether or not a person is actually present." Or. Rev. Stat. § 164.205(2) (2017).

Citation Clauses: Oregon statutes define both first-degree burglary, Or. Rev. Stat. § 164.225 (2017), and second-degree burglary, Or. Rev. Stat. § 164.215 (2017).

---

in a separate *citation sentence* that begins with a capital letter and ends with a period. If the citation supports only a portion of the sentence, it is included immediately after the relevant part of that sentence and set off from the sentence by commas in what is called a *citation clause*. Table B-3 provides examples of each.

Do not cite a client's facts or your conclusions about a case, statute, or other authority. The following sentence should not be cited: "Under the facts presented, our client's conduct would fall under first-degree burglary because a homeless family sometimes slept in the building he broke into." These facts and conclusions are unique to your situation and would not be found anywhere in the reference source.

3. Case Citations

Detailed rules for case citation are included in Rule 12 of the *ALWD Guide* and Rule 10 of the *Bluebook*. A full citation to a case includes (1) the name of the case, (2) the volume and reporter in which the case is published, (3) the first page of the case, (4) the exact page in the case that contains the idea you are citing (i.e., the *pinpoint* or *jump cite*), (5) an abbreviation for the court that decided the case, and (6) the date the case was decided.

a. Essential Components of Case Citations

Include the name of just the first party on each side, even if several are listed in the case caption. If the party is an individual, include only the party's family name. If the party is a business or organization, shorten the party's name by using the abbreviations provided by the manuals.

Between the parties' names, place a lower case "v" followed by a period. Do not use a capital "V" or the abbreviation "vs." Place a comma after the second party's name; do not italicize or underline this comma.

The parties' names may be italicized or underlined. Use the style preferred by your supervisor and use that style consistently throughout each document. Do not combine italics and underlining in one cite or within a single document.

EXAMPLE: *Glik v. Cunniffe*, 655 F.3d 78, 80 (1st Cir. 2011).

Next, give the volume and the abbreviation for the reporter in which the case is found. Pay special attention to whether the reporter is in its first, second, or third series. In the example above, 655 is the volume number and F.3d is the reporter abbreviation for *Federal Reporter, Third Series.*

After the reporter name, include both the first page of the case and the pinpoint page containing the idea that you are referencing, separated by a comma and a space. The first page of the *Glik* case above is 78, and the page containing the specific idea being cited is 80. If the pinpoint page you are citing is also the first page of the case, then the same page number will appear twice.[8]

In a parenthetical following this information, indicate the court that decided the case, using abbreviations provided by the manual. In the jurisdictional tables, court abbreviations are included in parentheses just after the name of the court. In the above example, the First Circuit Court of Appeals, a federal court, decided the case.

If the reporter abbreviation clearly indicates which court decided a case, do not repeat this information in the parenthetical. To give two examples, only cases of the United States Supreme Court are reported in *United States Reports,* abbreviated U.S. Only cases decided by the Oregon Court of Appeals are reported in *Oregon Reports, Court of Appeals,* abbreviated Or. App. Repeating court abbreviations in citations to those reporters would be duplicative. By contrast, *Pacific Reporter, Third Series,* abbreviated P.3d, publishes decisions from different courts within several states, so the court that decided a particular case needs to be indicated parenthetically. Thus, in the last example below, "Cal." indicates that the decision came from the California Supreme Court rather than from another court whose decisions are also published in this reporter.

EXAMPLES: *Citizens United v. Fed. Election Comm'n,* 558 U.S. 310, 340 (2010).
Mid-Valley Res., Inc. v. Engelson, 170 Or. App. 255, 259 (2000).
Ketchum v. Moses, 17 P.3d 735, 736 (Cal. 2001).

---

8. When using an online version of a case, remember that screen breaks do not mirror page breaks. This means that you have to skim the text to find an embedded page marker. For example, if the notation *81 appeared in the text before the relevant information, the pinpoint cite would be to page 81, not page 80.

Note that these court abbreviations are not the same as postal codes. Abbreviating the California Supreme Court as either CA or Calif. would be incorrect.

The final piece of required information in most cites is the date the case was decided. For cases published in reporters, give only the year of decision, not the month or date. Do not confuse the date of decision with the date on which the case was argued or submitted, the date on which a motion for rehearing was denied, or the publication date of the reporter. For cases available only online, give the month abbreviation, date, and year.[9]

b. Full and Short Citations to Cases

The first time you mention a case by name, immediately give its full citation, including all of the information outlined above. Even though it is technically correct to include the full citation at the beginning of a sentence, a full citation takes up considerable space. By the time a reader gets through the citation and to your idea at the end of the sentence, the reader may have lost interest. The examples below demonstrate this problem.

Assume that this is the first time the case has been mentioned in this document.

CORRECT   The intent of the legislature enacting a statute must be determined. *Day v. City of Fontana*, 19 P.3d 1196, 1198 (Cal. 2001).

AVOID   In *Day v. City of Fontana*, 19 P.3d 1196, 1198 (Cal. 2001), the court noted that the intent of the legislature enacting a statute must be determined.

After using a full citation once to introduce an authority, use short citations to cite to this same authority. A short citation provides just enough information to allow the reader to locate the longer citation and find the pinpoint page.[10]

---

9. The following citation provides an example of a case that is available on Westlaw, but not in *Federal Supplement*: *Torretti v. Paoli Mem'l Hosp.*, No. 06-3003, 2008 WL 268066, *1 (E.D. Penn. Jan. 29, 2008).

10. Note that entering a short cite into an online service will often take you directly to the page of the case you need to review. In other words, you don't have to use the full cite with the first page in order to retrieve a case.

When the immediately preceding cite is to the same source and the same page, use *id.* as the short cite. When the second cite is to a different page within the same source, follow the *id.* with "at" and the new pinpoint page number. Capitalize *id.* when it begins a citation sentence, just as the beginning of any sentence is capitalized.

If the immediately preceding cite is to a different source, give the name of one of the parties, the volume, the reporter, and the pinpoint page following "at." In general, use the name of the first party in the full cite; if that party is "United States," a state, or another common litigant, use the opposing party's name.

EXAMPLE: Open and notorious possession requires the claimants to prove the owners had notice that the claimants were asserting title to the disputed property. *Slak v. Porter,* 128 Or. App. 274, 278 (1994). The notice may be actual or constructive. *Id.* at 279. Owners have actual notice when they are aware that their claim of the land is being challenged. *See id.* Constructive notice is satisfied when claimants use the property in a manner considered to give the owner knowledge of their use and claim. *Hoffman v. Freeman Land and Timber, LLC.,* 329 Or. 554, 559 (1999). Construction of a fence is the classic example of open and notorious possession. *Slak,* 128 Or. App. at 279.

If you refer to the case by name in the sentence, your short citation does not need to repeat the case name, although lawyers often do. The last sentence of the example would also be correct as follows: In *Slak,* construction of a fence was recognized as the classic example of open and notorious possession. 128 Or. App. at 279. The format, *Slak* at 279, consisting of just a case name and page number, is incorrect. The volume and reporter abbreviation are also needed.

c. Prior and Subsequent History

Sometimes a citation needs to show what happened to a case at an earlier or later stage of litigation. The case you are citing may have reversed an earlier case, as in the example below. If you are citing a case for a court's analysis of one issue and a later court reversed only on another issue, you need to alert your reader to that reversal. Or, if you decide for historical purposes to include in a document discussion of a case that was later overruled, your reader needs to know that as soon as you introduce the case. Prior and subsequent history can be appended to the full citations discussed above; the history begins with an italicized abbreviation like *rev'g* or *aff'd*.

EXAMPLE: The Supreme Court has upheld the right to marry as a fundamental right. *Obergefell v. Hodges*, 135 S. Ct. 2584 (2015), *rev'g DeBoer v. Snyder*, 772 F.3d 388 (6th Cir. 2014).

D. Signals

A citation must show the level of support each authority provides. You do this by deciding whether to use an introductory signal and, if so, which one. The more common signals are explained below:

No signal
- The source cited provides direct support for the idea in the sentence; or
- The cite identifies the source of a quotation.

See
- The source cited offers implicit support for the idea in the sentence.

See also
- The source cited provides additional support for the idea in the sentence. (The support offered by *see also* is not as strong or direct as authorities preceded by no signal or by the signal *see*.)

E.g.,
- Many authorities state the idea in the sentence, and you are citing only one as an example; this signal allows you to cite just one source while letting the reader know that many other sources say the same thing.

E. Explanatory Parentheticals

At the end of a cite, you can append additional information about the authority in parentheses. Sometimes this parenthetical information conveys to the reader the weight of the authority. For example, a case may have been decided *en banc* or *per curiam*. Or the case may have been decided by a narrow split among the judges who heard the case. Parenthetical information also allows you to name the judges who joined in a dissenting, concurring, or plurality opinion. An explanatory parenthetical following a signal can convey helpful, additional information in a compressed space. Parenthetical information generally should not be given in a complete sentence, but should begin with a present participle (i.e., a verb ending in "-ing") that is not capitalized. When using this type of parenthetical, be sure that you do not inadvertently hide a critical part of the court's analysis at the end of a long citation, where a reader is likely to skip over it.

> EXAMPLE: Before striking a contradictory affidavit under the "sham affidavit rule," a court must find the inconsistency between the party's deposition and subsequent affidavit to be "clear and unambiguous." *Van Asdale v. Int'l Game Tech.*, 577 F.3d 989, 998–99 (9th Cir. 2009) (urging district courts to apply the "sham affidavit rule" with caution).

F. Quotations

Use quotations only when the reader needs to see the text exactly as it appears in the original authority. Of all legal audiences, trial courts are probably most receptive to longer quotations. For example, quoting the controlling statutory language can be extremely helpful. As another example, if a well known case explains an analytical point in a particularly insightful way, a quotation may be warranted.

Excessive quotation has two drawbacks. First, quotations interrupt the flow of your writing when the style of the quoted language differs from your own. Second, excessive use of quotations may suggest to the reader that you do not fully comprehend the material; it is much easier to cut and paste together a document from pieces of various cases than to synthesize and explain a rule of law. Do not use quotations simply because you cannot think quickly of another way to express an idea.

When a quotation is warranted, the words, punctuation, and capitalization within the quotation marks must appear *exactly* as they are in the original. Treat a quotation as a photocopy or scan of the original text and indicate any alterations or omissions. Include commas and periods inside quotation marks; place other punctuation outside the quotation marks unless it is included in the original text. Also, try to provide smooth transitions between your text and the quoted text. Quotations that have fifty or more words must be set off in indented blocks. Table B-4 compares a statute's text to a quote in an appellate brief.

Table B-4. Citing a Quotation

Statutory Text: In the case of a hospital that has a hospital emergency department, if any individual (whether or not eligible for benefits under this subchapter) comes to the emergency department and a request is made on the individual's behalf for examination or treatment for a medical condition, the hospital must provide for an appropriate medical screening examination within the capability of the hospital's emergency department, including ancillary services routinely available to the emergency department, to determine whether or not an emergency medical condition (within the meaning of subsection (e)(1)) exists. 42 U.S.C. § 1395dd(a).

Quotation in Appellate Brief: A hospital with an emergency room must provide every patient with "an appropriate medical screening examination within the capability of the hospital's emergency department ... to determine whether or not an emergency medical condition ... exists." 42 U.S.C. § 1395dd(a).

G. Noteworthy Details

The following citation details are second nature to careful and conscientious lawyers, although they frequently trip up novices.

- Use proper ordinal abbreviations. The most confusing are 2d for "Second" and 3d for "Third" because they differ from the standard format.
- Do not use superscript for ordinal abbreviations. The abbreviation 4th is correct, while the abbreviation 4th is not.
- Include space only between elements of abbreviations that are not single capital letters. As examples, there is no space in the reporter abbreviation "U.S.," but there is space in the court designation "D. Or." and the law journal "Animal L."
- Ordinal numbers like 1st, 2d, and 3d are considered single capital letters for abbreviation spacing. Thus, there is no space in P.2d or F.3d, but F. Supp. 2d has a space on each side of "Supp."
- In citation sentences, abbreviate case names, court names, months, and reporter names. Do not abbreviate these words when they are part of textual sentences; instead, spell them out as in the example below.

EXAMPLE: The Ninth Circuit held that Oregon's Measure 11 did not violate constitutional rights provided under the Eighth and Fourteenth Amendments. *Alvarado v. Hill*, 252 F.3d 1066, 1069–70 (9th Cir. 2001).

- When *id.* is used to show support for just part of a sentence, this short cite is set off from the sentence by commas and is not capitalized.
- Spell out numbers zero through ninety-nine and use numerals for larger numbers. However, always spell out a number that is the first word of a sentence.

Table B-5. Typeface for Law Review Footnotes

Item	Explanation	Example
Case	Use ordinary type for case names in full citations. (See text for further explanation.)	Legal Servs. Corp. v. Velazquez, 531 U.S. 533 (2001).
Book	Use large and small capital letters for the author and the title.	MEGAN MCALPIN, BEYOND THE FIRST DRAFT: EDITING STRATEGIES FOR POWERFUL LEGAL WRITING (2014).
Law review article	Use ordinary type for the author's name, italics for the title, and large and small capitals for the periodical.	Adell Louise Amos, *The Use of State Instream Flow Laws for Federal Land: Respecting State Control While Meeting Federal Purposes*, 36 ENVTL. L. 1237 (2006).
Explanatory phrase	Use italics for all explanatory phrases, such as *aff'g, cert. denied, rev'd,* and *overruled by.*	Legal Servs. Corp. v. Velazquez, 531 U.S. 533 (2001), *aff'g* 164 F.3d 757 (2d Cir. 1999).
Introductory signal	Use italics for all introductory signals, such as *see* and *e.g.* when they appear in citations, as opposed to text.	*See id.*

III. Citations for Law Review Articles

Under the *ALWD Guide* and the *Bluebook*, citations in law review articles use different formatting than is used for practice documents. Using the *Bluebook* to write citations for law review articles is considerably easier than using it for practice documents. As noted above, almost all of the examples given in the *Bluebook* are in law review format. Table B-5 of this appendix summarizes the typeface used for several common sources and gives examples.

Law review articles place citations in footnotes or endnotes, instead of placing citations in the main text of the document. Most law review footnotes include text in ordinary type, in italics, and in large and small capital letters. This convention is not universal, and each law review selects the typefaces it will use. Some law reviews may use only ordinary type and italics. Others may use just ordinary type.

The typeface used for a case name depends on (1) whether the case appears in the main text of the article or in a footnote and (2) how the case is used. When a case name appears in the main text of the article or in a textual sentence of a footnote, it is italicized. By contrast, when a full cite is given in a citation sentence in a footnote, the case name is written in ordinary type. But when a short cite is used in footnotes, the case name is italicized. Assuming you are submitting an article to a law review that uses all three typefaces, *Bluebook* Rule 2 dictates which typeface to use for each type of authority.

Law review footnotes use short cites generally the same as in other documents. The short cite *id.* can be used only if the preceding footnote contains only one authority.

IV. Editing Citations

To be sure that the citations in a document correctly reflect your research and support your analysis, include enough time in the writing and editing process to check citation accuracy.

While writing the document, refer frequently to the local rules or to the citation guide required by your supervisor. After you have completely finished writing the text of the document, check the citations carefully again. Be sure that each citation is still accurate after all the writing revisions you have made. For example, moving a sentence might require you to change an *id.* to another form of short cite, or vice versa. In fact, some careful writers do not insert *id.* citations until they are completely finished writing and revising.

Sometimes editing citations can take as long as editing writing mechanics. The time invested in citations is well spent if it enables the person reading your document to quickly find the authorities you cite and to understand your analysis.

Appendix C

Selected Bibliography

Oregon Research and Resources

Karen S. Beck, *Oregon Practice Materials: A Selective Annotated Bibliography*, 88 Law Libr J 288 (1996).

Lesley A. Buhman et al., *Bibliography of Law Related Oregon Documents* (AALL 1986).

Mary Clayton & Stephanie Midkiff, Oregon Practice Materials: A Selective Annotated Bibliography, in *State Practice Materials: Annotated Bibliographies* (Frank G. Houdek, ed., W.S. Hein 2005).

Stephanie Midkiff & Wendy Schroeder Hitchcock, *State Documents Bibliography: Oregon* (2009).

Oregon Administrative Law (Hans Linde et al., eds.) (OSB Legal Pubs. 2010), Supplement (2016).

Oregon Blue Book (available in print and online at www.bluebook.state.or.us).

Oregon Legal Research (website maintained by public law librarians from Clackamas and Washington counties in Oregon) (available at http://www. oregonlegalresearch.com).

General Research (tending to focus on federal material)

Stephen M. Barkan, Barbara Bintliff & Mary Whisner, *Fundamentals of Legal Research* (10th ed 2015).

Morris L. Cohen & Kent C. Olson, *Legal Research in a Nutshell* (12th ed 2016).

Deborah A. Schmedemann et al., *The Process of Legal Research: Practices and Resources* (9th ed 2016).

Amy E. Sloan, *Basic Legal Research: Tools and Strategies* (7th ed 2018).

Research Guides (LibGuides)

Lewis and Clark University, Oregon Legal Research Guide, http://lawlibguides.
lclark.edu/oregon.

State of Oregon Law Library Online Research Guides, http://soll.libguides.com/
c.php?g=409503&p=3173223.

University of Oregon, Oregon Legislative History Research Guide, https://research
guides.uoregon.edu/orleghist.

Willamette University, Oregon Law LibGuide, http://law.willamette.libguides.
com/oregon.

Advanced Legal Research

Joanne D.S. Armstrong, Christopher A. Knott & R. Martin Witt, *Where the Law Is: An Introduction to Advanced Legal Research* (5th ed 2018).

Specialized Research

Specialized Legal Research (Penny A. Hazelton, ed. 2014) (formerly edited by Leah F. Chanin).

About the Authors

Suzanne Rowe is the James L. and Ilene R. Hershner Professor and Director of Legal Research and Writing at the University of Oregon School of Law. She received her law degree from Columbia University.

Megan Austin is a Law Instruction Librarian at the University of Oregon School of Law, where she teaches legal research to law students, master's students, and undergraduates. She received her J.D. and M.A. from the University of Arizona.

Index

See *"Terms of art"* for pages where legal words or phrases are defined or are introduced for the first time.
Most index entries dealing solely with federal research sources and processes appear under the heading *"Federal research."*